THE PEOPLE'S CAUSE

A HISTORY OF GUERRILLAS IN AFRICA

BASIL DAVIDSON

THE PEOPLE'S CAUSE

A HISTORY OF GUERRILLAS IN AFRICA

LONGMAN

Longman Group Limited,
Longman House,
Burnt Mill, Harlow, Essex, U.K.

© Basil Davidson, 1981

First published 1981

British Library Cataloguing in Publication Data
Davidson, Basil
    The peoples cause.
    1 Guerrillas – Africa – History
    I. Title
    355.02'184   DT21.5

ISBN 0 582 64680.4 (csd)
          64681.2 (ppr)

Phototypeset in V.I.P. Baskerville by
Western Printing Services Ltd, Bristol
Printed in Great Britain by
Richard Clay (The Chaucer Press) Ltd,
Bungay, Suffolk.

Then Turi set out with the men of Vuga,
a very great army, young men and elders,
with his two war horns and his flute, and his signal horn.

Habari za Wakilindi
(traditional: Tanzania)

We are armed militants, not militarists

Amílcar Cabral
(modern: Guinea-Bissau)

CONTENTS

PART ONE   THE OLD TRADITION   1

  1 On guerrillas and their wars   3

  2 On method and technique   7

  3 The epic of Askia Nuh   10
    Professionals and volunteers
    The two sides at Mbwila

  4 Meeting the colonial invasions   21
    Sandile's men
    Beyond self-defence : towards new nations
    Commandos and concentration camps
    Abd al-Kader and the defence of Algeria
    The Mahdia and others

  5 'No misfortunes broke their spirit'   40
    Jacob Morenga : a guerrilla genius
    Revolt in the grasslands
    Revolt in the hills

PART TWO   THE LONG MARCH FOR RESURGENCE   55

  6 In the toils   57
    New weapons
    Old motives and new motives
    The challenge of nationalism

  7 The contest in the north   70
    After 1945 : the mailed fist
    Tunisia and Morocco : the pressures from below
    Algeria : the young men 'cut the knot'
    Insurrection
    A bitter war of liberation
    Politics decide

  8 The land and freedom armies   87
    The run-up to rebellion
    Finding a leadership
    The struggle in the forests
    Balance sheet

CONTENTS

 9 **The confusion in the Congo**   100
   Soumialot in Kivu and Maniéma
   Mulele in Kwilu
   Comparable cases ?

10 **Conditions of success or failure: a summary**   115

11 **Building movements of maturity**   119
   Advantages
   Obstacles
   Angola
   Mozambique
   Guinea-Bissau and Cape Verde

12 **On the wider scene**   139
   Eritrea
   Zimbabwe
   In the deep south

13 **A tentative typology**   149

PART THREE   ON STRATEGY AND TACTICS   155

14 **The strategy of people's war**   157
   An ideology of liberation
   Liberated zones
   Counter-insurgency *versus* political warfare

15 **Tactics and weaponry**   174
   Organisational development
   Ambush techniques
   Combined operations
   Weaponry
   Conclusion

   Guide to sources   193

   Index   199

LIST OF FIGURES

Fig. 3.1   Racine Tall, army commander for al-Hadj Umar   14
Fig. 3.2   King Alvaro III receiving Dutch ambassadors in the
           seventeenth century   16
Fig. 3.3   British troops entering Kumasi during the British invasion
           of 1874   20
Fig. 4.1   Carving of an African soldier with 'spark-and-gunpowder'
           musket   22
Fig. 4.2   An incident in the South African frontier war of 1848   25
Fig. 4.3   Boer fighters assembling at the beginning of the South
           African War   32
Fig. 4.4   The Amir Abd al-Kader, Commander of the Faithful and
           defender of Algeria against French invasion   34
Fig. 4.5   The Mahdi Mohammed Ahmed ibn Abdullah   38
Fig. 5.1   Nama fighters resisting German forces in German South
           West Africa   43
Fig. 5.2   Tale fort, Somalia   48
Fig. 5.3   Abd al-Krim al-Kattabi, founder and defender of the
           Republic of the Rif in northern Morocco   50
Fig. 5.4   Guerrillas of Abd al-Krim waiting to attack Spanish troops   52
Fig. 6.1   The Gatling machine-gun   61
Fig. 6.2   A British regiment boarding a steamer at Jebba, on the river
           Niger, in 1901   63
Fig. 6.3   'The fight at Ologbo', an incident in the British campaign to
           capture the ancient city of Benin in 1897   64
Fig. 7.1   Guerrilla fighters in the Algerian war of independence
           (1954–62)   79
Fig. 7.2   Guerrillas walking through napalm-bombed woodlands
           during the Algerian war of independence   82
Fig. 8.1   'General China', a commander of the Kikuyu 'land and
           freedom armies'   94
Fig. 11.1 Liberation fighters of the MPLA in eastern Angola, 1970   131
Fig. 11.2 Samora Machel, FRELIMO leader and military commander   134
Fig. 13.1 POLISARIO fighters escorting a column of Moroccan and
           Mauritanian prisoners of war   149
Fig. 14.1 A scene during the elections held by the PAIGC in liberated
           territory in Guinea-Bissau, 1972   164
Fig. 15.1 Men of a PAIGC *bigrupo* attacking the Portuguese military
           base of Buba, Guinea-Bissau, 1968   188

LIST OF MAPS

Map 3.1   The Moroccan invasion of Songhay in 1591   11
Map 3.2   The battle of Mbwila, Kongo, 1665   17
Map 4.1   British Kaffraria, South Africa   24
Map 4.2   Southern Africa at the time of the Anglo-Boer War, 1899–
          1902   29
Map 4.3   North Africa in the time of Abd al-Kader   35
Map 5.1   The Horn of Africa at the end of the nineteenth century 46
Map 5.2   French and Spanish Morocco   51
Map 7.1   North Africa and the Algerian and Moroccan wars of
          independence   72
Map 8.1   Kenya and the area of the 'Mau Mau' rebellion   93
Map 9.1   Central Africa; the Congo rebellions of 1964   101
Map 11.1 The former Portuguese colonies of Africa   119
Map 11.2 Angola   130
Map 11.3 Mozambique   133
Map 11.4 Guïnea-Bissau   136
Map 15.1 Typical ambush by Commandant 'Cowboy', eastern
          Angola, 1967   180
Map 15.2 Ambush on the Chiume-Ninda road, eastern Angola,
          1 May 1971   182
Map 15.3 Ambush on the Luvuei-Lutembo road, eastern Angola,
          22 November 1973   182
Map 15.4 Ambush on the river Lute, eastern Angola, 2 June 1973 183

ACKNOWLEDGEMENTS

The publishers are grateful to the following for permission to reproduce photographs in the text:

BBC Hulton Picture Library for pages 34, 38, 52, 61, 63 & 64; British Museum for pages 16 (from Davidson, *Africa – History of a Continent*) and 48; Camera Press for page 94; Basil Davidson for pages 131, 134 & 164; Werner Forman Archive for page 22; Keystone Press Agency Ltd for page 149; Museu de Artilheria, Lisbon for page 20 (from Davidson, *Africa – History of a Continent*); Zdravko Pečar – Yugoslavia for pages 79 & 82; Royal Commonwealth Society Library for pages 14 (taken from Mage, *Soudan Occidentale*), 25 (taken from Godlonton and Irving, *Narrative of the Kaffır War) and 43* (taken from Schwabe, *Der Krisg in Deutsch Südwest Africa*); John Sheppard for page 188; John Topham Picture Library for page 32; United Press International Inc. for page 50.

The cover photo was kindly supplied by Basil Davidson.

The publishers regret that they have been unable to trace the copyright holders of some of the photographs because of lack of information on addresses and apologise for any infringement of copyright caused.

We are grateful to the following for permission to reproduce copyright material:

The author's agents for an extract from a poem by Hilaire Belloc reprinted by permission of A. D. Peters & Co. Ltd; Centre de Recherche et D'Information for extracts from *Rebellions au Congo* edited by B. Verhaegan, 1964; Heinemann Educational and Monthly Review Press for extracts from page 152 of *Unity and Struggle* by A. Cabral, translated by M. Wolfers, copyright © 1979 by the PAIGC. Reprinted by permission of Monthly Review Press; Merlin Press Ltd for an extract from 'Report on the Further Liberation of Guinea' by Basil Davidson page 295 of *The Socialist Register* 1973; the author, J. Morais-Monty for extracts from *Luta de Libertacao, Exercito Nacional e Revolucao* published by Uniao dos Escritores Angolaros, Luando, Angola; the author, Z. Pečar for extracts from *Alzir do Nezavisnosti* published by Prosveta, Belgrade 1967.

PART ONE

THE OLD TRADITION

I have spoken the language of that which is not called amiss, The Good Old Cause

John Milton, 1660

We say *Good* because it hath a tendency to the securing of the people's just rights, liberties, properties, privileges and immunities against tyranny, arbitrariness and oppression. *Old* because anciently and originally all power was in the people.

Anon, 1659

CHAPTER ONE

ON GUERRILLAS AND THEIR WARS

Guerrilla or irregular warfare seems to be pretty well as old as recorded history, but its place is evidently larger than it used to be. A full review would have to be immensely long, but it would still confirm what this short history shows: that this kind of warfare, which should not for a moment be confused with terrorism, has been above all a political and social enterprise with specific characteristics. This book is about guerrilla or irregular warfare in Africa, but the African examples, as it happens, are reliable guides to a wider picture.

I have had to be selective in choosing examples, and, within the limits imposed by a broad survey, have had to omit many of great intrinsic interest, such as the long Libyan resistance to Italian invasion. Yet my study of these omitted examples does not suggest that their inclusion would have led to any change in conclusions about the nature and development of guerrilla warfare. On the contrary, their inclusion would have fortified my conclusions while extending the evidence. I should also stress, perhaps, that I scarcely touch upon the general history of warfare. Many large contests find no place here, while others are mentioned only in passing.

Even so, the subject is still a wide one, and its limits remain hard to define. When, for example, does guerrilla warfare become regular warfare, or indeed the reverse? Into what category are we to place regular armies which nonetheless rely on guerrilla tactics? Some definitions will be helpful, even if their answers to such questions may still be imprecise.

Mere size of fighting units or their loose organisation in 'irregular' or 'independent' bands was an early measure of definition. Coined in Spain during the Napeolonic wars of French invasion at the beginning of the nineteenth century, the word *guerrilla* meant simply a 'small war', a diminutive of the Spanish word *guerra*, a big or regular war. But guerrilla soon acquired a second meaning. It became used to define not the 'small war' itself, but the bands of Spanish peasants and soldiers who harassed the rear units and lines of communication of the invading French armies, and were often cruelly effective. For 'it was neither battles nor engagements against regular forces which exhausted the French army', affirmed a contemporary French observer, 'but the incessant molestations of an invisible army, who, if pursued, became lost among the people, out of whom he reappeared immediately after with renewed strength'. Long afterwards, during the huge contests of our own century, it would be the Chinese leader Mao Tsetung who would put that same description into modern garb, affirming that guerrillas are 'among the people like fish in water: the water can live without the fish, but not the fish without the water'. And other famous leaders of 'people's war' have said much the same.

Those Spanish bands of nearly two hundred years ago were called *guerrillas*.

3

So far as Africans have been concerned, these *guerrillas* were fighting units of a type known long before, whether in various parts of the African continent or in the countless slave revolts of the Caribbean, and, most obviously among the latter, in the long series of guerrilla wars fought for their freedom by African slaves and 'maroons' in Jamaica after about 1673. Those, too, form examples that I have been sorry to have had to leave out; the literature about them, fortunately, is beginning to be ample. But so far as the term itself is concerned, the earliest English usage of *guerrillas* seems to have occurred in a despatch to London by the British commander in Spain, the Duke of Wellington, when, during his campaign of 1809, he 'set the Guerrillas to work towards Madrid'. Two years later the Scottish poet and novelist, Sir Walter Scott, was writing in *Don Roderick* that

> The Guerrilla band
> Came like night's tempest
> And avenged the land. . . .

The individual members of these bands were known as *guerrilleros*. But the word never took in English, and soon the word 'guerrilla' came to indicate the actual man – or woman – who joined these bands. This is how the word has been used ever since.

Yet mere size or loose organisation are poor means of definition. Like other continents, Africa has lately known irregular wars that were anything but small in size, and whose forces were far from loosely organised. Definition by method may be more helpful. From this point of view, guerrilla wars are different from other forms of warfare because they are fought by small detachments which are constantly or repeatedly on the move. They avoid head-on confrontations with their enemy, because their enemy is more numerous and better armed or equipped. They adopt a range of specific tactics such as ambush and the sabotage of lines of communication. They rely largely on their own internal sources of supply and shelter. They have no great 'back up' organisation of logistical support. They are invariably fought by volunteers, the notion of a conscripted guerrilla being a contradiction in terms.

But guerrilla wars can grow into regular wars; so definition by method also leaves something to be desired. It may suggest, too, that our subject can properly include a whole range of types of violence, from outbursts of spontaneous fury to banditry or terrorism or various forms of political crime, such as are not considered in this book. They are not considered because they do not belong in it. And they do not belong in it because they fail to meet the requirements of a people's self-defence. What are those requirements? And why are they related to self-defence?

The historical record can best provide the answer. It shows that two factors have governed the nature of organised irregular warfare. One is that this warfare has always been defensive in its primary motive. The other is that this warfare has always acquired its military form from an emphatically political content: a political content, specifically, concerned with the fate of a whole community or people.

For all these reasons I shall generally use the term 'people's war', meaning by this nothing demagogic or doctrinaire but the driving force of men and women capable of leading large numbers of their fellow-countrymen in self-defence. In self-defence, that is, not of some purely sectional or selfish advantage: but, as the old defenders of the English parliamentary cause described it, in self-defence of their 'just rights, liberties, properties, privileges and immunities against tyranny, arbitrariness and oppression'.

Such wars may of course be fought offensively, and even must be from the standpoint of strategy and tactics. All successful guerrilla wars have been fought offensively from this point of view: that is, by seizing and retaining a tactical initiative and gradually transforming this into the strategic initiative which alone wins wars. All the same, the primary motive has not been offensive. It has been to defend a people and a way of life.

By no means all regular or 'large' warfare, however, has been offensive in its primary motivation, or sought to invade another land, to crush another people, to destroy a different way of life. Many such wars, essentially, have been wars of self-defence by kings, governments, states or military commanders. And in such cases the motivating difference between regular and irregular warfare has been sometimes hard to detect, with the one merging into the other, whether in strategy or in tactics: strategy meaning the overall plan, and tactics the detailed ways in which the plan is carried out. There is the interesting fact that the 'father' of modern military thinking, the Prussian general and patriot Karl von Clausewitz (1780–1831), prescribed for regular warfare a principle of action which every successful leader of irregular warfare, whether he knew the work of von Clausewitz or not, has followed as a guide.

Von Clausewitz argued that the stronger strategic position would always be held by the side which fought from defensive, not offensive, motives. This side could and then should aim at three major targets; hitting these would bring success. These targets were, firstly, the forces of the enemy; secondly, the enemy's lines of supply and other rear resources; and, thirdly, the enemy's will to fight. Now this prescription carried von Clausewitz directly into non-military issues, into emphatically political issues, since the third of his decisive targets raised the question of who was fighting for what, and why? Von Clausewitz came to believe that if you could press such questions on an aggressive enemy's troops, while you yourself were fighting from defensive positions, then you could attack and undermine his morale.

It was along this line of thought that he produced his famous definition of warfare, more complex in his original German but long since simplified by common adoption: that 'war is the continuation of politics by other means'. If your politics were right, in other words, you would win: if not, you would as surely lose. Now von Clausewitz arrived at this definition, in the 1820s, after specific consideration of the strategy and use of his own country's regular army. But it was widely applied afterwards. Above all, it was applied to irregular warfare, and especially to those irregular wars, guerrilla-type wars, which acquired a revolutionary content in our century: a content, that is, concerned not only with defeating an aggressive enemy – whether external or internal – but also with the ending of 'tyranny, arbitrariness, and oppression'. Again we see that the ideas and motives of true guerrilla warfare – as distinct from banditry and the like – have all confirmed our two factors of definition: such warfare has been emphatically political in its purpose, and primarily defensive in its motive.

5

More could be argued to the same end, but let us now summarise. This study is concerned not with the history of wars of African dynasties and states, professional armies and their actions, but with specific forms of armed resistance to aggression: forms, above all, in which more or less large numbers of ordinary people have joined together in voluntary defence of their homes and lives, their cultures and their common interests.

It remains true, of course, that regular or non-guerrilla wars of resistance – including African wars of anti-colonial resistance – could and did win the active support and participation of large numbers of ordinary people. There again the boundary between 'regular' and 'irregular' was often blurred. In the 1870s the king of Asante put his national army into the field against an invading British army, and this was regular warfare; and every reader will be able to think of other such examples. Yet the king of Asante's army was actively supported by the people of Asante, and much of its ability to fight depended on that. The king's army fought to defend Asante against the British, and the people backed it to defend their nation. This was both regular warfare and a people's war.

But chiefly we are concerned with cases of warfare that were in no sense regular, although they were often extensive. These were armed resistances to governments, regimes or comparable powers felt by large numbers of ordinary people to be so unjust, arbitrary and oppressive as to call for self-defence by a counter-violence. In such cases, as we shall find in the historical record, counter-violence has ranged from brief revolts to highly sophisticated campaigns which, sometimes with outstanding success, have 'continued politics by other means'. And in the latter cases the politics in question also call for a definition. They may be called 'the politics of armed struggle'. They will bulk large in the later chapters of this study.

This 'politics of armed struggle' can be seen as a range of responses, a continuum of motive, which has varied greatly over time, and has moved or developed according to its own dynamic. It is in considering this range or continuum over time that we shall be able to discern the pattern, even the typology, on which an objective study of the history of irregular warfare may be able to depend.

CHAPTER TWO

ON METHOD AND TECHNIQUE

Anyone whom the duties and destinies of life have ever caused to fight with irregular armed forces against regular armed forces will be likely to have several thoughts in mind when meditating on the experience afterwards: if, that is, he or she should enjoy the good fortune to survive for long enough to meditate. One thought will be that war is always evil and, sanely, can never be considered otherwise. Another will be that certain forms of warfare, defensively conceived but offensively conducted, may nonetheless be able to extract some good from that evil. A third will be, as we have seen, that these forms of warfare must from first to last be a form of politics if any good is to be extracted from them. But a fourth thought, coming hard upon the third, will be that the military strategy and tactics must be right.

But what does 'right' mean here? Again we are into problems of defining what is elusive, changing, highly particular to time and place. Just where, in fact, are the crucial elements of strategy and tactics which decide between disaster and success? And how are these matters to be weighed, historically, against the subjectivities of bias, interest, and the rest? It has seldom been a question that men have asked in the moment of action. Then there was nothing, very likely, save a tough awareness of the hard slog ahead, the endless marching and counter-marching, the need for swift clashes, sudden but sufficiently decisive at the point of ambush or encounter, so that the next move should be possible as well as planned by choice rather than imposed by necessity: all that and more of the same, and then the hunger and the weariness offset only by morale, belief, the solidarity of companionship, or else accompanied, if these should fail, by the darkening shadow of defeat.

These subjectivities also had their part in a most objective reality. They too need to be weighed in the balance. On one side there was the demand that men and women should rise above themselves, take inspiration from their cause, grow larger in companionship. On the other side there were the miseries of hardship, danger and solitude, the temptations to withdraw into neutrality, the longing for food and sleep in safety when no such safety, let alone food or even sleep, was anywhere to be looked for or even to be hoped for. All this, for better or for worse, was 'in the situation'. So were other demons which assail, the demons of the forest or the wilderness that are not the demons of the ancestors but the demons of doubt, distrust of absent comrades, nagging fears of intrigue, surges of despair, the ever-repeated question of knowing what best to do and how best to do it, the anger at enemy reprisals that can distract judgment, the fury at the injustice of an enemy still too strong to be frustrated: all these and others like them strive against morale, belief, and the solidarity of companionship. Those who would understand the obscure history of this warfare must keep them all in mind, however difficult that may be.

Such subjectivities form part of the problem of knowing how much can be asked of soldiers by their commanders; they are part of the answer to the problems of arriving at a right strategy and tactics. And what is extraordinary about these 'people's wars', or at least about the successful ones, the ones conducted by a right strategy and tactics, has been just how much could be asked of their soldiers and could be given by these men and women. Some of the great liberation struggles of the Second World War produced feats of human steadfastness and endurance that had seemed impossible to their enemy, and yet were done by men and women whose origins were humble and obscure, whose arms were poor and insufficient, whose bellies were caved in hunger, whose nerves were stretched to breaking point, and yet whose morale still held firm. Some of the great liberation struggles of recent years in Africa produced feats of the same order, even if the outside world has scarcely cared to notice them or award the credit that is certainly their due.

What a right method and technique can mean in these circumstances was very brilliantly demonstrated, for example, by Samora Machel's 'right hook' through western Mozambique in 1972–73, the blow that finally destroyed the Portuguese army's last hope of defeating FRELIMO, Mozambique's liberation movement. There have been few more effective matchings of long-range strategy with short-range tactics. It asked enormously much of FRELIMO's fighters and peasant militias, and yet, as it proved, not too much. While feinting on his long left flank in the provinces of Delgado and Niassa as well as containing offensives by a powerful colonial enemy, Samora launched other units under veteran commanders on a long and extremely difficult offensive mission right down through the western province of Tete into the central provinces of Manica and Sofala. Huge problems of deep penetration had to be solved, as well as of porterage of ammunition. Yet the mission succeeded and the forward units, moving ever further into the heart of Portuguese-held territory, were then reinforced by fresh units and supplies. Soon enough the fighters of FRELIMO were firmly installed far into the south and pressing on again.

This success offered a classic demonstration of the effectiveness of the method and technique prescribed so long before by von Clausewitz. Samora's fist on his 'right hook' through Tete into Manica and Sofala smashed into unsuspecting enemy garrisons, marching columns, and convoys of supplies. Secondly, it placed some of his best units hard across the rear lines of supply and communication of the colonial armies, while, at the same time, cutting similar lines between the Portuguese and their allies in Rhodesia (Zimbabwe). Thirdly, and decisively, it struck at the enemy's morale. For the enemy, the 'impossible' had happened: only a little earlier the Portuguese commander Kaulza de Arriaga had boasted that he would end the war with victory within a few months, and yet here he was in 1973 with his back to the wall, outfought and outmanoeuvred.

This singular defeat marked the beginning of the end, and was a powerful factor in preparing the Portuguese armed forces' *coup d'état* of April 1974 which overthrew the fascist dictatorship in Portugal and declared for 'decolonisation and democratisation'. How directly this was so was confirmed in May 1974 by the Portuguese chief of staff himself, General Costa Gomes. 'Our armed forces,' he told a press conference in the capital of Mozambique (then Lourenço Marques, now Maputo), 'have reached the limits of neuro-psychological exhaustion'. It was a singularly clear demonstration of the effectiveness of this politics of armed struggle and its military operations.

Not all such struggles have shown a like success. Some have shown none at all, while others have ended in disaster. The record, as we shall see, is long and various. Here, at the end of this brief introduction, I want to add a few words on the way this record is examined.

Three chapters complete Part One. The first of these looks at the distant history of our subject, together with a few examples in so far as the records enable them to be examined. The purpose there is to provide a desirable 'time depth', a necessary 'history of duration', as a background to recent examples. It is a background that can be little more than sketched, for its history is obscured by centuries and tangled in motivations not always possible to grasp today. Even so, it is a background that we need to look at.

The two concluding chapters of Part One are devoted to successive phases in more recent history, phases in which irregular warfare, with more or less of the content of 'people's war', has repeatedly held an important place. These are:*

1 primary armed resistance to European invasion and conquest before and during the early colonial period;
2 secondary armed resistance after formal or real conquest by this or that external power: ranging, in period, from around 1900 or soon after down to the 1930s.

Coming down the years towards the present, Part Two continues into the period of armed struggle for independence as this developed after the Second World War (1939–45). The aim there is in no sense to offer a catalogue. Any such catalogue would be so lengthy as to be unwieldy and confusing. Treated in such detail, the history of irregular warfare would slip through our fingers as surely as guerrillas disappearing in the watches of the night. It will be more useful to select examples of success and failure such as are characteristic of other cases, are reasonably well recorded, and are capable of displaying some or other part of the pattern and dynamics of this history.

Part Three moves into a more general consideration of the politics of armed struggle, as defined above, and into a detailed consideration of method and organisation, tactics, weaponry, and other technical matters.

Lastly, a Guide to Sources keyed to successive chapters and pages of the book will provide a list of the sources I have quoted or drawn upon, and a brief review of the relevant literature.

* For discussion of the terms 'primary' and 'secondary', see pp. 19–20, 39, 40, 151.

CHAPTER THREE

THE EPIC OF ASKIA NUH

Here we reach towards the ancestry of guerrilla war in Africa and begin, if not at the beginning, at least a fair way back.

In 1591, heading for the great trading cities of Timbuktu and Gao on the middle sector of the river Niger, there came out of the Sahara Desert a tired and thirsty troop of some 3 000 Moroccan fighting men and as many porters, cooks, and camel grooms. They had made an impressively swift march across the wasteland from Morocco, and meant to seize control of the great Songhay empire of the Western and Central Sudan, so that their master, the sultan of Morocco, could win wealth and prestige.

This small invasion force expected a strong defence by the armies of Songhay, but its leader, a Spanish Christian in Muslim service called Judar, had strong hopes of success. Most of his men were trained musketeers, and his baggage train carried ten mortars able to fire stone balls; while the Songhay, as Judar knew, had no firearms. And something could also be hoped from the factor of surprise.

News of this approaching invasion did in fact reach the Songhay emperor and his generals in good time, but they were slow to react, perhaps believing that Judar's force would never be able to reach the Niger. Orders to destroy or foul wells on the invasion route were despatched but were not carried out. Small units were sent to harass the invaders on the last stages of their march to the Songhay capital at Gao, but were not effective. A pitched battle of defence was going to be necessary, or so it was agreed on the Songhay side.

It occurred on about 12 March 1591, at Tondibi, some 50 kms north of Gao, and proved decisive. On one side the Songhay emperor, Askia Iskaq II, had the advantage of numbers: according to the author of the *Tarikh al-Fattash* (completed in Timbuktu some 60 years later but drawing on the testimonies of people who had been present at the battle) the Songhay had 18 000 cavalry and 9 700 infantry, all armed with swords or spears. The invaders were thus outnumbered by some ten to one, but besides their firearms they had unity and discipline. No doubt, too, they had an additional determination that came from knowing that for them there could be no retreat: these invaders must win, or they would die.

The battle was short but bloody. The Moroccans had drawn up their 3 000 fighting men in close ranks with their backs to the river Niger, and, records the *Tarikh al-Fattash*,

> as soon as the Songhay army came within range, the Moroccan infantry dropped to their knees and prepared to fire. Now, the Askia had brought a thousand cattle with him and ordered these to be driven between his

own front ranks and those of the enemy; so that these cattle would take the impact of the musket firing while his own infantry, driving·the cattle ahead of them, came to hand-to-hand grips with the Moroccans. But the musket volleys panicked the cattle and turned these back into the Songhay infantry, crashing into them and killing many of them. . . .

Continuing to reload and fire, the Moroccans soon had the Songhay in confusion, and, thanks partly to divided councils among the Songhay commanders, confusion became rout. Judar pushed on into Gao where he and his troops stayed for seventeen days. In Gao malaria struck them hard, so Judar turned back northward and entered Timbuktu, a city believed to be healthier. Here the Moroccans made their headquarters, and here they stayed.

So far, this was regular warfare. But the commanding Songhay general, the Askia Nuh, was not yet beaten. Rallying such men as he could and fighting

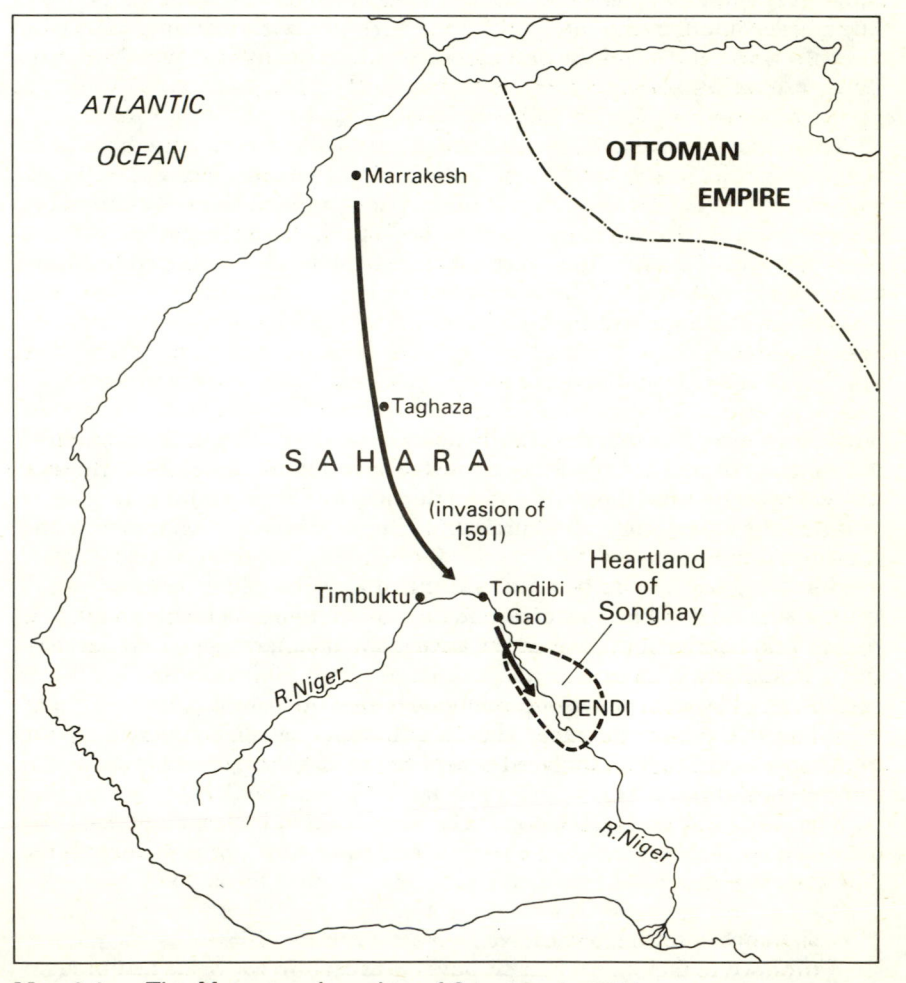

Map 3.1   *The Moroccan invasion of Songhay in 1591.*

rearguard actions, Nuh withdrew southward into the wooded lands and marshes of Dendi, the Songhay homeland. The initial Moroccan commander, Judar, foresaw the problems this would pose and advised his master, the sultan in distant Marrakesh, that the invaders should be content to plunder the Songhay cities and seize their trade. But the sultan wanted more. He sacked Judar from command and sent out a replacement, Mahmud, with orders for large-scale conquest. Mahmud decided to pursue Nuh and destroy him in battle.

Nuh was too good a general to be taken in such a trap. Avoiding major encounters with the pursuing Moroccans, he drew them into ambushes or forced them to fight in small detachments, and on ground of his own choosing. 'Many stiff battles were fought', says the *Tarikh as-Sudan*, another Timbuktu history completed at about the same time as the *Tarikh al-Fattash*, 'and in spite of the small number of his partisans, Askia Nuh achieved results that Askia Ishaq (the emperor defeated at Tondibi) had failed to score with forces much larger, even a hundred times larger'. And here we are clearly concerned with guerrilla warfare, such as the peasants of Spain were to fight against Napoleon two centuries after.

Nuh maintained his guerrilla war until he died in battle two years later, bringing Songhay resistance virtually to an end. He is worth remembering in the annals of people's war. 'A fine horseman, strong, very brave, and handsome to see', as the *Tarikh al-Fattash* described him from those who knew him, Nuh comes with a powerful impact through these distant records.

Those who wish for a fuller account of the Songhay-Moroccan conflict may turn to one or other of the standard histories; for this is not the place to give it. But some comments will be useful.

PROFESSIONALS AND VOLUNTEERS

The nature of warfare has depended upon the nature of the human community at any given point: on its social or class structure and its mode of government, on its economic development and conflicting interests, and on its level of culture – using this word 'culture' in a wide reference to technological and ideological factors.

The Songhay empire by 1591 was the product of a long development of centralising rule, military control, and the exploitation of peasant labour. The older empire of the 'lords of gold', of ancient Ghana, had begun that development many centuries earlier; the still larger empire of Mali had carried it further, giving way to Songhay power only in the 15th century. A 'core people' – Soninke in the case of Ghana, Mandinka in that of Mali, Songhay in that of Songhay – found itself well placed to control the long-distance trade as well as to exploit local resources of labour and land. Each of these 'core peoples' and its rulers thereupon set out, successively, to dominate a large zone of trade, tax and tribute. That was the chief object of their enterprise: not so much to bring neighbouring peoples under direct rule, as to exploit their labour.

So long as these neighbouring peoples paid their 'dues', they were more often than not welcome to conserve their separate identities and cultures, and even their autonomy. They might have to accept governors from the 'core people' of the empire which enclosed them; but the governors were concerned with little more than raising tax or tribute and putting down resistance to paying these. Using such revenues, the imperial rulers were able to build strong armies whose success could also draw on technological advances. The kings could buy or make expensive weapons. They could maintain more or less permanent or fulltime troops of soldiers, another costly innovation.

We see this in the case of ancient Ghana. Writing in about AD 1150 (about 545 of the Age of the *Hijra*), the Arab annalist al-Zouhri remarks that the people of Ghana – he means its 'core people', the Soninke – 'make expeditions against neighbours who have no use of iron, and who fight with bars of ebony', so that the Soninke 'can defeat them because they fight with swords and lances'. Then came another military innovation: the use of cavalry, taking its major development in the 15th century. All the important savannah rulers, by that time, disposed of troops of cavalry which developed, in the military balance of those days, the overwhelming power of tanks in recent times.

Such innovations depended on the fulfilment of two conditions. One was that the users had the wealth to buy and maintain horses and cavalry equipment such as quilt-armour and the rest. The other was that the cavalrymen became professionals. The mass of such armies might be 'called up' from core or subject peoples, and trail by thousands into battles where the sheer weight of numbers could decide the day. But any such 'call up' was slow, unwieldy, and unreliable. To police and patrol the trade routes, put down revolts, punish tax offenders, and ensure military intelligence over the huge distances enclosed within these empires, small but strong forces of cavalry appeared indispensable. Yet these had to be always available, permanently 'on call', ready at a day's notice to move and fight. In short, they had to be professionals.

So it was in all the great states of those times, whether in Africa or elsewhere. The armoured professionals became the masters of the field. Where to find them? A general answer was to buy mercenaries or take men reduced to servile status and turn them into full-time soldiers. That is what the sultan of Morocco had done. Half his troops were European mercenaries, mostly from Spain or southern France (although his chief artilleryman on the invasion of Songhay was said to have been English): that is, they were volunteers or men captured in war with the Christians and reduced to Muslim slavery. And it strikes a strangely modern note, comparing those old mercenaries of the 16th century with other Europeans who have lately come to Africa to fight for pay, to read that the purses of those killed by Songhay guerrillas, say the old *tarikhs*, were found to be 'full of gold coins'.

Now this army of mercenaries was good at pitched battles and the like. It could and did deal hardly with the 'call up' of Songhay infantry and cavalry, even if some of the latter were professionals too. Its muskets, of the primitive type known as arquebus, were hopelessly inaccurate at ranges of more than a hundred metres or so, and dangerously slow to reload; they were also very heavy, and generally needed to be fired by resting the barrel on a metal tripod stuck into the ground. Yet they made a great deal of noise, were weapons generally never before seen in the Western Sudan, and had their effect.

But Askia Nuh took the measure of these mercenaries. He saw that they liked their pay, but not the price they had to give for it, especially when this came to toiling through unknown country in search of an enemy who refused to stand still. 'The Moroccan troops', the *Tarikh as-Sudan* tells us, 'suffered a lot.

They got very tired. They were attacked by hunger. They fell victims to the sicknesses of the country. The water they drank infected their intestines, spreading dysentery and killing many besides those who died in battle.' As well as all that, they were invaders and lonely. In sum, their morale collapsed.

This alone would have done Askia Nuh's business and that of his successors. But the nature of the Songhay empire fatally intervened. Seeing the 'core people' in bad trouble, the subject and exploited peoples of the empire rose in revolt. All those who resented having to pay tax or tribute in goods or labour services, as well as all those who lived on the frontiers of the empire and looked

Fig. 3.1   *Racine Tall, army commander for al-Hadj Umar in the western Sudan during the 1860s (after a drawing by the French traveller Mage). As the men in the background and the spurs on his boots indicate, Tall was a cavalry commander, used to rapid movement and fast-moving raids in the wars of jihad or conquest led by al-Hadj Umar. But his heavy musket shows that he and his men also fought on foot; the musket is a typical ball-firing and smooth-barrelled weapon of the period, fired by triggering a flint spark into a little 'pan' of gunpowder at the rear-end of the barrel.*

for a chance of loot – Fulani and Bambara, Dogon and Tuareg – saw the defeat of the Songhay as their chance of liberation or profit. The records say that they seized this chance with eager hands. What remained of Songhay power was swept away on tides of insurgence. 'Everything changed', laments the *Tarikh as-Sudan*: 'Danger took the place of safety, poverty supplanted wealth, and instead of the calm we had known there was violence and disaster. People fought against each other everywhere; and everywhere there was looting and robbery. War spared neither life nor property. Disorder became the rule. . . .'

This was to see matters from the Songhay standpoint, or at any rate from the standpoint of the learned men of Timbuktu; and no doubt the *Tarikh*'s 'everywhere' is much exaggerated. We may be sure that many rural peoples saw it differently. If there were some who suffered, there were others who gained or believed they had a chance to gain. Little is known of the confusions which followed Songhay collapse; but we shall be wise to reject any picture of 'tribal chaos', and to interpret the upheavals of subject and exploited peoples, of neighbouring raiders, as having perfectly rational motives, however much they may have hurt the previously established order. The latter vanished from the scene. The Songhay might be able to rally their own chiefs and people, the beneficiaries of the old empire, and even find temporary allies among neighbouring peoples, such as the Borgawa, who evidently thought that a weak Songhay neighbour was much preferable to a strong Moroccan one. But what the Songhay commanders could not do was to raise any general resistance among the exploited social classes or peoples of their old regime.

Various themes are obvious here. They will recur down the years. Attacked from outside, a given people closes its ranks no matter what its previous internal conflicts of interest may have been, and develops a people's war out of a defeated regular or 'state' war. Once this happens, conflicts between diverse strata among the defenders – between rulers and ruled, 'élites' and 'masses' – can temporarily disappear. New leaders appear: we know nothing of the Songhay peasant heroes of the anti-Moroccan guerrilla war, but peasant heroes there must have been. There emerges a sense of unity that may even prelude a change in the balance of class forces within the given society. With defeat, this unity vanishes again.

But the situation which promotes Songhay unity is also one that promotes the unity of other peoples, and the empire finally breaks down as one revolt after another shatters the imperial system. The national defence of the Songhay is matched by the self-defence of exploited peoples or classes of people. The themes of a people's war are sounded – resistance to invasion, resistance to exploitation – but there is no common ground on which they can develop. There is no chance of restructuring the old imperial system. Instead, there is a dispersal of power. The Bambara set up their own kingdoms. Fulani groups embark on new experiments in statehood. Others follow suit. A unifying ideology has yet to come: whether a multi-ethnic class ideology, or a multi-ethnic national ideology. Later, Islam will largely play this rôle in the Western Sudan (as elsewhere), but Islam in the 16th century is still weak or absent outside the trading cities.

All this has useful lessons for the history of our own times. The distant origins of nationalism can be perceived: in the resistance led by Askia Nuh; in the subsequent rise of kingdoms among neighbouring peoples. The complexities of response made by various sectors of an invaded society can be examined, again foreshadowing the experience of later time. The empire of the Songhay had often known a conflict of interests between the rural peoples of the countryside, not yet Muslim or rarely so, and the people of the cities, led as these were by Muslim traders and Muslim scholars. When invasion came by the Moroccans, who were also Muslims, the traders and scholars of Timbuktu saw it as offering advantages, and, as a ruling group, they generally welcomed it. They lived to repent of this, as such 'collaborators' often have; but that was afterwards.

In this Songhay experience, furthermore, we see the difficulty of separating forms of defensive regular warfare from forms of irregular warfare. In what degree, for example, were the ideas and motives of the Songhay 'regular troops' who responded to their chiefs' appeal, and fought the battle at Tondibi, different from those of the Songhay guerrillas who fought on under Nuh and others after Nuh? How far did the army of the Borgawa, going to the aid of the Songhay in face of Moroccan invasion, differ in the spirit of its fighters from the peasant fighters of the subject peoples who identified the Songhay, and not the Moroccans, as their enemy? We can only guess at the answers. But what appears beyond question is that old wars of self-defence, and the attitudes or 'tradition' they established, have thematic links with modern wars of self-defence.

Fig. 3.2 *Kings defended their states from European invasion, whenever they could, by diplomacy and trading treaties, and took to arms only when peaceful efforts failed. Here is King Alvaro III, of the Kongo kingdom (afterwards part of Angola), receiving some Dutch ambassadors early in the seventeenth century. The Dutch soon went away, having bigger interests in the Far East; but the Portuguese made war on the Kongo kingdom and eventually conquered it. (From a contemporary print.)*

There is space for one other suggestive example, once again emphasising the ways in which 'regular' and 'irregular' warfare could go together.

THE TWO SIDES AT MBWILA

On a day of driving rain in 1665 the old kingdom of Kongo (what today is northernmost Angola) saw another decisive battle. This settled the fate of that kingdom as surely as Tondibi had settled the fate of Songhay.

It was a kingdom which had emerged some three centuries earlier under the rule of local chiefs who, growing stronger, formed an aristocracy topped by a king elected from a number of royal candidates. As in Songhay or other such kingdoms, armies were raised by 'call up' of peasant fighters through subordinate chiefs whenever war or massive shows of force seemed necessary; but here, as yet, there were few or no professional soldiers. 'The sovereigns of these countries' round the mouth and lower reaches of the river Congo, a French observer explained somewhat later but in circumstances that were similar, 'maintain no regular troops. Whenever a king decides to make war, his Makaka, minister of war and army commander, sends orders to the princes and governors of provinces, telling them to call up troops.' These troops were peasants obeying their chiefs; once the campaign was over, they went off home again. Casualties were evidently small.

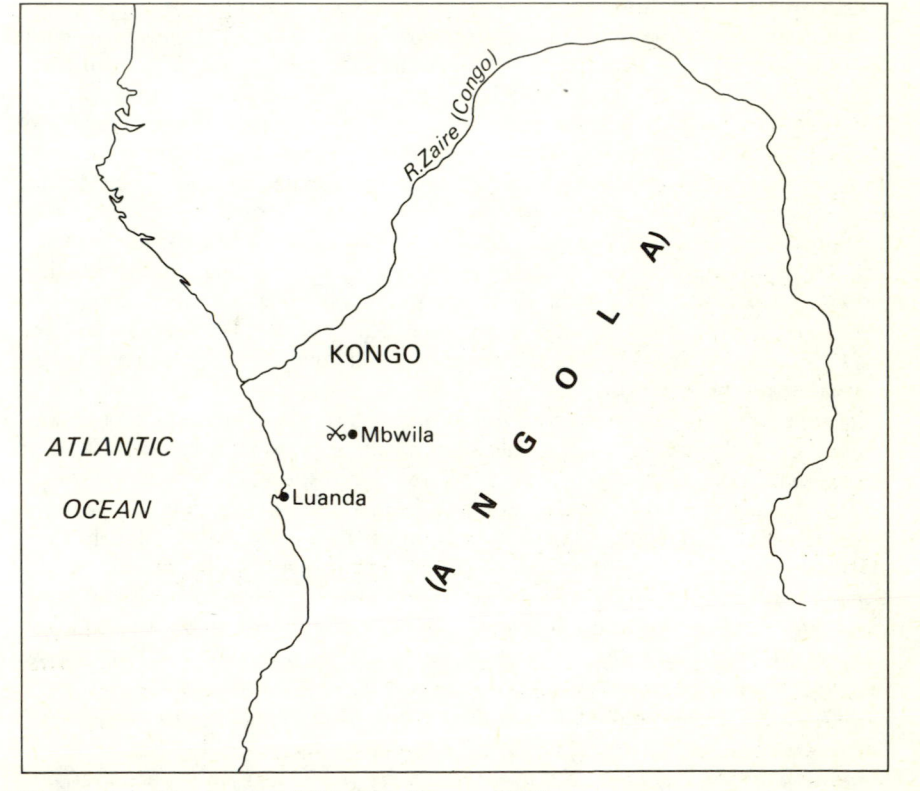

Map 3.2 *The battle of Mbwila, Kongo, 1665.*

Circumstances altered with the coming of the Europeans, in this case chiefly the Portuguese. These settled in small numbers at favoured points along the coast, and were generally welcomed because they could open new channels of trade. But the Portuguese, like others of their kind, wanted more than a share in trade; increasingly they wanted control of the country and its resources. In wanting this they naturally fished among local peoples for conflicting interests such as could bring them allies. Since the trading interests of the people of the seaboard were by no means always the same as the trading interests of the inland people – indeed, the two were the guardians of different monopolies – such conflicts were not hard to find or promote. They opened the way for Portuguese domination of both seaboard and interior peoples. For this, however, much fighting was first required; and the battle in the driving rain, that day of 1665, was a foremost part of it.

Pursuing their aim of conquering the inland country, still independent of their rule in 1665, the Portuguese commander on the seaboard at São Paolo de Loanda (the Luanda of today) led an army to overthrow the reigning Kongo monarch. On his side the latter, whose Christian title and name was King Antonio, called up his own army to defend the kingdom. The two armies fought it out at Mbwila, and Antonio's forces were defeated, signalling a disaster for the Kongo kingship from which Antonio's successors were never able to recover. In the context of our study here, it is worth asking exactly who was fighting whom, and why.

Africans and Portuguese fought on both sides. The Portuguese invasion force is said to have consisted of 200 soldiers from Portugal, 150 local Portuguese from the seaboard, 100 African musketeers and some 3 000 African bowmen. Antonio's army was much more numerous in spearmen but he too had some 400 musketeers; of the latter, half were Africans and half were inland Portuguese traders and settlers. These Portuguese, whether from the seaboard or the inland country, had no doubt all come from Portugal in the first place; but now they were so clearly divided in their interests and loyalties that they were ready to make war on each other. And it must have been much the same on the African side. The bulk of Africans on both sides possibly belonged to the same ethnic groups, Kongo for the most part or groups closely related; yet they were so clearly divided in their interests and loyalties that they were ready to make war on each other.

Once again we find a diversity of motives. Antonio called up his people to defend his kingdom, his Kongo nation or nationality, in circumstances and in terms that make us think of the people's war that responds to an outside threat to homes and freedom. And it appears from the evidence that they fought valiantly. King Antonio himself was slain on that grey and sodden field of Mbwila, and his severed head was carried back in triumph to Luanda by the victorious Portuguese commander. But the battle had swayed back and forth for hours, and the invaders had come near to defeat. Antonio's call to arms before the battle can tell us something too. We have it in its Portuguese version, or at any rate in the version which has survived in the Portuguese records. It must have sounded very differently in kiKongo, but in Portuguese it went like this:

Listen to the mandate given by the King sitting on the throne at Supreme

Council of War: it is that any man of any rank, noble or base, poor or rich, provided he is capable of handling weapons, from all villages, towns and places belonging to my Kingdoms, Provinces, and Domains, is to go, during the first ten days following the issue of this royal proclamation, to enlist with their Captains, Governors, Dukes, Counts, Marquises, etc., and with other justices and officials who preside over them .'. . to defend our lands, goods, children, women and our own lives and freedoms, which the Portuguese nation wants to conquer and dominate. . . .

What did all that mean to Kongo peasants? We scarcely know, except that many rallied and fought: whether as 'regulars' or as guerrillas may be hard to say. For here too we seem to catch, however distantly, the echo of that later appeal and response which would eventually remove the invading Portuguese and their colonial system, even though in circumstances entirely different and in scope far wider, three centuries later.

Such examples teach a familiar lesson: to understand the present, one needs to understand the past. They could be multiplied by many others. Their lessons reappear time and again in the long period of the slave trade. Then the interests of one ruling group clash in the search for captives with the interests of neighbouring ruling groups; or else, reaching an accommodation between these interests, they combine together in a joint commercial enterprise. In those enterprises it was the relatively weak peoples who suffered, the 'small' peoples who lived on the fringes of strong political systems, those who were least equipped to defend themselves. And among these we may be sure, even if the records seldom tell us in more than tantalising brevity, that threatened peoples produced many heroes in wars of self-defence which, by the nature of things, were another prelude to the big guerrilla wars of later periods.

With the opening of colonial types of aggression, this need for self-defence by whole peoples as distinct from 'dominating core peoples', or ruling groups or classes, became a general one. That is why many of the wars of self-defence of the opening colonial period took on the character of guerrilla wars, of people's wars, as well as of wars of 'regular' self-defence. Now it was not only fringe peoples, 'small' peoples threatened with enslavement by stronger neighbours, who had to fight for their liberty or else go under: now the whole continent, save for one or two favoured regions, came under an external threat. And logically, now, early foreshadowings of nationalism, of the sense of national community over and above social divisions or class conflicts, begins to acquire new shape and substance. Logically again, this is when the concept of self-defence grows slowly into the concept of wars of national liberation: quintessentially, of people's wars.

Historians have distinguished between types or phases of resistance to attack from outside. Usually, the early resistances were made by states with strong kingships or central governments, while the later resistances were more often made by states or communities without such centralising powers. These two types of resistance have been called 'primary' and 'secondary'.

Such neat labels have their value, but can seldom fit neatly into the real circumstances of life. The resistance of kingships sometimes overlapped with that of village communities following the oracles of their ancestors; or else both types, 'primary' and 'secondary', appeared together. The primary–secondary phasing may be useful as an aid to analysis, but it needs to be seen against the actual development of society. Some armed resistances arose in defence of existing states or nations – or of nationalities and ethnic groups dismissed by the invaders as 'tribes', or, more contemptuously still, as 'primitive tribes' – and were concerned with restoration, with fighting to retain what had existed before the invasions began. Other resistances were waged by peoples, by nationalities (again 'tribes', in European parlance), who were on the way towards becoming structured states, self-identified nations. For them, the invasions provided another spur to the development of a sense of nationalism, of national community, such as was scarcely present in earlier times. They were fighting for restoration, but also, with time, for a new form of community.

Fig. 3.3 *British troops entering Kumasi, the capital of the Asante empire, during a long and hard-fought campaign of British invasion in 1874. At their head, on horseback, is the British commander Sir Garnet Wolseley who, having taken Kumasi, returned with his men to the coast (of what was then Gold Coast, and now Ghana). This was a regular, not guerrilla, war between a mixed British, West Indian, and local African force on one side, and the Asante army on the other; but many of its features were of a guerrilla-war nature.*

CHAPTER FOUR

MEETING THE COLONIAL INVASIONS

'I look for some reason why I should obey you and find not the smallest. If friendship is what you want, very well, I am ready for it now and always, but never to be your subject.' Thus wrote a chief of the Yao of southern Tanzania, Masemba, to German invaders in 1890. It was the reasoned response of chiefs and kings.

Against Masemba the Germans had tried with three military expeditions to crush his inland monopoly of trade, and to prevent him from buying rifles from coastal importers. They tramped up country from their seaboard bases. Their columns were small but strong, well disciplined and well armed. But the Yao met them with partisan tactics, attacking and withdrawing, ambushing, relying on their knowledge of the terrain. Now the Germans were ready to talk. Masemba should accept their overlordship, and they would reward him.

Masemba's reply continued: 'I am sultan here in this land. You are sultan there in yours. But listen: I do not say to you that you must obey me, for I know that you are a free man. As for me, I will not come to you, and if you are strong enough to do it, then come and fetch me.' The German conquest followed, but not easily.

Such was the common response of those years. Kings and chiefs replied with offers of partnership; when these failed before a new imperialism that wanted territorial possession, as well as commercial gain, they moved to defensive warfare. Sometimes, as in Masemba's case, this defensive warfare was of guerrilla type. The cases are too numerous to list; several are famous in history. A few kings were so placed as to be able to make alliance with the invaders on terms which appeared to suit them well: the Ganda king in southern Uganda was one of those who did this, going into partnership with the British against his neighbour, the Nyoro king. But most found themselves obliged, like the Baule in Ivory Coast against the French, to move from defensive diplomacy to defensive warfare.

The period of this 'primary' resistance was a long one. It took the French some thirty years to subdue the rulers of the Western Sudan, and about as long for the British to do the same in Asante. In prolonged and often ragged wars which ranged from guerrilla skirmishes to pitched battles, the invaded peoples defended themselves. The Europeans, though with better and more numerous firearms, did not always win the pitched battles. At Isandlwana in 1879 the Zulu triumphed over professional British regiments. In 1896 an Italian expeditionary army was shattered by the Ethiopians at Adowa.

Yet weight of armour generally carried the day. These state or national wars are not our subject, but one example may be useful.

In the Niger Delta, for example, the initial clash came usually from a

British ambition to destroy African trading monopoly on the mainland, and add this to British trading monopoly at sea. By the late 19th century, several enterprising royal traders commanded the landward monopoly just as the British, moored on 'hulks' in estuaries and creeks or operating from Lagos Island, commanded the seaward monopoly. Among these royal traders, each with his own military power, were Ja Ja of Opobo and his neighbours. Among these neighbours was Chief Nana of Ebrohemi on the Benin river.

In Nana's case, as with others, the clash had its diplomatic prelude. Seeking to use him as one of their 'points of entry', the British recognised Nana as the governor of the Benin river. Governor for whom? For us, argued the British. But Nana thought otherwise: he held that he was sovereign in Ebrohemi. In 1894 the British became impatient of Nana's claim to sovereignty. They wanted territorial possession or its equivalent in 'indirect rule'.

Fig. 4.1 *Old African carving, possibly of the 18th century and now in a Dutch museum, of a soldier taking aim with a 'spark-and-gunpowder' musket. Such muskets, mostly made in Europe, became common in the period of the overseas slave trade, and were used both in self-defence and in raiding for captives.*

They sent in a small force, commanded by Rear-Admiral Bedford, to deal with him. But Nana turned it back. So the British replied with a stronger expedition and a naval component. This was eventually successful after overcoming some opposition.

Nana's defence showed years of preparation and evinced, according to Bedford, 'a considerable amount of intelligence . . . the guns (in Nana's defences) were admirably placed to meet any attack from the direction expected . . . and were well and strongly mounted'. Not just a few guns, either. Bedford's troops counted 106 cannon ranging from 3-pounders to 36-pounders, including 'a large number of 9-pounders, very good-looking cast-iron guns' evidently made in local workshops.

Nana's powder magazine contained 1 500 kegs in good order, and was protected from bombardment by sheet iron, timber, and earthworks. There were stores of ammunition made up of iron balls and tubular bamboo frames filled with bits of broken iron pot, an ingenious form of early shrapnel. So why was Nana's fortress so easily taken by an invading force hampered by the creeks and terrain of the Benin river? Mostly, it appears, because Nana's troops did not have their heart in it when the fighting started. Most were conscripted slaves who evidently saw no sufficient difference between one master and another. They had little desire to fight for Nana.

And here too the lesson of this history was to become a general one. Invariably, the kings and chiefs went down before colonial power not only because they were weaker in military strength and hitting power, but as much, and sometimes even more, because they were kings and chiefs. They fought for interests which the people whom they sent to fight did not sufficiently share: or, in the case of Nana's troops, did not share at all. In the end, against colonial power, only those forms of warfare were going to prevail in which the people who were sent to fight were those who volunteered to fight, and volunteered because they identified the interests they were fighting for as their own interests. It was to be the prescription for what we have called people's war.

SANDILE'S MEN

There were wars of resistance in which the people who were sent to fight had volunteered to fight, and fought hard, because they were convinced that they were fighting for their own interests. The records of southern Africa are especially rich in examples.

In 1652 the Dutch East India Company, having previously failed to seize the old Portuguese base on Mozambique Island up the eastern coast, fixed on the Cape of Good Hope as their chosen 'relief and relay station' for Dutch ships going to the Indian Ocean and returning thence. They put ashore a few Dutchmen with orders to stay there and grow vegetables. Slowly spreading, this little colony soon needed more land and labour. These the colonists took from local Africans, a people called Khoi, whose ancestors had lived here since remote Stone Age times. They took the land of the Khoi and enslaved its owners.

With a population enlarged from Europe, as well as with children who were the fruit of unions between male colonists and female Khoi, the colonists then pushed further into neighbouring lands. For a long while they met with no opposition save from the Khoi, and the Khoi were too weak to be able to stop them. But soon after the middle of the 18th century the colonists ran into a stronger resistance. This was offered by iron-using communities of farmers belonging to the great family of Bantu-language speakers who had begun to populate most of central and southern Africa about two thousand years earlier. In the southern parts of what was to become South Africa these Bantu-speaking communities or states belonged to long-established Sotho and Nguni peoples. They were numerous, more strongly organised than the Khoi, and able to defend themselves.

The colonists from the Cape reached out for the land and cattle of these communities. There began a long period of violence and counter-violence. Small scuffles on either side at first: but gradually, as the pressure of the colonists grew stronger, the scuffles turned into wars. Known as 'Kaffir Wars' in the European records,* these were initially between the colonists (including, later, British troops) and the Nguni peoples along the east bank of the Great Fish River. European histories list nine 'Kaffir Wars' between 1779 and 1877, after which the main thrust turned northward against the Zulu and their subjects in Natal.

These so-called 'Kaffir Wars' belong closely to our subject. The states of these Bantu communities were generally unorganised for regular warfare, whether in defence or offence, before the rise after 1800 of Dingiswayo and then of Shaka who built the Zulu nation. They had no professional troops. They fought by variants of 'call up' and mass levy. Defending themselves against the colonists and British troops, they adopted variants of guerrilla warfare.

The relatively little-known case of Sandile seems directly relevant here.

The 'Kaffir War' of 1850–53 was a big affair in a region then known as

---

* The word Kaffir derived from the Arabic term for a pagan, *kafir*, but was generally used by Europeans or local Dutch to describe all Africans, no matter of what religion. Here is was being used to describe the Xhosa and their neighbours.

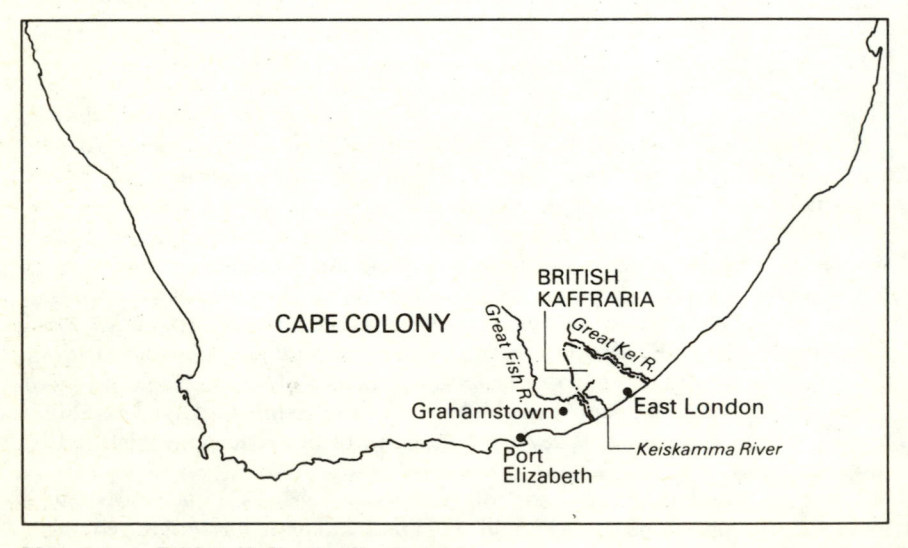

Map 4.1   *British Kaffraria, South Africa.*

British Kaffraria. This was in the far south-east of present South Africa, and bordered on the Kei river. As usual, the roots of the conflict lay in an attempt by the local African inhabitants, Xhosa-speaking people, to reduce or if possible prevent the further spread of white settlement with its accompanying seizure of land and cattle. As was customary in these circumstances, a British 'punitive expedition' was despatched from Europe.

About 500 troops under the British commissioner for Kaffraria, a certain Lt.-Col. Mackinnon, marched off against the local African 'rebel', whose name has come down through the records as Sandile. They expected an easy victory. Tramping along with no care for what Sandile might be up to, they came into a narrow gorge 'where the men could only proceed in single file'. Sandile and his men, well placed in ambush, were waiting for them. Their ambush, 'most resolutely maintained for a considerable period', killed twelve British soldiers before the rest of the 'punitive force' could reach the head of the gorge.

Worse was to follow for the British troops. Some of the police accompanying this force were Africans in British service. These now joined the 'rebels' and took their guns with them. This outraged the colonists. Unreasonably: because, as one of the colonists wrote later, the defectors had 'repeatedly and openly said: "We are willing to follow spoor and catch thieves, but we will never *fight* against our own people"'; and the word 'fight' is underlined in the original. Being asked to do just that, they changed sides; and the war got bigger. Sandile's force, resisting a domination they had never accepted even if the colonists preferred to call them 'rebels', soon numbered some 14 000 men

Fig. 4.2 *A fierce episode in the South African frontier war of 1848, as depicted in a British drawing at the time. Xhosa fighters, probably of Sandile's guerrilla forces, have attacked an encampment of British 'military settlers' as they were called along this frontier of strife. It can be seen that the guerrillas have guns as well as spears.*

25

under arms, many with guns; and nearby peoples who still hesitated might now join them. The colonists had to make their familiar answer. They called for troops from Britain. These came, and the war finally came to an end in 1853 with Sandile's defeat. Disunity on the African side could yield no other outcome.

The European stereotype of this war, as of others like it, gave a picture of disciplined and orderly British troops facing 'tribal hordes'. The actual records show things differently. Sandile's units, attacking the little British forts in Kaffraria, had to face shelling as well as small-arms fire. Only disciplined and well-conducted fighters withstand such bombardment, and continue to advance. Sandile's men did both.

'There were forty-three shells fired from one of the 24-pound howitzers', reported the British commandant of Fort Hare during one such attack, 'and I allow you to guess the loss when the enemy were as close as I describe. . . .' Another British report illustrates the military scene, however strangely some of its detail may read today. 'The number of Kaffirs who attacked the fort', it runs,

> cannot be estimated at less than *five thousand*, nor were they a disorganised multitude, but bodies of regularly marshalled assailants, moving in columns, and protected by clouds of skirmishers.
>
> Previous wars had taught them the deadly effects of shell, and how to avoid them. It is represented that when these were seen whizzing through the air, and the probable place of striking determined, the masses near that spot all fell flat upon the ground, jumping up immediately after the instrument of death had exploded. . . .

These guerrillas, in short, had learned the value of discipline as well as unity. They went their way into defeat, as many before them and more after. But they as surely belonged to the military tradition that would in due course survive beyond defeat.

BEYOND SELF-DEFENCE : TOWARDS NEW NATIONS

Others took the lesson of unity much further. Foremost among them were peoples of the Nguni group in what was to become Natal and Swaziland. Among these there set in a process of conscious nationalism which, as it developed, became qualitatively new.

Historians have disagreed on the reasons for this process. Some have argued that the organisational structure of African life, in this case in Natal, had outgrown its usefulness. Growth of population had induced a competition for grazing land which customary procedures could no longer deal with. If violent rivalry was to be overcome, new forms of unified control were required. Other historians have thought that this competition for land was influenced not by growth of population but by the ever-advancing 'frontier' of white settlement and its seizure of African land and cattle. Perhaps the right answer is a combination of all these explanations. In any case, one thing was evidently clear to the men of those times. As the white 'frontier' pushed forward, the peoples remaining to the north of it were faced by a choice: either they reorganised their communities so as to strengthen their means of self-defence, or they too must accept defeat and subjection.

The facts add their commentary. A paramount chief of some of the Nguni, a man who took the ruler's name of Dingiswayo, set out to unify a series of neighbouring communities. A notable innovator, Dingiswayo proceeded to build a long-service army organised in companies and sections under appointed commanders. He imported muskets from wherever he could buy them. He embarked on a campaign of unification. To Henry Fynn, an Englishman who became his friend, he explained his reasons. He said that 'he wished to do away with the incessant quarrels that occurred among the [Nguni] tribes, because no supreme head was over them to say who was right and who was wrong'. He said that 'it was not the intention of those who came first into the world that there should be several kings equal in power, but that there should be one great king to exercise control over the little ones'. Dingiswayo thought that force would be required, and he used it; but, says Fynn, he proceeded by methods of diplomacy and conciliation so long as these were feasible. He disciplined his troops so that they should indulge in no plunder or wanton destruction.

What Dingiswayo began around 1800 his foremost military commander, Shaka of the Zulus, continued after 1816; with Shaka the unifying design became very clear. By this time the warnings from the south were sharp and many. The third 'Kaffir War' had come in 1799, the fourth in 1812, the fifth in 1818, and each had shoved the frontier of white settlement and expropriation further to the north. Each had hit hard at communities unable to unite. Each had shown the superiority of guns and practised regiments.

Inter-African warfare, so far, had been relatively sparing of bloodshed. As the oral records combine to show, battles were demonstrations of force rather than bloody massacres. Victory went to the stronger side by weight of numbers in the field. Or selected champions might fight it out in front of the assembled multitudes, and the winner would decide the day. Few were killed, wounded were exchanged, there would be compensation for the side that had lost the more. Even the favoured weapon showed as much. The 'sides' lined up and launched long throwing-spears for as long as any man still held one. Shields made sure these spears killed few.

Dingiswayo went beyond such temperate tactics. He introduced muskets with more killing power at greater distance. Shaka went further still. Matching his warfare to the general ferocity now common in European practice, he built a tough army of long-service regiments and spread his power over neighbours, often with terribly destructive consequences. Whether or not from watching Europeans, he changed Zulu methods of warfare. But Shaka did not adopt guns. Instead, he displaced the long throwing-spear with a short stabbing-spear, and taught his men to get to close quarters. He tightened discipline, introduced new formations, and vastly improved their mobility.

These methods were overwhelmingly effective. They crushed all African resistance. They scattered white raiding bands. Many years later, at Isandl-wana, they destroyed a British expeditionary force. Even so, would Shaka have done better with guns? He thought not. They were hard to buy; it was harder still to acquire powder and ball. Besides, he argued to Fynn, the stabbing-spear and hide shield 'were in many ways more advantageous' than guns. 'The shield', he said in Fynn's account,

> if dipped into water previous to an attack, would be sufficient to prevent the effect of a ball fired whilst they were at a distance, and in the interval of loading (by the whites) they (the Zulu regiments) would come up to us at close quarters: we, having no shields, would drop our guns and attempt to run; and, as we could not run as fast as (Shaka's soldiers), we must all inevitably fall into (Zulu) hands. . . .

The method failed in the long run, but it certainly had its power at the time.

Pinned between the hammer of Shaka's regiments and the anvil of white seizure of their land and labour, many local peoples strove to find escape. Onwards from 1820 there developed a period of conflict and confusion, in this far south-eastern region, which became known as *Difaqane*, 'the wars of wandering'. Threatened peoples or fragments of peoples sought to find sanctuary and defend themselves on the Zulu pattern. The Basuto nation emerged in this way; further northward, so did the Swazi.

Among other examples of the same process there was the singular one provided by the white community, initially of Dutch descent, which the British called 'Boers', a Dutch word meaning 'farmers'. Penetrating northward over many years, and reinforced after 1830 by fresh waves of migration, this people evolved its own dialect or *taal*. This was the dialect of Dutch which duly became a language, Afrikaans, the language of the Afrikaner (or Boer) nation, whose sense of national or separate consciousness seems to have emerged in southern Africa at about the same time as the emergence of the Zulu, Basuto, and Swazi nations.

Yet the inner processes in play were not the same. King Moshweshwe of the Basuto, for instance, strove to weld his scattered seSotho-speaking fragments into a unity, a prospective nation, as a means of adjustment to new ideas and opportunities as well as new dangers. He welcomed European missionaries as a source of useful knowledge. He repeatedly avoided war by diplomacy. Among the Afrikaner farming community there were, of course, individuals who saw ahead and tried to move their community into new ideas. But they were not dominant. What dominated that emergent nation was not a forward-looking drive for adjustment to the future but an attempt to stay in the past, to preserve a way of life which depended upon white supremacy and black enslavement.

It was supported by a peculiar variant of Calvinist Christianity. This taught that the Boers, now beginning to think of themselves as the Afrikaner nation, were God's chosen people, while the African peoples whose land and labour they took were 'destined' to be slaves. It was a mythology of extreme racism reinforced by a sense of guilt. However little they might be prepared to admit the fact in public, the Afrikaners knew that a significantly large fraction of their nation were the fruit of unions between Boer farmers and their female slaves. Discrimination by ruling whites against all non-whites in South Africa took shape long ago. Thus behaving, they guaranteed that the northward-shifting 'frontier of settlement' should remain a zone of violent dispossession of African land and labour. This pulled the British after them, for the British were determined to keep the upper hand, and to regulate peace between all contending groups. So, gradually, there evolved a 'lesser contradiction' alongside the basic white–black confrontation: a contradiction, that is, between the Boer drive for independence and the British drive for overall control. This 'lesser contradiction' became explosive after diamonds were found in Griqualand West, and then gold was discovered in rich deposits in the Transvaal, where the Afrikaners had established an independent republic (together with another, that of the Orange Free State, further to the south). War broke out in the early 1880s but was inconclusive in resolving this 'lesser contradiction'. Resuming their drive for overall control of the resources of the region, and powered now by a most aggressive imperialism, the British provoked a major war in 1899.

This Anglo-Afrikaner war was fought for white supremacy, whether of the Boers or the British, in the Transvaal and the Orange Free State, for the British had retained their control of the other two provinces of South Africa, Natal and the Cape Colony. It has a central place in the general history of southern Africa. But it also has a place in the history of guerrilla warfare. Many of the techniques and counter-techniques then evolved were to be repeated and re-adapted in other such wars right down to the 1970s.

COMMANDOS AND CONCENTRATION CAMPS

In 1881 the Boers – or, as we should now call them, the Afrikaners – had astonished themselves as well as the British by defeating strong British regular

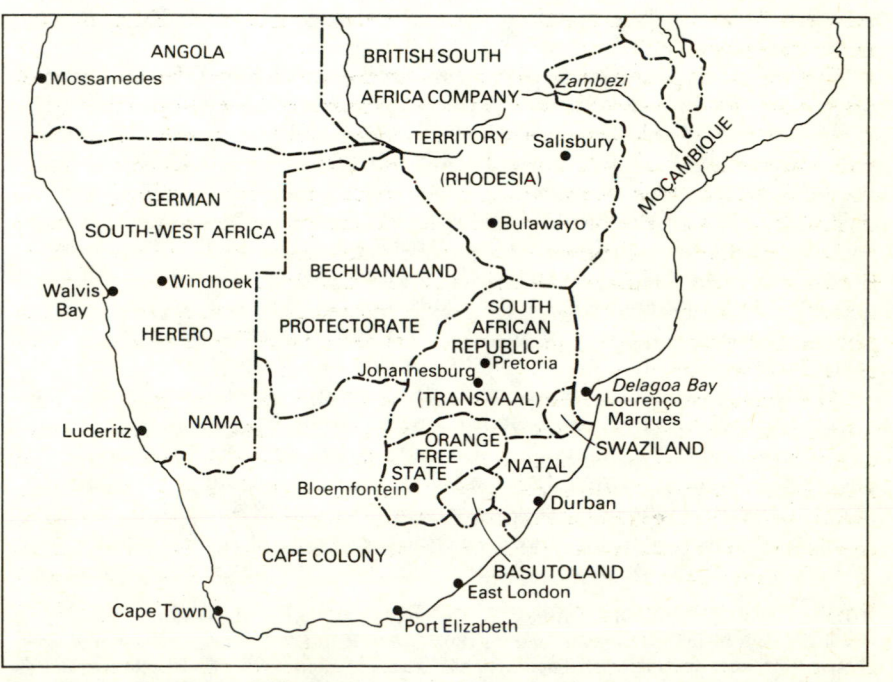

Map 4.2   *Southern Africa at the time of the Anglo-Boer War, 1899–1902.*

forces at Laing's Nek and Majuba. Then came the big mineral finds, and British pressure was renewed.* War began in 1899, initially as the result of a Boer ultimatum provoked by a variety of British probes. It continued until 1902, ending with a Boer defeat which the British, by ensuring that white supremacy should be guaranteed by law, turned into an eventual Afrikaner victory. In this way the British removed the 'lesser contradiction' – sufficiently, at least – so that joint British and Afrikaner exploitation of African land and labour should continue in the future; which it did.

Early successes went to the Afrikaners. Given their mode of settlement – with each man's farm, ideally, being 'out of sight of his neighbour's smoke' – they formed no regular army. Instead, each farmer or burgher took horse and gun and joined a unit of volunteers. These units they called commandos. Of varying size but always great mobility, these commandos consisted of tough riders who were also good marksmen. For a long time they baffled Britain's slow-moving columns of an infantry trained for the wars of an earlier time.

The Afrikaners began with some 85 000 of these armed and mounted burghers organised in many commandos, but capable of joint operations when they had good commanders. Their leaders believed they could fight the British to a stalemate and then, with international diplomatic support (principally, as they hoped, from imperial Germany), force the British to accept the independence of their two republics of the Transvaal and Orange Free State. To that end they embarked at once on forceful operations. These were highly successful in the outset, though difficult to conduct. The burghers proved to be resentful of military discipline, doggedly attached to the ox-drawn wagons which contained their worldly goods but slowed their movements, and always liable to cling to the defence of their own locality at the expense of their neighbours. But they were formidable under their best leaders. These cut off British convoys, attacked unsuspecting British columns, extracted themselves from huge British pincer-movements by skilful use of terrain, and often displayed a stronger morale than that of the imperial forces.

The British, on their side, made huge military errors but persisted. At the height of their imperialist self-assurance, they were ready to expend whatever blood and money victory might demand. They found that it demanded much of both. By the war's last stages, the British had brought some 450 000 troops from the homeland, a scale of effort of the kind not to be seen again in Africa till the Portuguese colonial wars of the 1960s. Besides this force, they also had on their side a very large number of Africans, not only as enrolled or conscripted porters, guides, scouts, and so forth, but also as fighting men.

The initial British and Boer attitude to African involvement was that it should be prevented, the argument being that if the Africans took part in the war this would imply some kind of African share of interest, and might even lead to claims that Africans should have a say in the eventual peace settlement. As it happened, many Africans were determined to fight for one reason or another, chiefly that while they disliked the prospect of British rule they still preferred it to the prospect of Boer rule. By 1902 the British commander

* Diamonds were first located in the Griqualand West in 1867, and the British annexed the diamond fields in 1871. Ten years later, in 1881, British defeats led to British recognition of the Transvaal as an independent Afrikaner republic. Then came the first big gold discoveries of 1884 in the Transvaal.

Kitchener admitted that he had armed some 10 000 Africans and Coloureds, although a British parliamentary opinion put the true number at 30 000. The fact, in any case, was that the British could scarcely have fought the war at all if they had refused African assistance, non-combatant or otherwise. The Boers also accepted or conscripted African assistance, though were more strongly opposed to allowing any of 'their' Africans to carry arms.

It was during the latter part of 1900 that the Boers developed a phase of purely guerrilla warfare, being no longer able to face the British in pitched battles. Hugely outnumbered, the Boer commanders still found ways of preserving a guerrilla initiative, knowing that so long as they held this initiative they could survive, and, in surviving, hope to fight the British to a standstill. The calculation was reasonable. But it failed for two essentially political reasons. One was that they failed to break out of their isolation: no diplomatic or other aid came from outside. The other was that they failed in any form of political warfare, and above all in relation to African opinion.

But before they failed these burghers wrote an epic in the annals of this type of warfare; and one, moreover, that deserves to be studied even by those with every distaste for Boer ideas and policies. Here is one of their best commanders, a guerrilla leader called Christiaan Rudolf de Wet, in a book published immediately after the war, explaining 'to the uninitiated our methods of checking the advance of the enemy':

> The burghers who had the best horses would remain behind any rise or kopje (small hill) they could find in the neighbourhood. When the enemy approached and saw ahead of them two or three hundred burghers they would halt and bring their guns (artillery) to the front. When they had got the guns in position, they would bombard the ridge behind which the burghers were stationed. But as our men had no wish to remain under fire, they would then quietly withdraw out of sight. But the English would continue bombarding the hill, and would send flanking parties to the right and left. Sometimes it would take the English several hours before they could make sure that there were no Boers behind the rise. It was tactics such as the above that gave my burghers, who were handicapped by the condition of their horses, time to retreat.
>
> It sometimes happened, in these rearguard actions, when the position was favourable, that the enemy were led into an ambush, and then they were either captured or sent racing back under our fire to bring up their guns and main force. . . .

Facing such tactics the British generals invented, in their essentials, all those techniques of 'counter-insurgency' which later years would see applied by imperial armies in many countries across the world. After the middle of 1900, unable to destroy de Wet's commandos and their like, they went for the jugular vein of all guerrilla forces: their sources of food, shelter, and civilian information about the enemy. They burned down farms and villages. They destroyed crops and cattle. They seized Afrikaner women and children who had remained at home in undefended farms while their men were fighting in the field, and these they imprisoned in what were called, for the first time, concentration camps. By the end they had taken upwards of 116 000 civilians into these camps, where many of them and many of their children died of fever or famine. And when none of this was enough to destroy the commandos, the British generals proceeded on another plan, and this too would find many copies in later years.* They built a complex grid of blockhouses and wire fencing across the grasslands where the commandos lived and fought, seeking in this way to prevent commando movement so that major British forces could surround and crush them. De Wet wrote of them:

> Erected at intervals varying between a hundred and a thousand metres, depending on the terrain, these blockhouses were sometimes round, sometimes angular, erections. The roofs were always of iron. The walls were pierced with loop-holes four feet from the ground, and from four to six feet from each other. Sometimes stone was used in the construction of these walls at other times iron. . . . Between the blockhouses were fences, made with five strands of barbed wire. Parallel with these was a trench, three feet deep and four to five feet across at the top, but narrower at the

---

* It is always difficult to know the actual origins of this or that method. Thus the Spanish army in their colonial war in Cuba of the 1890s are said to have used 'fortified lines' to contain and isolate Cuban guerrilla forces, and, along with this blockhouse system, to have introduced a *reconcentrado* method by which large numbers of Cubans were driven into 'fortified areas where they died in great numbers'. Were the British commanders aware of these precedents?

Fig. 4.3 *Afrikaner (Boer) 'burghers' gather as volunteers, in 1899, to defend their Transvaal Republic from British invasion. Though the Afrikaner forces began their war by attacking the British in the style of regular warfare, they soon fell back on guerrilla tactics by fast-moving 'commandos' on horseback.*

bottom. Where the material could be procured, there was also a stone wall . . . sometimes there were two lines of fences. . . . There was thus a regular network of wires in the vicinity of the blockhouses – the English seemed to think that the Boer might be netted like a fish. . . .

De Wet and others like him laughed at this attempt to catch them. They proved that they could cross these obstacles more or less as they wished, and called the policy of building blockhouses 'the policy of the *blockhead*'. True or not, the British generals had to move another step towards later times: they adopted the tactics of 'counter-insurgency'. They began to do what they had scorned to do before: fight this elusive enemy with his own methods, by night-marching, by night-attacking, by copying African scouting skills, by training their troops to shoot as marksmen. The 'commandos' of the future were on the scene.

Such methods were combined with weight of numbers, and prevailed in the end. Reduced to some 20 000 fighters, and with the British in occupation of all their towns and large urban settlements, the Afrikaners now discovered that they might be able to save the substance of their cause. This was confirmed in 1902 at the Peace of Vereeniging, but as early as March 1901 the British commander-in-chief, Kitchener, had given an assurance that helped to end Boer resistance. He told the Afrikaner leaders that

As regards the extension of the franchise (the right to vote in subsequent elections) to Kaffirs in the Transvaal and Orange Free State, it is not the intention of His Majesty's Government to give such franchise before representative Government is granted to those colonies, and if then given it will be so limited as to secure the just predominance of the white race. . . .

And so the Afrikaner nation, fighting for a future that should conserve and continue the past, was able to console itself for its losses. Immensely stronger forces had defeated them, but now the British proceeded to give them everything of substance that they had failed to win for themselves. They lost their nominal independence, but they saved a racist system. The real losers were the Africans.

This Afrikaner nation had failed in the political culture and creativeness required to transform a guerrilla war against Britain's imperial armies into a liberation war, such as could yield progress for all the peoples of the region. That is another story. More generally, the nation-building process which was afterwards to become a central feature of the colonial scene proved to be a progressive feature, and, eventually, a liberating feature.

This process of evolving nationalism was long and complex, and belongs to a wider history. Yet we need to follow it in outline, for its stages have much to do with the development of guerrilla warfare.

ABD AL-KADER AND THE DEFENCE OF ALGERIA

There is perhaps no better 'bridge to understanding' between past and present, in the context of this subject, than the French invasion of Algeria and its consequences. In one sense this invasion of the 1830s was simply another chapter in the ancient record of empire building. But in another sense it marked the passage to the values of a different world, the one that we inhabit now.

Much about it belonged to an age that is far away. Of the initial fleet of some 600 vessels which conveyed the French invasion force across the Mediterranean Sea in 1830, a force composed of some 38 000 men and 4 000 horses with all their stores and arms, only six small ships were under steam; all the rest relied on sail. Its commanders were among the best that France could produce; yet most of them were graduates of military academies presided over by the Emperor Napoleon, and one or two of them had served in the campaigns of Napoleon which had ended in 1815. Yet out of this old-fashioned enterprise there came, in due course, a colony of a type not seen before: a colony, very early on, in which the outlines of 20th century colonialism were already manifest.

The Algeria invaded by France was in large degree an independent country, although, in principle and to some extent in practice, it was also a province of the Ottoman Turkish empire. Generally, and in some contrast with their

Fig. 4.4 *The Amir Abd al-Kader, Commander of the Faithful (Amir al-Mumenin) and defender of Algeria against French invasion after 1830. Abd al-Kader proved himself a master at guerrilla warfare, and his memory is honoured in modern Algeria as a great patriot. This portrait shows him in middle-age, after the French had at last overcome the long resistance that he led.*

Tunisian neighbours, the Algerians had resisted Turkish assimilation. Down the years from the original Turkish conquest of the 16th century, there had evolved a sentiment of local sovereignty within this loosely-governed empire. Turkish garrisons occupied most Algerian towns, where they were tolerated by long custom and common religion. But their influence outside the towns was small or absent.

Otherwise the Algerians were Arabs and Berbers of many lineage groups, clans, and divided loyalties, being united by little save living in the same country and by Islam. Did they already form an Algerian nationality? Had they the consciousness of forming an Algerian nation? There is little to make one think so. Yet a new consciousness came out of this old invasion. The challenge of an aggressive French nationalism produced the response of an awakened Algerian nationalism. This was to be the new nationalism, as we shall see later on, which would eventually destroy the new colonialism.

The French expected an easy conquest, and began by making one. They took the ancient city of Algiers with little trouble. They were able to occupy other ports and extend their control to a small zone inland from Algiers. So far, and misleadingly for the French, this was only the defeat of Turkish garrisons grown fat and feeble from years of doing nothing. The real war had yet to come.

It began around the middle of 1832, nearly two years after the arrival of the French. It developed on two fronts. In eastern Algeria the forces of an armed resistance were gathered under a leader called Ahmed Bey. But the resistance which began in western Algeria proved more important. In May of 1832 a resistance force of some 12 000 men was got together near Mascara in the hills south-east of Oran, the chief city-port of western Algeria. In November, preparing for action, the leaders of this force chose a single leader to command them all. This was the celebrated Abd al-Kader, named Amir al-Mumenin (Commander of the Faithful) at this time. Although no more than 24 years old, he at once proved his worth. It is no illusion that makes Algerians of today think of Abd al-Kader as the symbolic founder of their nation.

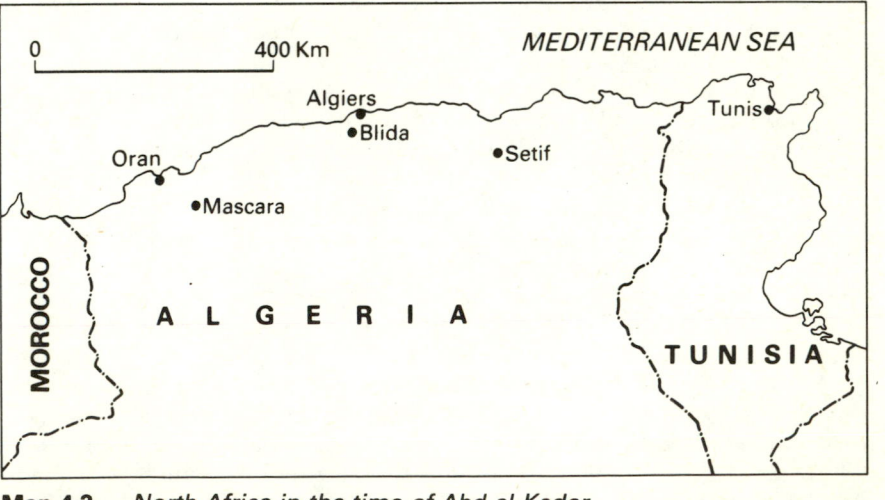

Map 4.3   *North Africa in the time of Abd al-Kader.*

Now the Amir's little army of 1832 was ready to fight and even to accept a single commander; but it was badly organised to fight well. It consisted of volunteers from no fewer than thirty-two clans or lineage groups, many with long-felt enmities between them. Left like that, it could easily fall apart. And this falling apart was likely to be hastened by the prevailing idea of how to fight, which was to go out in a compact body and assault the enemy head-on. This was precisely what the French generals with their many muskets and artillery were hoping the Algerians would do. The Amir had other ideas.

For Abd al-Kader was more than a figure in the old tradition, a man of the past. He was certainly that, being a Commander of the Faithful such as previous centuries had known. But he was also a modernising figure. His mode of warfare shows this best. To begin with, he imposed unity of command right down through his forces. This enabled them, badly to begin with but better as time went on, to carry out combined operations by units in different places. In this and other ways he foreshadowed the future. His standing army of from five to ten thousand men fought by guerrilla tactics against a numerically far stronger enemy; and they fought for nearly ten years with repeated success. The French commander, the Duke of Orleans, summed up their methods after they had taken Blida from his forces. 'They operated', wrote the Duke, 'with small groups of horsemen who moved as fast as mosquitoes in their assaults on French positions . . . denying our army all rest or sleep. . . . Impossible to pin down, they celebrated their victory by taking the town of Blida. . . .'

Mobility, daring, strong local support: these were all elements in the Amir's successes, but good intelligence as well. 'He is well informed on everything', continued the Duke of Orleans. 'He knows just what goes on inside our camps and what our generals are thinking, while they on their side have no idea of what is happening with the Arabs.' But the Amir also matched this partisan warfare by political warfare, constantly playing on French fears and ambitions, repeatedly 'making war as a continuation of politics by other means'; while, at the same time, he promoted the participation of the Algerian clans in a joint effort at building a new administrative and social order in the territories they defended from the French. Such was the innovating drive of this young man, still under thirty, that he was even able to construct workshops capable of making muskets.

From 1832 to 1839 the new Algerian state took shape over most of western and central Algeria, and began to reach eastern Algeria as well. Only then, but especially after 1841, did the tide of war turn against it. By this time the French had sent 100 000 troops across the Mediterranean. They had also installed a commander, Marshal Bugeaud, who had learned about 'counter-insurgency' against the guerrillas of Spain during Napoleon's wars. Bugeaud broke up his dense columns and static garrisons, and sent in strong mobile units against the Amir's forces. Cut off from outside aid by way of Morocco, faced with an outbreak of new disunities on the Algerian side and discouraged by his losses, Abd al-Kader finally gave up in 1847.

Yet in Abd al-Kader and his fifteen-year resistance we already find the dual themes of people's war that will command the liberation struggles of a century later. One theme is armed resistance to an invader, the fight to restore a threatened or a lost independence. The other theme goes further. It demands more than a return to the past. It looks to a different future. Combining to fight invasion, this Algerian resistance of disparate clans and groups can be seen as the founder of a sense of common nationhood, even of a new social order. Defeated and driven underground, this theme of unity and renewal will constantly grow stronger under the pressures of colonial subjection: until, 122 years later, it will acquire maturity in the flames of a new resistance which will not be defeated.

We shall meet this duality of theme and motive all the way down the record of these years. It can be expressed as restoration on the one hand, and as reorganisation on the other: or, later in its development, of reform combined with, and then contrasting with, what is more than reform: what becomes, in structural terms, revolution.

Little more at first than the hint of a possible dynamic, a fragile 'atmosphere of thought and expectation', a far-off glimpse of development, this dual theme of resistance will act as the great lever of cultural change in the period of colonialism. It will bridge the gulf between 'traditional' and 'modern'. It will take hold of all those things the Europeans bring that can be useful, and will transform new ideas of nationalism into new weapons of self-defence.

The stages of this history still require much study. But their outline is sufficiently clear. We can use it as a basis for advance.

THE MAHDIA AND OTHERS

In 1881 a *faqih* of Dongola, far up the Sudanic Nile, declared himself to be the *Mahdi* awaited by Islam, the God-sent leader whose task was to restore the reign of faith and justice and presage the Day of Judgment. This learned man, Muhammad Ahmad ibn Abdullah, was accepted by the Muslims of Sudan. Rather in the manner of Abd al-Kader fifty years before in Algeria, he set about removing the loose colonial control to which the Sudan was then subjected, that of Egypt and its local (sometimes European) governors; and then set about constructing a new state. He brought the wide province of Kordofan quickly under his control, using for this purpose units of Muslim volunteers, *mujahiddin* or 'fighters of holy war'; Darfur and Bahr al-Ghazal provinces followed, while other units pushed the Mahdi's power to the northward.

After the Mahdi's death in 1885 at the age of 44, he was followed by the Khalifa Abdullahi, who built a more consistently organised army and continued to build a new state: the state which was the forerunner of the Sudanese nation of today. But imperialism was now closing in, and the Khalifa's troops were destroyed by the British at the Atbara river (8 April 1898) and finally at Omdurman (1 September 1898).

The case of the Mahdia may seem peripheral to an inquiry into guerrilla warfare, for its troops seldom adopted Abd al-Kader's tactics and were eventually destroyed in a pitched battle against modern firearms. Yet the Mahdia was only one of a whole series of Muslim 'reforming movements', as they have been called, which have revealed this duality of theme discussed above. In one dimension of its ideology and action, the Mahdia did indeed look to the past. It looked above all to that 'golden age' of the Rightly Guided Caliphate which had followed the rise of Islam in the seventh century AD; and the Mahdi himself was held to announce the coming end of man's time on earth. In this respect the Mahdia was 'messianic' or chiliast, and so were its *mujahiddin* with their fervent courage. In another dimension, more clearly under the Khalifa than under the Mahdi himself (for by this time the Mahdi had died and man's time on earth continued), the *mujahiddin* defended a reorganisation of Sudanese society. They looked to a different future in the world they knew, as well as to the promised world of Heaven.

There were many such reforming movements, and all of them had resort to warfare of one kind or another. They had begun a century earlier with the establishment of the Muslim states of Futa Jallon, Bondu and Futa Toro in the western Sudan. They had continued with the *jihad* or 'holy war' of another western Sudanese reformer, al-Hajj Umar; with that of others who followed; with that of Uthman ibn Mohammad known as Dan Fodio, the Learned, and the overlordship of Hausaland established by him and by Mohammed Bello, another Commander of the Faithful. And then they merged, almost imperceptibly, into wars of resistance to European invasion: wars that lie largely outside our field of interest here because they were fought by more or less regular armies using more or less regular tactics, even if, often enough, they also used the tactics of guerrilla warfare. Yet the duality of theme – restoration on one hand, renewal or reorganisation on the other – runs through them all. We need to see this, for it links 'the old tradition' with all those new types of armed resistance, above all guerrilla forms of resistance, which the colonial period would provoke.

Fig. 4.5 *The Mahdi Mohammed Ahmad ibn Abdullah, famous Sudanese leader of the 1880s against foreign rule of the Sudan, who died in 1885 before he could complete his work. He set about uniting the various Muslim peoples of the northern Sudan into a new state with a strong religious loyalty. His work was continued by the Khalifa Abdallahi, but British colonial invasion followed in the 1890s.*

Colonial imperialism, at the end of the 19th century, was at its high tide. New systems of highly productive capitalism in Western Europe had built wealth and power for expansion. This expansion ran into self-defensive warfare by kings and chiefs and their armies. These fought until defeated. Then new responses became necessary. But with kings and chiefs defeated, or set aside, or absorbed into colonial systems, these new responses had generally to come from new sources of protest.

There followed that wide range of responses which compose the history of African rejection of colonial rule: whether by revolts, prophetic movements, evasions, strikes, as well as many forms of accommodation to colonial systems: and then by the development that will eventually win the day, the development of nationalism. More and more strongly, the responses become the work of new class formations which, in turn, are partly the fruit of colonial policies and their impact on rural masses, and, later on, the urban masses. Beginning as the possession of the 'educated few', nationalism will thus find, by the 1950s, a wider audience and following. And this wider following, this mass following, will then give to nationalism the attractive power and influence which, whenever fighting becomes necessary, can and sometimes will transform protest and resistance into higher forms of mass political participation.

But earlier forms occurred in the long colonial period before the Second World War. They are sometimes called 'secondary resistances' in contrast to the still earlier 'primary resistances' which Africans offered to the colonial invasions. So far as the history of armed struggle in an anti-colonial context is concerned, the term has little value. The fact is that invaded peoples continued to resist but within changing forms of resistance. The following chapter offers examples of these changing forms in the pre-Second World War period. These examples have been selected, from a large number of cases, to depict a variety of geographical and other conditions under which Africans were able to develop guerrilla warfare.

CHAPTER FIVE

'NO MISFORTUNES BROKE THEIR SPIRIT'

If resistance was to begin afresh, now that kings and chiefs were defeated, who should organise and lead it? Generally, new forms of armed resistance called for new types of leadership as well as new motives. Men (and sometimes women) from social groups and situations outside the ranks of traditional authority now took the lead, and on behalf of causes very different from the self-defence of this or that traditional authority.

Old kingships had oppressed people, taxed or bullied them, exploited them, enslaved them. Now the resistance to that kind of experience was re-focused, as it were, by the fact that oppression came 'from outside', grew heavier, was applied more widely. Resistance acquired, necessarily, the undertones of a patriotic response, even if the loyalties of modern nationalism had still to develop. Standing outside the ranks of traditional authority, or at least on their margin, new leaders could appeal for new unities. Those who responded to this appeal could identify their struggle with the defence of their own interests: group interests, potential mass-class interests.

This is why the so-called 'secondary resistances', those that began after the invasions had occurred, always had their modernising element, their search for a more or less radical reorganisation of society. This search might be confused or unrealistic. It might take the form of messianic movements promising a Day of Judgment when Justice should return and all wrongs be righted. It might take the form of anti-witchcraft movements concerned with rooting out the sources of this new evil, this colonial rule. It might take many forms.

It might be, or at least begin with, straightforward recourse to counter-violence against the violence of the new systems. Many such examples could be mentioned. There is the famous example of Ndebele and Shona resistance to newly-established white settler rule in what became the British colony of Southern Rhodesia. In the 1830s the Ndebele had migrated from what is now Natal, as a result of the *difaqane*, into Shona lands north of the Limpopo. For years after that, they had regularly pestered the Shona for tribute in cattle and other goods. But this had generally been the violence of neighbouring societies which otherwise lived alongside each other and generally accepted each other's right to self-identity, and cultural freedom, no matter how the shift and drive of history might thrust them into rivalry.

The Ndebele exploited the Shona, but they seldom attempted to eliminate Shona independence or suffocate Shona-speaking culture. And we have seen the same in other cases: for example, in that of the Songhay empire. Most of its constituent peoples were exploited by the Songhay lords and their subordinates, and were visited by punitive expeditions whenever they protested.

Boatbuilders had to provide ferry services. Blacksmiths had to deliver spears or other iron gear. Cultivators had to hand over a proportion of their crops; and every year the Minotaur in Gao took young men and maidens for sale into enslavement. All this belonged to the mode of exploitation which circulated goods and services in those days. But it did not involve the suppression of whole communities. When the Songhay empire fell it was seen that all its constituent peoples had conserved their cultural identity, their command of their local economies, their sense of community and the subjectivities of self-confidence which these gave. They were able to continue with the development of their own history.

The violence of the colonial systems was of a different nature, not only for its scale and ruthlessness, but also, and still more tellingly, in its demand that constituent peoples should lose their own history. Communities should be severed from their roots and die, not because their cattle or other goods were seized by raiding neighbours, but because their land and even themselves were to pass into permanent possession of the colonising power and its settlers. Reacting to this, new unities were found by threatened peoples. In 1896 the Ndebele rose against settlers who had seized their land; a little later the Shona followed suit. Whether or not they followed the same leaders, such as Nehanda and her like, these two peoples fought the same war of self-defence with the same motives. Those of their chiefs or leaders who stayed 'in the past' and refused the challenge were thrust aside, but those who spoke for resistance and unity were followed. And once again, as this resistance continued, the theme of far-reaching social reorganisation made itself heard. A guerrilla war against expropriation became, in its latent outlines, what we have defined as a people's war.

Perhaps still more clearly, the same development occurred nine years later in the German colony of Tanganyika (which passed to British control in 1919). There, in protest against some of the more painful consequences of colonial rule, notably taxation, neighbouring peoples sought and found a unity they had not known before, or thought desirable before. Numbering upwards of one million, perhaps a quarter of Tanganyika's population at that time, these peoples joined together under the symbol of *maji maji*, the god-empowered water through whose acceptance each separate people could join with its neighbours for purposes of self-defence. Thus combined, they opposed their counter-violence to the violence of the colonial system. Fought by guerrilla bands, highly mobile, skilled in their use of terrain, this resistance survived every German effort to destroy it. After two years of fighting with success (from July 1905 to late in 1907), the *maji maji* movement was destroyed only by famine. It is by no means fanciful to see in this new unity the foreshadowing signs of a future nationalism.

Could such resistance occur only in forests or mountains or other such suitable terrain? The *maji maji* fighters had dense bush and complex river systems on their side: were such features necessary to success? Later it was to be argued that they were. But the record shows otherwise. Turning more directly to guerrilla operations, we shall now look at three examples in different types of terrain. They show that terrain was invariably important, but also that it need not be decisive.

JACOB MORENGA : A GUERRILLA GENIUS

The great rising against colonial intrusion and expropriation in Zimbabwe (Southern Rhodesia) during 1896–97 was repeated, scene for bloodstained scene, in Namibia (South West Africa) eight years later. Here the terrain consisted largely of open plains and low rolling hills with little or no woodland cover. This looked unpromising for guerrilla warfare, and was made the more so by the great flanking wastelands of the waterless Kalahari. Yet the Herero and the Nama and their neighbours proved it otherwise. Their ultimate defeat came at the hands of a vastly superior force, but only after two and a half years of fighting.

First, the Herero took to arms in the middle of the country, reacting against their wholesale loss of land and cattle to German settlers and of their freedom to German colonial rule; and then, some nine months later, the Nama to their southward joined in. As usual, the local settlers and their colonial government called for reinforcements from Europe, and these came in large numbers. Still unable to achieve mastery, the Germans turned to other methods. As the German colonial archives demonstrate in great detail, the colonial power introduced all those terrors against civilian populations which a later age would call genocide. Women were hanged and children shot. Wells were poisoned. Great masses of unarmed peoples were herded into the waterless deserts of the east. When all was over, silence reigned. Official German estimates found then that 15 130 Herero remained alive out of a former total of some 80 000 and 9 781 Nama out of about 20 000.

Only a skilled guerrilla leadership able to rely on popular support could have sustained those years of a resistance, fought over open terrain, where food for men and fodder for their horses was always hard to find, and no forests or mountains could offer any shelter. Yet the Herero and the Nama found at least half a dozen guerrilla leaders capable of meeting the challenge of these plains; among them, none was more remarkable than Jacob Morenga.

His story remains to be written from the memory of his own people; almost all that we know of him comes from German and British colonial records. English-language newspapers in the neighbouring Cape Colony of South Africa interviewed him several times during this anti-colonial struggle. They called him the 'black De Wet', the best of the Boer guerrilla leaders whom the British had lately taken so long to beat. It was the most handsome compliment they knew how to pay him.

Morenga joined the Herero rising in the middle of 1904 with a handful of well-horsed Nama volunteers whom he led in initially small attacks on German police posts and army patrols. Here again, in other words, we find the unifying theme of anti-colonial resistance; Morenga was Herero, but Nama accepted his command. Gradually he strengthened his punch, and at Haartebeestmund, in 1905, was able to corner a considerable German force, killing many and forcing the rest to withdraw. Unable to corner him in return, the German command thereupon went over to its policy of outright terror against the civilian population, on whose support 'commandos' like that of Morenga had often to rely for food, shelter, and information.

A German settler who was sickened by what he saw of this policy of terror wrote an article, for which he was arrested by the German authorities, in a South African newspaper. He told of the following incident:

> It happened near Haartebeestmund, where our people arrested fifty women and thirty-eight children, but were unable to get a single word out of them as to the whereabouts of Morenga. I don't know whether it was for this reason, or from the difficulty of carrying prisoners with them, but all of the arrested persons were shot. . . .

There was much testimony to the same effect, and from many sources. Identifying Morenga and others like him as their defenders, these peoples fought alongside him in their own way, and took their sufferings as a price that had to be paid. Well might Morenga have said of them what another famous leader of guerrillas would say nearly seventy years later. Asked in 1971 how his people of Guinea-Bissau could resist the Portuguese colonial system without having any mountains to shelter in, Amílcar Cabral replied in words that went to the heart of the matter: 'Our people', he replied, 'are our mountains.'

Meeting this mass resistance, the German command hesitated. From December 1905 till February 1906, moreover, it ran into supply problems

Fig. 5.1 *After Germany had invaded Namibia some 90 years ago, the Herero and Nama people fought a long guerrilla war in defence of their land and freedom. Some of their commanders, like Jacob Morenga, became famous for their skill and courage. Here is how, at the time, a German artist imagined the desperate and daring action of a handful of Nama fighters faced by far bigger German forces.*

which held up offensive action. Morenga and other guerrilla leaders used this interval to redouble their own effort. The records show they were often successful. Too weak to withstand pitched battles, they relied on speed, evasion and the food which their people continued to give them in spite of all reprisals. Then in March the Germans put in a major offensive sweep, and Morenga with his men had to retreat over the border into the Cape Colony of South Africa. There they camped some nine kilometres from the border on the British side. The Germans followed in 'hot pursuit', killing twenty-three of Morenga's men but failing to kill Morenga himself.

To this German incursion British authorities mumbled no more than an embarrassed protest; and so the Germans made two further incursions. At this point still with some illusions on the score of British friendship, Morenga applied for British protection; but it was not the end of the story. Already two and a half years old, the war continued as before, with some 10 000 German troops unable to master the resistance of very much smaller African forces. Yet weight of numbers and armament gradually told, together with the total absence of any friends abroad. One by one the African commandos under Johannes Christian, Abraham Morris and Simon Kopper were overcome or scattered; but there was still Morenga. Responding to his request for protection against German incursions across the Cape Colony frontier, the British refused to hand him over to the Germans, now clamouring for his head. Instead, they put him into prison. Then, after a year, they let him out again under the condition that he was to be subject to British police control.

Instructed now on the real nature of British intentions, Morenga made his way to a remote region of the frontier and there, as soon as his presence became known, volunteers again began to join him. 'His appearance there', reported a German colonial official to Berlin, 'worked like an electric shock, and right up into the north [that is, the Herero country] we could notice its effect upon the natives. . . .' All recall of German troops to Europe was stopped at once, and a large force was assembled to deal with Morenga. Twelve companies of infantry, three field batteries, four detachments of mountain artillery (although there were no mountains), and four machine-gun sections were sent against him, together with some of the latest 75 mm. cannon received from Germany.

Even the German emperor, Kaiser Wilhelm, took a hand. He ordered his senior man in 'South West' – that is, in Namibia – to put a price of 20 000 marks on Morenga's head, and, in any case, to destroy Morenga and his men 'without mercy'. German civilian administrators on the spot objected to this imperial order on the grounds that they would be better advised to try to negotiate with Morenga, rather than destroy him, something they despaired of being able to achieve. But the German emperor held firm.

Happily for them, the Germans had their British imperial neighbours. Morenga and his men were still on the fringe of British territory, and the British now sent troops to arrest them. To one of their officers, Morenga said that he would in no case surrender to the Germans, but, if compelled, only to a Major Elliot, a British officer whom he knew. Elliot accordingly came up with troops on 20 September 1907, but fighting broke out: Morenga himself, his brother and two nephews, were killed. The Germans knew how lucky they were, as their official records show. For they regarded Morenga as the most skilled opponent whom they had had to face since 1904 when the Herero-

Nama rising had begun. An officer of the German general staff, a certain Captain Bayer, was one of those who generously recognised Morenga's merits. This guerrilla leader, Bayer wrote afterwards,

> by means of criss-cross moves, clever surprise attacks, and, above all, through the influence on his followers of his outstanding personality, prolonged the war and did us incalculable damage. . . . His conduct of the war had something grand about it and in its form was far superior to that of all the other native leaders. Altogether he was an outstanding soldier to whom we as the enemy do not wish to deny our respect,

As with other men of his kind and situation, Morenga has to be seen not as an isolated 'terrorist' or 'adventurist', but as the leader of people who freely gave him their support, bitterly though they had to pay for doing so. How far he should also be seen as a modernising figure, capable of conceiving and leading towards new forms of integration and unity, must remain an open question. He died too soon; and after his death the Germans fastened on 'South West' a colonial grip which nothing could loosen until the German empire had collapsed in Europe. And when that empire had collapsed in Europe its power in 'South West' was taken by a white South African replacement; and this replacement proved, if anything, more repressive than the Germans. Only in the 1970s would the seeds sown by Morenga and his companions begin to foretell a different harvest in Namibia.

REVOLT IN THE GRASSLANDS

The dividing line between 'primary' resistance to invasion, and 'secondary' resistance or revolt after the imposition of colonial control had taken place, is often hard to draw, if only because colonial control often remained little more than nominal, so far as outlying areas were concerned, for years after its proclamation. The real difference lay rather in type of leadership and motive. Somali resistance to British, Italian and Ethiopian colonial control offers a case in point as well as another chapter in the military history of our subject.

During the 1880s and early 1890s, three outside powers were concerned with the partition, between them, of all that part of the Horn of Africa occupied since time beyond memory by Somali clans. No frontiers existed save those accepted – and often disputed – by Somali herdsmen as they moved in seasonal transhumance across plains that reach from the foothills of ancient Abyssinia to the shores of the Indian Ocean. No central authority in this vast country unified the local rule of chiefs or petty kings. When outside powers began to move in, each could deal with or destroy the local authority that it found.

Pursuing this course, the Ethiopian empire-builder Menelik took the old trading hill-town of Harar in 1887 and pushed his troops eastward along the escarpment to Jijiga, an important place for watering and assembling camel caravans in all the western country of the Somali. In the same period, far to the east again, Italian troops landed on the ocean coast, and, after some setbacks, pushed a short way inland. For their part the British, concerned with control of the Red Sea straits of Bab al-Mandeb, were determined to obtain the northern Somali coastland, while remaining well content to support the Italians and the

Ethiopians, both of whom they regarded as convenient junior partners, in sharing out the rest. The Germans, Britain's great rivals in East African partition, were thus excluded; apart from the little enclave at Djibouti, so too were the French.

A number of agreements between the three partitioners fixed on paper the

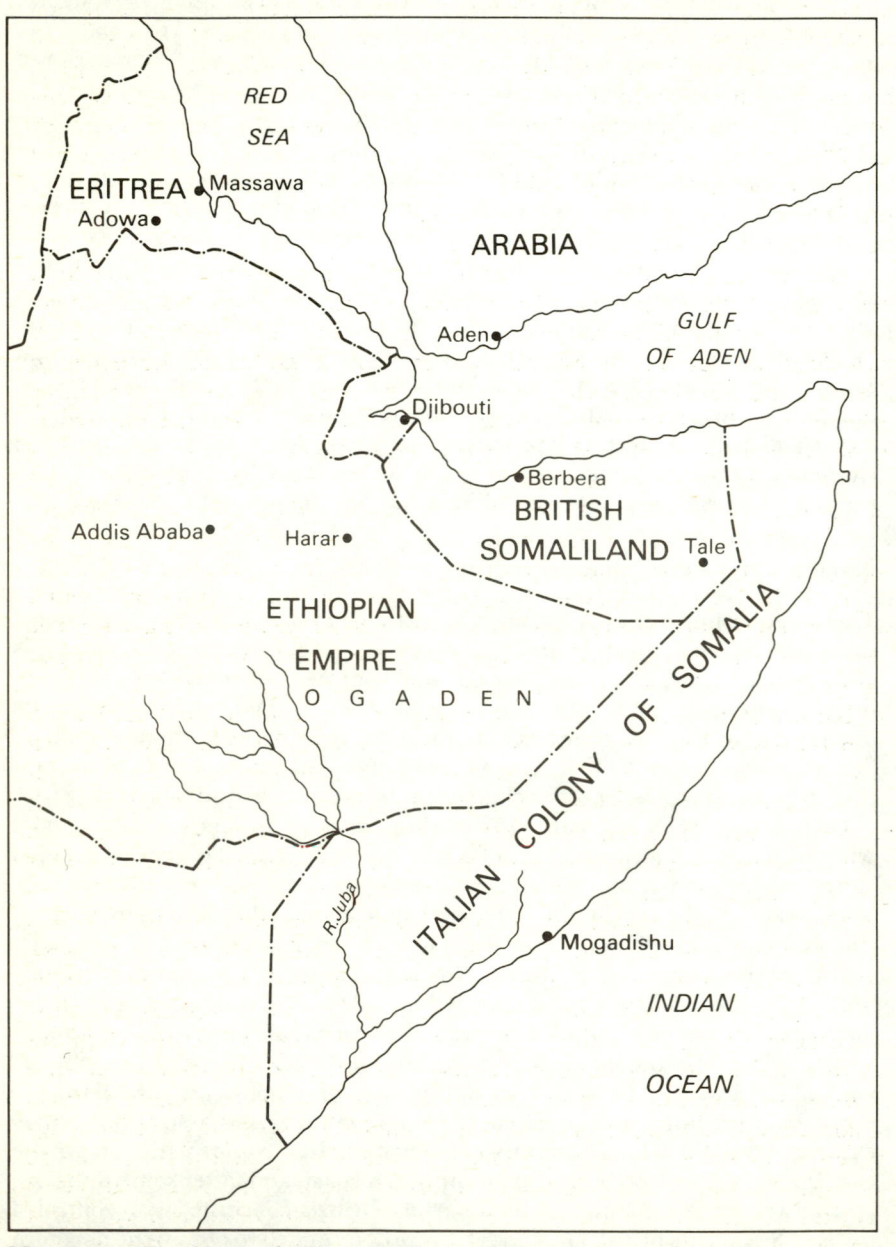

Map 5.1   *The Horn of Africa at the end of the nineteenth century.*

frontiers of a British colony in the north (Somaliland); of an Italian colony in the east and south (Somalia); and of an Ethiopian colony in the west (Ogaden). Later adjustments were made on several occasions, but the partitioners were substantially agreed by 1897 on the frontiers thus drawn. To all this the Somali clans offered repeated resistance but never a united one. They were picked off one by one because they possessed no single focus for combined resistance. At this stage, one may say, there existed among them a sense of Somali community or nationality, of *Somaalinimo* as they themselves called it, but no Somali nation in the sense that would develop later. But there now appeared a focus and a crystalliser of united thinking and action. He emerged in 1899, aged about twenty-five or perhaps a little more but already recognised as a *wadad* or 'spokesman of Islam'. This man, Mohammed Abdille Hasan, proclaimed revolt, at first against the British, with a force of some 5 000 fighters of whom two hundred had guns.

The revolt of the Sayyid Mohammed, as his people came to know him, never gained the support of all the Somali clans. Some stood aside; others joined one or more of the colonial powers against him, with each clan seeking its local advantage. Yet the Sayyid's was certainly an all-Somali movement in the mind and teaching of its leader, and it gathered enough support in all three colonies to endure for twenty-one years. From another angle it may be seen as a Somali equivalent of the Mahdia in the Anglo-Egyptian Sudan, or even as a variant of that whole complex of Islamic resurgence which had begun in the 18th century. For the Sayyid's war evidently combined the idea of *jihad*, of holy war against unbelievers, with the idea of reorganisation for self-defence in the coming world of nation-states. 'The novelty of the Sayyid's movement', Andrzejewski has suggested, 'was the ideal of creating an Islamic state which would give a political entity to the nation which had long been in existence. For he was well enough travelled to know what the colonial powers did to nations not recognised officially as sovereign states'.

Known to themselves and their enemies as the army of the Dervishes, a term borrowed from the Mahdia of a few years earlier, the Sayyid's men proved formidable. They adopted the tactics of high mobility, guerrilla raiding, occasional set battles when the odds were on their side; and they had much success in each. Between 1900 and 1904 the British alone were obliged to mount four campaigns against this army of the Dervishes, but without securing any clear decision.

The Sayyid naturally tried to divide his three enemies, and in 1905 was able to make a separate peace with the Italians. A lull in operations followed, with sporadic but indecisive fighting in Somaliland and Ogaden. By 1910 the British had become reluctant to embark on any further expeditions against this elusive enemy, and withdrew their forces to the coast at Berbera. Exploiting these gains, the Sayyid opened a new chapter in the development of what he now saw, increasingly, as a Somali state which should become a political nation capable of being recognised as such. And in 1913, moving further in this direction, he called on stonemasons from the Yemen, across the straits in southern Arabia, to come and build a fortress for him that should also be a political capital. Based on this central point at Tale, he then developed a network of lesser forts which could dominate much of the inland country.

The Sayyid's fortress at Tale was a political departure from the mobility of guerrilla warfare, but deserves a special mention here in that it was perhaps the most ambitious structure of its kind that any African power south of the Nile valley had ever raised. Its chief feature was a high enclosing wall surmounted by thirteen well-designed fortress-turrets, suitably revetted and arranged for defensive fire; outside this wall there stood three isolated but very strong covering forts. Here the Sayyid established his headquarters and developed his diplomacy in a political war of letters exchanged with his colonial opponents; and from here, as his organisation developed, he maintained a severe discipline aimed at holding firm even against traditional Somali impatience with any 'orders from above'. Left to himself, the Sayyid could now have turned his attention to the development of a unitary Somali state. But he was not left to himself.

The British were willing enough to recognise his military eminence, but not a Somali sovereignty which rejected their own. Sooner or later the Sayyid would have to be eliminated. The effort came the sooner through the influence of British defeats on British prestige. With some 6 000 men under arms, and most with rifles, the Sayyid repeatedly won the day. At Dub Madoba in August 1913 he lost 395 fighting men in a pitched battle with the British, who met the Dervish onslaught with Maxim and other automatic weapons; but the British lost their commander and thirty-four others and were obliged to retreat. In March 1914 the Sayyid's men even raided the British seaboard base of Berbera.

Early in 1914 the British accordingly resumed their policy of occupying the

Fig. 5.2 *One of the longest guerrilla wars of resistance to colonial invasion was fought by Somali clans united under the forceful leadership of the Sayyid Mohammed Abdille Hasan. They had much success, and the Sayyid began to lay the foundations for a future Somali state. In 1913 he called for skilled stonemasons to come from Arabia to build a network of defensive forts, the greatest of which was at Tale, shown here. Tale fort was destroyed by British aerial bombardment in 1920.*

inland country. Their initial operations were almost at once reduced by the enormous distractions of World War One (1914–18). But they persevered, and had much weakened the Sayyid by the end of that war, so that in 1918 he was probably down to few more than a thousand troops. Exhausted by the world war, the British now wanted a quick kill. In 1919 the cabinet in London approved a plan for joint ground and air assault on the Sayyid's strong points. Assisted by bombing from the air, his chief forts were taken from him one by one, finally losing that of Tale itself; and the Sayyid was reduced to flight with a few companions into the mountains of the Arussi country near the head-waters of the Shebelle river. There, abandoned even by these companions, he died in November 1920, more than two decades after raising his standard.

Yet in this example one may again see the relevance of past history to what has come after in our own times. The Sayyid died alone and in defeat; and then, with his resistance beaten down after so many years and the man himself removed by death, 'a proud and liberty-loving people', in the words of one of the Sayyid's British opponents, 'witnessed the subjection of the only represen-tatives of their race who were not prepared to admit allegiance to any of the four alien nations' – for the French, at Djibouti, were now in the partition game as well – 'among whom the Somali country had been parcelled out'. Even so, the passing of the 'Mad Mullah', as the British called the Sayyid with a mixture of astonishment and respect in the light of his stubborn skills against overwhelm-ing force, proved not to be an end but a beginning. That was hard to perceive at the time, but there were some who saw it. For the Sayyid, wrote that same Englishman with a prescience remarkable for as early as 1923, 'in the heads of his fellow-countrymen . . . will live for ever as a national hero'.

And so it has proved to be, for the Sayyid today is venerated by the Somalis as the founder of their nation. Though in many ways a man of the past, he had moved towards a modernising unity beyond the narrow clasp of Somali clannishness. Perhaps it was his very stubbornness that ensured his living influence after death. Faced by colonial powers bent on his destruction, again in the words of that Englishman in 1923,

> he was never apparently tempted to abandon his ideals and come to terms. Even when he seemed to have lost everything but his personal freedom, he scorned and scoffed at the extremely favourable peace terms that were offered him. Instead of seeking comfort and repose for his declining years . . . he preferred to start once more to regain all that he had lost. No misfortune broke his spirit.

REVOLT IN THE HILLS

Just how far the Sayyid's ideas of national unity were perceived by those who fought his long campaigns, or were even clarified in his own mind, will remain controversial. Such ideas came to be expressed more clearly as the colonial enclosures continued. Another guerrilla resistance, this time in the hills, already displayed that same development in the years immediately after the Sayyid's death. This was the revolt of the Amir Abd al-Krim in the hills of northern Morocco. His brief 'Republic of the Rif' was another forecast of the future.

By 1912, when Abd al-Krim was thirty-two, Spain had secured a small sector of northern Morocco, inland from its long-occupied Mediterranean foothold of Melilla. Meanwhile France, infiltrating steadily after 1900, had

Fig. 5.3 *Abd al-Krim al-Kattabi, 'the Learned' was the founder and defender of the Republic of the Rif (1920–26) in northern Morocco. An outstanding pioneer of 'people's war', he matched political vision with military skill, and hoped that his small mountain republic could show how to build a mighty federation in an independent Maghrib (Morocco, Algeria, Tunisia). He and his forces won victories over the Spanish and French colonial armies. They were overwhelmed in the end, but the ideas for which Abd al-Krim fought were not forgotten.*

secured the acceptance by all its rival powers in Europe of a 'right' to occupy and eventually control the rest of Morocco, and the Moroccan sultan had been obliged to accept this too. Morocco was thus divided into a small Spanish 'zone' and a much larger French one. Both rapidly became colonies of direct Spanish or French military rule.

History had long given the Moroccans a sense of community and even of nationhood, although their social structures, like those of the Somali, were embedded in ancient clan or other divisions. They did not take kindly to this new subjection, and showed their resentment of it by countless acts of resistance, whether in the French or Spanish zones. Yet by 1920 it appeared that the colonial powers had everything sufficiently under their control. All that remained was to keep the lid of 'protectorate rule' – in practice, a direct military or police rule – safely fastened down. Having crushed initial risings and 'primary resistances', the colonial powers believed this would be easy, for were they not immeasurably strong? Abd al-Krim shattered their complacency.

As a literate official of the Spanish administration, Abd al-Krim saw reality from the inside. For him, at least, the Spanish were not immeasurably strong. He decided that revolt was not only desirable, but also possible, in that same year of 1920 when the colonial powers, even the Spanish, seemed at the height of their military strength in Africa. He regained his native hills of the Rif, a wild zone of rocks and gorges which reach across the southern part of what was then the Spanish colony; and there he prepared for war. Learning of this, the Spanish army went after him but without success. Meeting his troops in battle at Anual in July 1921, the Spanish suffered a disaster. Though with immensely stronger forces, they were crippled by heavy casualties,* and lost

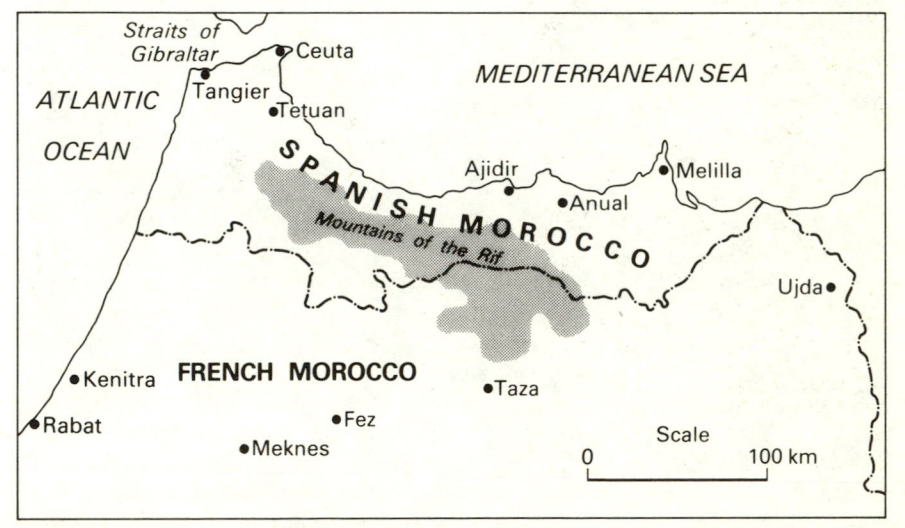

Map 5.2 *French and Spanish Morocco.*

---

* French military sources said that 60 000 Spanish troops met 3 000 Rif fighters, and that Spanish dead left on the field counted between 13 000 and 19 000 men. The Spanish official report listed 13 192 killed.

practically all their weapons, amongst which were some 20 000 rifles and 400 machine-guns.

Thus reinforced, Abd al-Krim swept the Spanish out of about a hundred administrative posts in the Rif, and seized the plains town of Nador. He could now begin to build an independent state. French military sources say that he was able to call on a total of 75 000 fighting men, but never in fact used more than 30 000 and often fewer still. These he organised in units of between 2 000 and 2 500 men commanded by trained and disciplined long-service fighters, many of whom had seen active service in the French armies of World War One. Each of these units, or *mehallas*, was in turn divided into smaller units of a hundred men apiece, and these were again organised in platoons or companies of between twenty-five and fifty men. Devised for a war of high mobility by guerrilla tactics of ambush, night attack, and evasive use of terrain, this stout little army avoided pitched battles or 'set piece' warfare. It had repeated success.

Yet Abd al-Krim's political initiatives are still more interesting. There took shape in the Rif a state whose institutions gave scope to new social groups and forces. What was still usable in the old tradition was merged with innovations whose accent was on equality, unity, and youth. Altogether there

Fig. 5.4 *Men of a guerrilla* mehalla *of Abd al-Krim's fighters, during the war in the Moroccan Rif (1920–26), await their moment to attack a force of Spanish troops. This rare photograph shows the mountain terrain that was used so well by the fighters of the Rif, giving them concealment and the tactical initiative against slow-moving colonial forces marching along valley roads and through narrow passes.*

emerged a striking forecast of what was to happen, at a more mature level, in the liberated zones of future wars of anti-colonial independence. 'There are no privileged classes any more' in the Rif, a French observer concluded in 1925, when this little state was barely four years old, and 'all this may be seen in a determined effort at social levelling and unification'.

Something new was clearly on the scene. Among those who marked it well were specialists of French military intelligence. A confidential report of the French Army's *Deuxième Bureau* reported in that same year of 1925 that

> Abd al-Krim is not a *rogui* (a bandit or warrior leader) competing for the throne. He is not a *mahdi* come to renew Islam. He is a nationalist seeking to liberate the territory. He is a patriot aiming to throw off a foreign yoke.

More could be said to the same effect. Here, beyond question, was a modernising pioneer.

Once in command of the Rif, Abd al-Krim had the realism to perceive that 'enough was enough'. He could take on and beat one colonial power, but not two: the Spanish, but not the French as well. It seems from available sources that the mountain republic he formed in the Rif may have had, in his mind, the character of a forerunner of an eventual Moroccan state. But he limited his war of independence to the Rif, and refrained even from driving the Spanish out of Melilla. And having beaten the Spanish, he sought peace with the French, sending emissaries to their commanders in the ancient city of Fez, asking for French recognition, and repeatedly saying that he did not want war with France.

The French were in two minds about how to reply. Their commanders in Fez were inclined to counsel patience and the granting of at least an unofficial recognition to the Rif republic. But their commander-in-chief, Lyautey, reacted differently to Spanish defeats. He decided to advance his own units from Fez and Taza into the southern foothills of the Rif. Here they clashed with Rif units bent on controlling the same foothills as part of the defensive periphery of their republic. That was in 1924. Reacting to this French move, which he evidently interpreted as a prelude to further French advances, Abd al-Krim was pushed into offensive action. Was it his fatal error? Could he, in fact, have avoided war with France? In any case, offensive action followed.

His units set upon the French and drove them southward to the very gates of Fez and Taza. These decisive towns the French were able to hold only by the last-minute arrival of reinforcements; and how far Lyautey had underestimated Abd al-Krim's army may be seen by French losses in arms. The Rif army took from them some 5 000 rifles, 60 000 grenades, 200 machine-guns and 35 mortars. Beyond all this and their seizures from the Spanish, Abd al-Krim's army now possessed some 250 cannon, taken chiefly from the Spanish, and five aeroplanes, two captured and three delivered (interestingly, by French pilots) after purchase in Algeria. This was still a guerrilla war on the Rif army's side, but by now it was very much a war of modern times as well.

A war of modern times in other ways, too. There occurred in France, and to some extent in Spain, the same political reactions as later wars of independence would provoke. While French public opinion appeared to know little of what was going on, and to care even less, there were those who took an interest. Formed in 1921, the young French communist party and some other left-wingers at once declared support for Abd al-Krim's war of anti-colonial independence, and were as quickly denounced by rightwing and centrist political parties and trends as 'fake internationalists' who were really, as was said at the time, in the service of 'the Russian game'. The actual colonial issue vanished into the whirlpool of European politics. That is a story too complex to be told here, but the upshot, as on later occasions, was never in serious doubt. Their national pride wounded, the colonial powers and the bulk of their public opinion cried out for vengeance.

Huge armies were assembled to the tunes of an outraged patriotism, chiefly in France but also in Spain. These armies eventually totalled 800 000 men, mostly French. In and after August 1925 they were launched in immense waves against the little Rif republic with its twenty or thirty thousand fighters, and by June 1926 these were overwhelmed. Abd al-Krim surrendered rather than continue a war which threatened now to destroy the very people he had sought to defend, and passed into French imprisonment. Deported to the French island of Réunion in the Indian Ocean, he was held there for twenty years. Only in 1947 did the French allow him to leave for Europe, whereupon he jumped ship at Suez and found refuge in Egypt. There he died, in 1963, at the age of 82.

And there, too, he added a characteristic footnote to his own story. In 1954 there began an Algerian war of independence while Morocco, next door, was able to achieve independence in 1956. The king of Morocco and his independent government invited the old warrior to come home with full honours. Abd al-Krim refused, saying that there could be no freedom for him in Morocco so long as Algeria remained unfree. But another and more distant figure had already composed the epitaph that history may award the defender of the Rif. Abd al-Krim, said the Vietnamese leader Ho Chi-minh, was 'a national hero, the forerunner of people's war'.

With Abd al-Krim we have left the 'old tradition', and embarked on a period which has seen its culmination in the liberation wars of recent years.

PART TWO

THE LONG MARCH FOR RESURGENCE

If you want peace, I am also content.
But if you want peace, Go from my country
to your own!

> · Sayyid Mohammed to the colonial
> invaders, Somalia 1904.

The cycle of repression getting ever
tougher, and the rebellion ever stronger,
will ruin all your efforts at pacification

> Germaine Tillion to General Parlange,
> Algeria 1955

CHAPTER SIX

IN THE TOILS

Thus foretold in all the regions of the continent, anti-colonial resistance took its difficult course through colonial years which led to the rise of modern nationalism after 1945. More than before, the phenomena of armed response became intertwined with other responses. Most of these were the reverse of violent. But even when perfectly non-violent, they can still be seen to have responded to the violence of the colonial systems. It seems unlikely that one can begin to understand the responses of colonised peoples unless this dimension of colonial violence is held in mind. Certainly there were many peaceful places and periods, social advances, aspects of useful change: all great episodes have their contradictions. Yet the fact of colonial violence, with its continual provocation of a counter-violence, lay hard upon the heart of the experience.

A few favoured colonies knew little violence once the conquests were made, but most colonies knew much. There were colonial administrators who could look back upon 'their time' as one of peace and tolerance; there were others, and more, who could do nothing of the kind. These spoke rather of the peace they had imposed on 'everlasting tribal warfare', but seldom of the cost in casualties. Admiring audiences at home were asked to sympathise with a thankless 'burden' of ending strife among hapless multitudes who, if left on their own, must for ever scar the wilderness with murder and distress.

Some colonised peoples will have seen matters in much the same light: those, for example, still caught in the violence sown by the slave trade and its consequences. But it is not likely that many did. For the majority, the evidence is rather that the violence of the colonial conquests and of the 'pacifications' which followed were disruptively traumatic: even when the worst was past, its shadow and its threat remained. The hound of that violence might be kennelled, but could always break its chain and leap.

And if this was how they felt, the reason was not of course because pre-colonial Africa had been especially peaceful. On the contrary, it was probably as little peaceful as pre-imperial Europe. A multitude of nationalities and social groupings thrust against each other or developed together in a multitude of frictions. We have looked at a little of that. Yet the violence of the colonial invasions and systems was of a different scale, nature, and duration. It was not the internal violence of peoples and communities who work their way into new forms of society or productive system. It was the external violence of an all-inclusive dispossession: even if, as we know, it varied greatly in intensity and scale.

The colonial illusion of 'everlasting tribal warfare' fed on the facts of counter-violence to the systems, but had seldom anything to say on the violence which provoked that counter-violence. Concerned with realities, secret French intelligence could detect a patriot in Abd al-Krim; French public opinion, for the most part, could speak only of an upstart savage. Good English nationalists might be outraged by the spectacle of 'native rebellion'; few of their leaders ever cared to explain just why the 'natives' had rebelled. Or, if they did explain, they were shouted down. 'I have from the first regarded the rising of the Sudanese against Egypt as a justifiable and honourable revolt', said stout-hearted old Gladstone when speaking of the Mahdia. The Sudanese, he asserted on another occasion, were 'a people rightly struggling to be free'. It made no difference to the outcome. For 'the ready clamour of headlong philanthropists, political party men, and the men who think England humiliated if she ever lets slip an excuse for drawing her sword', in short the public opinion of a rising imperialism, made sure that England drew her sword on this occasion too.

A history of guerrilla wars must in any case stress that these, now, were chiefly a matter of new responses to a new violence. If the peoples of the Zambezi valley took up arms against the Portuguese, as others against other colonial intruders, this was not because warfare had become their natural or preferred condition, or because, left to themselves, they must fail to live in peace. On the contrary, as a Tawara leader explained more than half a century ago:

> The reason is that the Portuguese take our children away every day by force. I pay taxes, my people go to work. Now they send policemen who ravish our women. That is why we are fighting the Portuguese.

If the peoples of southern Tanzania joined in the *maji maji* war against the Germans, it was not because they were in the business of war as a regular thing. On the contrary, as an 18-year-old girl had told a missionary some years before the beginning of the *maji maji* resistance:

> Here at Chiwata there is a court every Wednesday, and many people are beaten and some are imprisoned by order of the German government. But we, who have for so long been used to govern ourselves, find the laws of these Germans very hard, expecially the taxes.

Or, as a man who had been a boy during the rising recalled afterwards on the conditions under which forced cotton-cultivation took place:

> The cultivation of cotton was done by turns. Every village was allotted days on which to cultivate . . . Thus you might be told to work for five or ten days . . . Then after arriving there you all suffered very greatly. Your back and your buttocks were whipped, and there was no rising up once you stooped to dig . . . [He explains that this forced cultivation interfered with every family's own farming, especially in the crucial phases of reaping and replanting.] And during this very period they still wanted you to leave your home . . . That was why people became furious and angry. The work was astonishingly hard . . . but its wages were the whip on one's back and buttocks. And yet he (the German) still wanted us to pay him tax.

After *maji maji* was crushed, the Germans accused its participants of being so backward as not to understand 'the benefits of agriculture'. This same old man recalled that the fighters

> hated the rule which was too cruel. It was not because of agriculture, not at all. If it had been good agriculture which had meaning and profit, who would have given himself up to die?

'Pacification' continued because it had to: partly to put down resistance, but also to extend conquest. After 1903, Tamuno has told us of southern Nigeria, 'a "pacification" programme became a yearly occurrence during the dry season', with each 'campaign' adding to British control. 'Practically the whole of Central and Eastern Provinces of the British protectorate in southern Nigeria', said a provincial commissioner called Bedwell in 1910, 'has been either taken or settled by force of arms'. In 1900, Crowder records, the French committed more than 8 000 troops and a supporting budget of more than one million francs to the further extension of their conquests in West Africa.

These were early exploits. Later ones repeated them. In 1925, for example, the Belgian colonial manual for administrators records an official circular of a year earlier, to this effect:

> Military displays [*promenades* in the circular's discreet language] are among the most effective of the methods that may be used to remove from the natives any will to resist; to induce them to fulfil their legal duties in all fields; and to introduce and sustain among them the habits of work . . . They are, in fact, a use of force which, in spite of their pacific character, is of a nature to impress the native vividly, and to give him a strong notion of our power.

And the circular goes on to reveal, however unintentionally, the nature of the system as it actually worked on the ground. It warns that:

> If supplies of food out of proportion with the inhabitants' resources are demanded of certain villages, or if their inhabitants are pestered by ceaselessly repeated demands for porters [meaning, for the most part, head-portage], they will obviously lose their goodwill and take flight when they hear of soldiers coming. That is why officers entrusted with the task of making a military display must agree their itinerary with the territorial administration in question.

Continuing through the 1920s and early 1930s, these situations of imposed violence were repeated in the later colonial period, and above all during World War Two when the drive for colonial production of food and raw materials was greatly reinforced. There is no way of measuring this growth of colonial violence, whether in the extraction of labour or in the repression of protest. A general impression from the records is that the early 1940s were, if anything, more violent than the 1930s.

A broad history of the colonial period would notice many differences of emphasis and method between the occupying powers. Some were self-confident and relatively rich, and could show a tolerance and even a benevolence that the relatively poor and weak, such as the Portuguese, were unable to afford. Essentially, all the systems sprang from a similar ideology: all of them worked on the assumption that Africans were an inferior humanity. All of them, in short, used racism as an instrument of policy. What it would be immoral to do to other Europeans or their 'equals', it could still be perfectly acceptable to do to Africans.

Beyond this underlying similarity of approach and method, there was another division in colonial policy and structure. This was between colonies where no large or consistent European settlement occurred, and colonies where it did. Violence and corresponding counter-violence were relatively small in the non-settlement colonies, once the conquests and 'pacifications' were complete. But they were relatively great in the second type; and it was in these, as we shall see, that the major examples of anti-colonial counter-violence occurred.

NEW WEAPONS

These major examples need to be considered against their formative background. Part of this was the nature of the new violence. It was more destructive than anything known before. Its weapons ensured that. Aerial bombing was used only after World War One, the earliest effective case, I think, being the bombing of the Sayyid Mohammed's Somali forts in 1920, though Italian bombing of Libyan resistance followed soon after, foretelling the still greater use of Italian bombing against Ethiopian resistance in 1935. But artillery had long been used, becoming much more destructive with the introduction of light fast-firing cannon such as the 75 mm. piece committed against the Herero and Nama after 1904. Yet the real killers of the wars of 'pacification' were machine-guns.

The Gatling was the first of these. Designed by an American inventor, Richard Jordan Gatling, in 1862, this was the best of several hand-cranked machine-guns which came into use during the second half of the 19th century. Claimed to be capable of firing up to 350 rounds per minute, at least if nothing jammed, it was superseded in 1884 by the first fully-automatic gun. Coming just in time for the wars of imperialist partition in Africa, this was the work of another American inventor, Hiram Stevens Maxim. Such was the superiority of the Maxim gun that other inventors tried at once to copy or improve on it, none more successfully than a third American, John M. Browning, whose ingenuity was to father several weapons of this lethal type. But the Maxim was the machine-gun of colonial supremacy. Just how greatly it was relied on led the English poet Hilaire Belloc into a sarcastic dig at British imperial complacency that became famous in its time:

> Whatever happens, we have got
> The Maxim gun, and they have not.

Shot-guns and various forms of ball-firing firearm were of course no strangers. They had been used since the 16th century, and increasingly during the turmoils of the Atlantic slave trade. Huge numbers were spread around the continent by the time of colonial partition. Breech-loading and groove-barrelled rifles, coming in around 1870, were hard to get. When captured, they presented problems of ammunition supply that were usually impossible to solve. Captured machine-guns presented even greater problems; as well as quantities of ammunition, they called for a level of technological knowledge rarely available until after World War One and the return of African soldiers from service in European armies. The Maxim and its kind were always, before that development, the monopoly of the invaders. Even after World War One the same monopoly held firm, except for a few cases (one of which, the war in the Rif, we have noticed). Only after World War Two, with the return of another generation of African soldiers from service in European armies, and with the rise of anti-colonial outside powers, did this position change.

Whether with new weapons or not, the resistances were widely spread; and this, too, forms part of the background to the examples we shall examine. Many of the men who fought in major wars of resistance after 1945 could

Fig. 6.1 *The earliest of machine-guns was the Gatling, named after its American inventor; and here is a drawing of one such gun, evidently 'somewhere in Africa', no doubt because this was where it was much used in the early period of the colonial invasions. But the Gatling was a heavy piece of equipment, and had to be fired by hand-turning a crank. It was soon superseded by somewhat lighter and more automatic machine-guns, of which the most effective in those days was the Maxim, again named after an American inventor.*

remember parents or grandparents who had fought in earlier resistances. Counter-violence had long become an old tradition; now it became a new one too, and began to foreshadow the liberation struggles of the future. A catalogue of such resistances would have to be immensely long. Among others, for example, Pélissier has shown that Angola's record of violence and counter-violence was almost continuous down to the 1930s and even later, so that the major liberation struggles of the 1960s were separated from the last resistances to 'effective occupation' only by a score of years or little more. And the history of anti-colonial risings and upheavals in Mozambique, to go no further, is no less rich in interesting examples.

In Mozambique, for example, Isaacman has listed no fewer than twenty-seven anti-colonial risings, from small to large, between the years 1878 and 1904 alone, not counting another twenty-three revolts on settler-owned plantations or a host of lesser manifestations of the same nature. Leading these were men whose names are still remembered in Mozambique: Kadungure, for example, who took the praise-name of Mapondera, 'he who overcomes the stronghold of his enemy', and who followed his father Gorenjama whose reputation as a warrior in eastern Rhodesia (now Zimbabwe) was already famous in the region. Mapondera opposed the spread of colonial rule throughout the 1890s and was himself overcome only in 1902. Others followed him, notably in the widespread Barue rebellion of 1917, made by a coalition of resisters whose strength was too great for the Portuguese alone, and was defeated in the end only with the aid of mercenaries and British reinforcement. Here, too, we may see a foreshadowing of the future. For this was a coalition of resisters, Isaacman tells us, whose member-peoples were able to 'join in a multi-ethnic mass movement based on a sense of common oppression and African identity', true forerunner of FRELIMO and its companion movements in other colonies of the 1970s.

Across these years the experience was a varied one. Yet it seems unlikely that there was any single colonial year without risings or revolts. Those that were large, almost invariably brought troops from Europe and bloodstained battles. Another example from the Portuguese colonies may at least be mentioned here, for it has otherwise remained little known. In that same year of 1904 when *maji maji* was preparing among the peoples of southern Tanzania, and the Herero went to war against the German dispossessors of their land and cattle, troops were shipped from Portugal to deal with 'dissidence' in southern Angola. This was by the Cuanhama, themselves the relatives of the Ovambo of northern Namibia ('German South West') and therefore neighbours at one remove from the Herero.

On 25 September an advance party of 500 Portuguese troops with two pieces of field artillery was routed by Cuanhama fighters with the loss of 137 white officers and men and 168 African mercenaries. Only in 1915, and this time with an expeditionary force of 11 000 men including 4 000 Portuguese troops, was the colonial power able to recover from disaster, and fasten its rule upon this 'dissident' people. Even then it required a three-day battle and much other fighting. Here again the weapons' imbalance was probably decisive. The Cuanhama had plenty of rifles and appear to have used them well; but the Portuguese had no fewer than sixteen machine-guns.

OLD MOTIVES AND NEW MOTIVES

In all these outbreaks of counter-violence, whether during the two world wars or the twenty years between, the underlying motives emerge as strikingly the same: resentment against this or that act of colonial rule, but also, even though often in a 'secondary' sense, the will to recover a lost independence. However little the colonial power in question might care to recognise the fact, the first motive led directly to the second. What changes, in this respect, is the way in which the will to independence is conceived. For a long time it remains the will to recover the independence of the past. The Cuanhama showed this in their defence against Portuguese intrusion. Many 'secondary resistances' did the same. Most had an essentially similar structure of thought and attitude.

An instructive example is that of the 1916 rising against British power in the Iseyin-Okeiho region of Yorubaland (western Nigeria). Though ostensibly an anti-tax resistance it was inwardly, Atanda has explained, a rising against the colonial system in defence of local institutions of self-rule. Among its specific grievances were opposition to forced labour extracted by the British, the right of women to seek and obtain divorce, and a colonial decision that villages must dig latrines.

Such grievances, from the colonial standpoint, were deplorable signs of 'native' refusal to progress. Forced labour, it was argued, was little more than

Fig. 6.2 *Men of the 1st Northern Nigeria Regiment board a steamer, at Jebba on the river Niger, at the outset of the British campaign of 1901 to crush resistance to colonial rule by the Aro of eastern Nigeria. The Aro fought back, chiefly by guerrilla tactics, and were defeated after only half a year's campaigning in the country east of the Niger Delta. After that the British pushed into northern Igboland, where they met with further resistance until 1910.*

the transfer of customary labour services which had been freely accepted in pre-colonial times: now these services were for the building of roads and other useful things by means of which the blessings of colonial rule could flow more easily. Divorce for civilised (that is, European) women might be very wrong, and worst of all when women asked for it: but if 'native' women in their moral darkness wanted it, then why not let them have it? As for latrines, were they not a very hallmark of progress?

Resistance took shape because these Yoruba conceived matters differently. They pointed out that pre-colonial labour services had been freely given, but had seldom lasted for more than a day or so, while those who gave them were fed by the communities for which they laboured. Colonial forced labour was another thing altogether. To begin with, it was extorted by violence or the threat of violence. Secondly, 'people had to work in gangs on a rotational basis, each gang spending a fortnight at a stretch'. Thirdly, 'no feeding was arranged by the administration. Consequently, the labourers, though unpaid, had to provide for themselves.'

Women's right to divorce scarcely needs argument today. But it was introduced by the British into a Yoruba society which found it disturbing; and it was introduced, moreover, not by an explanatory campaign but by a simple decree from on high. Iseyin husbands suddenly found that any wife could

Fig. 6.3 *'The fight at Ologbo', a typical colonial drawing of the period, showing British troops on their 1897 expedition to take the ancient Nigerian city of Benin. Under British officers, many of the troops were Hausa recruits to the West African Frontier Force, raised initially by the Royal Niger Company and afterwards taken over by colonial government. Here they are shown firing at Benin defenders in the surrounding bush; the power of the machine-gun, of Maxim type, is graphically rendered.*

secure a divorce merely by paying the necessary summons fee. As Atanda records:

> In fact, the administration made a plan to forestall any family interven-
> tion by setting up a place of sanctuary in the head chief's official
> residence for women intending to seek divorce. This was known as the
> *dipomu* (hold-the-post) system. And many men in the Okeiho and Iseyin
> area became horrified by the prospect that on their return from their
> farms after a day's work, they could be welcomed home with the news
> that any of their wives had gone to 'Hold the post'.

It seems that most of the men involved found this decree an act of social upheaval, and they responded accordingly.

The latrine question was another innovation which was resented because it was imposed, but also because its value was not understood. In these ways it was like the vaccination question. The Iseyin objected to vaccination, Atanda explains, 'largely from the feeling among the people that the vaccine looked very much like pus which had been extracted from a swollen sore'. They needed an explanation, in other words, which had not been provided: the requirement to vaccinate apparently 'came down' unexplained. Told in the same way to dig latrines, the Iseyin refused, arguing that they would have to dig them outside or even inside family compounds whereas, by custom, they had looked after this need in the nearby bush. Being then fined for not digging latrines, the Iseyin developed a hatred of the things. So the Iseyin duly went to war against forced labour, divorce, and latrines, and were punished for their wickedness. Their main force walked into British fire-power, including the Maxim gun, and suffered badly. Public executions followed.

There were many such affrays. The famous 'women's riots' in Eastern Nigeria during 1928–30 offer another instructive case. Large numbers of women rose in defiance of colonial rule, attacking government offices and men in government service, chasing chiefs out of sight, looting and burning down court-houses. They carried on like this for two months, and were checked only by military action. A sorely troubled administration then found that its troops had shot and killed fifty-five women and wounded some fifty others. How could this have happened? Various explanations were put forward. The women had followed fanatics; the women had lost their heads; the women were bent on theft. Hearing of these events far away in the Ivory Coast, French officials even 'discovered' that the forces of international com-munism, 'la Troisième Internationale', might have had their finger in the pie.

But the actual reasons why the women revolted, as Ikime and others have explained, were simple to understand if, that is, colonial administration had been in any position to understand them. Taxation of males had begun in Eastern Nigeria two years earlier in 1927. In 1928–29 the word went round that another census was to be held, this time of women. The previous census had heralded the taxing of men; this one, evidently, heralded the taxing of women. Besides, several administrative voices (including those of 'warrant chiefs' appointed by government) had said that 'the Government had ordered (them) to count women and domestic animals "so that they would be taxed"'.

This was believed, and found outrageous. As a witness explained to the inevitable commission of inquiry which followed the disturbances:

> Since the taxing of male adults started, there has been no peace in the land. A lot of men are in bondage in the hands of the chiefs. They pawn themselves in order to get the five shillings to pay their tax. Women have reason to be annoyed. They realise that as their husbands become slaves in order to obtain five shillings to pay their tax, the situation will be worse if women have to pay tax.

Aside from such fears, it was generally held that counting was a cause of death. Counting men might be obnoxious, since it led to taxing them; counting women would be disastrous. The future of the community could be at risk. As one woman said to the commission of inquiry: 'We women are like trees that bear fruit. You should tell us why women who bear seed should be counted'. Far from plotting for red revolution, these Aba women were evidently thinking about sheer survival.

Gradually, as the colonial experience went on, old motives merged with new motives. The recovery of a lost independence led to a wish for more than recovery: for new forms of independence, new freedoms, even new unities. One reason for this was that the colonial experience, however painful, could be singularly instructive. Its very disruptiveness undermined old certitudes, destroyed old complacencies. Besides, being imposed by force, the experience had to be absorbed, and the process of absorption, seeking to extract some good from loss, could be innovating too. There came a range of 'other forms' of resistance to which historians have attached the label of 'accommodation'.

Even where peoples still resisted violently, they were led to question their motives and the reasons for their defeats. Their resistance had an impact on their culture. As the last colonial years would most clearly show, resistance could also be a determinant of cultural change, the maker of a new range of ideas and objectives, even the prelude to a shift from concepts of reform to concepts of revolution.

Onwards from World War Two, above all, a new diversity of ideological development reflected the structural influence of the colonial systems. New social groupings and potential social classes appeared upon the scene. There were colonies in which large numbers of rural people had moved into the production of new crops for export, or else of old crops which became, with colonial demand, more yielding of cash. Such were cocoa and groundnuts, to mention only two. By one or other accommodation to colonial demand, rural society became more complex, different in structure, and generally with a widening gap between those who possessed something and those, more numerous, who possessed nothing. To groups of entrepreneurs increasingly competent in the use of capital for productive purposes, there were counterposed groups of producers who, being migrant or immigrant workers, became increasingly proletarianised: became deprived, that is, of any share of ownership in the process of production.

There were other colonies in which dispossession by extensive European farming settlement or plantations gave rise to a rural impoverishment which could be met, as men believed, only by a 'flight from the land' which they no longer controlled for their own use. There came a vast migration from the country to the towns, which increased enormously during and after World War Two. Whether in one way or another, the Africa of 'the old tradition' became increasingly a lost or nostalgic memory. Old forms of security, old beliefs, old loyalties went increasingly by the board, swept irresistibly away by the colonial hurricanes.

Meeting these dislocations and new structures of interest or opportunity, there were still those who preached a 'return to the past', prophets who foretold that resistance would 'bring back the ancestors', sects that held to a stubborn belief in the value of 'withdrawal or retreat'. After World War Two all these remain upon the scene. Yet, increasingly, they are overtaken by new forms of self-defence.

Trade unions or their prototypes appear in the vast urban jungles that are now so common, sprawling in slums and 'shanty towns' around the periphery of colonial cities. Strikes, demonstrations of protest, a variety of new movements of 'deruralised' opinion occur, become larger, add their impact to a sense of deepening crisis. And now, surging from all this groundswell to a mounting tide, there comes the rise of modern nationalism. It is the greatest of all the forms of self-defensive 'accommodation' to the provocations of colonialism, of European nationalism; and it will give rise to the greatest conflicts.

THE CHALLENGE OF NATIONALISM

The history of this rise of modern nationalism in Africa is rich and complex. A few points of general relevance will be useful here.

Whenever disposed to justify their invasions and conquests, colonising Europeans had said to Africans, if not always in as many words, that peoples deserve to be free in the measure that they are able to be recognised as nations. Being organised only in 'tribes', Africans were not or not yet deserving of freedom. They should therefore cease to be 'tribes' and grow into nations. The few in Africa who accepted that proposition, the pioneering nationalists of 1900 and after, had long preached the same lesson. They had accepted the European model of the nation-state as the necessary pattern, and, broadly, they had accepted the colonial systems as a necessary means of achieving it.*

But for a long time the nationalists preached in vain. The colonial powers would not listen to them. Their own peoples tended to see them as little different from spokesmen for the very systems against which they protested. Then came World War Two and its shattering consequences. In 1941 Britain and the USA agreed to an 'Atlantic Charter' of war aims. Among other things this stated that all subjected peoples should be free, after the war was won, to choose the governments they liked best. Understandably, the British meant to restrict this promise to the 'occupied' or subjected peoples of Europe invaded by Nazi Germany or Fascist Italy. But the Americans, just as understandably, had no interest in upholding the competitive empires of the British and other powers in Africa or Asia. On the contrary, their interest lay in dismantling those empires so that American trade and capital could gain easy access to them. They accordingly insisted that the promise of the Atlantic Charter

* I am telescoping a lengthy development: for a longer analysis, readers may care to turn to my *Africa in Modern History* (1978); us edition entitled *Let Freedom Come* (1978).

should apply to all peoples, including the peoples of colonised Africa. Post-war decolonisation was now firmly on the agenda, even if the colony-owning powers often preferred to insist that it was not.

And decolonisation duly began, at first in India and some other Asian countries, and then in Africa during the 1950s: nationalist pressures ensured as much. These pressures were the outcome of a new and potent convergence of effort. This was a convergence between the 'educated few' who saw in nationalism the only political means of escape from colonialism, and, increasingly, masses of urban and rural people for whom the perspectives of nationalism became a promise of relief from misery. There followed the period of mass nationalist movements and charismatic leaders, combining in a force which soon achieved successes.

In a few colonies, notably in British West Africa, these successes could be scored with a minimal use of counter-violence, or even with none at all. That was partly because these colonies had few or no European settlers. Wherever colonies had many European settlers, no progress could be made without large applications of counter-violence. These added new chapters to the history of guerrilla warfare, as to the history of much else. Generally, the process of decolonisation could never be a peaceful one; but the white-settler colonies were those in which the biggest wars had to be fought.

Yet these were not the only new chapters added to the history of warfare in the period of decolonisation down to the present day. Other and formally 'post-colonial' conflicts have to be taken into account as well. They too were many; and it is easy to see why. For the convergence between the 'educated few' and the 'masses' which had given force to nationalism was soon followed by a divergence.

· Possessing their nation-states, the 'educated few' and all who could share or hope to share their gains found themselves with interests, whether as groups or as individuals, that were no longer the same as the interests of the 'masses'. As a gap in power and privilege between 'the few' and 'the many' appeared and grew wider, the new states became the arena for new upheavals. And in the measure that the 'opposing sides' were now formed in opposing social classes, responding to the formative pressures of economic and social change during the colonial period, there developed a violence and counter-violence which increasingly took the form of class conflict.

This was variously seen in the immediate outcome. In little states greatly subordinate to their former colonial 'metropoles', most obviously in the case of small countries which emerged from direct French colonial rule, the 'educated few' and their local partners were content to do little more than take over the political and economic structures left by the colonising power, and operate these in agreement with the former colonising power or with other such powers. They were content, it has been argued, to act as a 'sub-bourgeoisie' or middle-class of beneficiaries who could one day hope to become an independent bourgeoisie. In this way an 'external governing class' was replaced by an 'internal governing class' whose success, like that of its predecessor, depended on preventing structural change. This was what African critics began to call 'neo-colonialism', or, as others have said, 'the continuation of imperialism by other means'. An old system of dependence was followed by a new system.

The scene varied greatly, but the results were much the same. The democratic intentions of parliamentary rule clashed with the bureaucratic realities of administrative dictatorships formed during the colonial period, but carried over into independence. And matters were further confused by the eruption of old disputes and rivalries which colonial rule had repressed. Now these also burst upon the scene, adding their troubles. Against all this the parliamentary institutions of the 'European model' proved unable to survive. They crashed or decayed beyond recognition, and were as rapidly followed by a wide range of expedients: sometimes by one-party regimes which soon became no-party regimes, sometimes by military governments, sometimes by individual tyrannies.

Yet gradually, in these years, a new trend became apparent. What I have called 'ideas of reform' were followed by what we may term, if with reservations, 'ideas of revolution'. The notion that you could make progress merely by tinkering with the 'European model', adjusting here or readjusting there, was now contested by a different notion. This was that the 'European model' – the model, that is, of a parliamentary system devoted to building an indigenous capitalism – would have to be scrapped in favour of a different model.

This different model would have to be an African development of a non-capitalist system, and eventually of some kind of socialist system. It would have to serve the interests of 'the masses', and not, as in the 'European model', the interests of the 'privileged few'. Onwards from the 1960s, in short, there was the developing concept of an independence controlled by all those groups or social classes which composed the vast majority of any population, and used in their interests. We have, with this, the emergence of 'mass-class' movements and regimes in contrast with 'élite-class' movements and regimes.

That is a simplified picture. Even so, it may state the essentials of a history of 'post-colonial conflict' which is clearly far from ended. Most of its phenomena, perhaps needless to say, were or are inherent to decolonised countries and continents. There could be no easy passage from a long subjection, and it would be naive to judge matters otherwise. What is significant, this being so, were not the monstrous apparitions like Idi Amin and Bedel Bokassa, nor even the persistent intrigue and manipulation by outside powers and interests, but the determined attempt at renewal and then the gradual appearance, here and there, of men and movements capable of dominating the confusion and the violence.

Much of all that belongs to a wider history. But some of it comes directly within our scope, and by no means the least interesting part of it. We now turn, in any case, to the development of guerrilla war in the general period of decolonisation.

CHAPTER SEVEN

THE CONTEST IN THE NORTH

It will be useful to begin with the great insurrections in North Africa, in the Maghrib,* not least because this region has been said to be so divided from the rest of the continent as scarcely to share the same history. Whether in their nature or their development, these insurrections offer further evidence to the contrary. Much the same could be said of Egyptian history in this period of resurgent nationalism.

Set alight in Tunisia during 1952, the flames of war passed rapidly into Morocco and Algeria, and a whole decade was to pass before their embers cooled. What pioneers such as Abd al-Kader and Abd al-Krim had begun was now continued on a scale that involved millions of men and women. Met by colonial repressions of an intensity and recklessness such as an older world had not known, these contests became immensely destructive of lives and human welfare, even of sanity or any tolerance, and drove both sides into depths that spared no wretchedness or evil. Yet those who took part or suffered in this defensive warfare were able, in the end, to extract from it the independence of their countries: of Morocco on 2 March 1956, of Tunisia eighteen days later, and of Algeria, coming last and tested hardest, on 3 July 1962.

AFTER 1945 : THE MAILED FIST

France's political parties emerged from the defeats of World War Two in a mood to make concessions to colonial demands. But the mood was brief, save on the left, and was made briefer still by the influence of oversea settlers and a colonial bureaucracy which meant to restore the substance if not the form of the French empire. Some concessions were granted. Statutory forced labour was abolished. Colonised peoples were enabled to elect a number of representatives to the restored parliament in Paris. Colonial dictatorship had to work with a weakened hand.

But the hand was still a strong one. All real power stayed in Paris. There might be talk of 'federal union'; any talk of independence was stifled or stopped by force. What this could mean was seen in Algeria and Madagascar, the two colonies where claims for independence had been made even before World War Two, as well as in the 'League Mandated Territory' (then a 'UN Trusteeship Territory') of Cameroun. A first clash in Algeria came in May 1945, just as the great war in Europe was ending, and left many thousand dead.† Two

---

* Tunisia, Algeria, Morocco.
† Officially, in this clash of 1945, 103 Europeans and 1 500 Algerians were slain. But French Army sources put the total of Algerians killed at 8 000, while the Algerians themselves claimed that the true total of their dead was 45 000.

years later, in 1947, the same scene was repeated on a larger scale in Madagascar. Insurrection there, affecting a large part of the island, was put down with overwhelming force, and again the toll of African dead went into thousands, even tens of thousands.* A third insurrection, in Cameroun, saw a repetition on a smaller scale in the late 1950s.

As the restored French state grew stronger and more confident, the greatest contest developed in North Africa. Here the French had two 'protectorates', Morocco and Tunisia, each ruled more or less directly by a colonial administration, and a third country, Algeria, with a somewhat different status, most of populated Algeria being regarded as an integral part of France itself. All three had big European settler communities, mostly French, and biggest of all in the old colony of Algeria. In all three countries the acute nationalism of the European communities had proved a stimulus, by 1940, to the emergence of Tunisian, Moroccan and Algerian nationalisms.

These local nationalisms matured rapidly during World War Two. Conceived initially by the 'educated few', they now found reinforcement from masses of urban and then rural people for whom, as elsewhere, nationalism was seen as a promise of escape from poverty and coercion. The end of the war brought the same convergence as elsewhere. The 'protest nationalism' of the educated few was now given force and muscle by the 'social demands' of the masses; and both forms of resistance flowed towards the same objective of winning independence. Given French policy and settler racism, this was going to be hard to get. But no alternative seemed to offer any hope of progress or relief. The question therefore was: how to get it?

TUNISIA AND MOROCCO : THE PRESSURES FROM BELOW

The answer came first from Tunisia, although, as soon grew clear, the same combination of ideas was already at work in Morocco and Algeria. It proved to be guerrilla war.

As far back as the 1920s the educated few in Tunisia – a small commercial and professional grouping linked to a traditional ruling hierarchy – had formed a 'party of constitutional protest'. This was the Destour (Constitution); its very cautious leaders bid for a junior partnership with the French, but nothing came of that. There accordingly evolved during the 1930s a more radical party, the Néo-Destour (New Constitution) with a wider following and less limited demands. Much came of this, but, for the time being, only a stronger colonial repression. Meanwhile, with the development of new social groupings in response to the colonial system, there had emerged a Tunisian trade union movement aimed chiefly at the defence of Tunisian urban wage-workers. Spasmodic combination developed between the nationalists of the Néo-Destour and this trade union movement, but, for a long time, no effective convergence. The two 'bodies' remained apart in their aims and attitudes, as in their standards of living.

Protest developed further with the Great Depression of the early 1930s and its consequences for wage-levels and employment. Responding to this, repression became tougher, but any real confrontation was delayed by World War

* Once again there are no agreed figures of dead. French estimates at the time spoke of 80 000 or 90 000, most of whom died by famine as a consequence of the repression.

Two (1939–45). From 1940 until 1942 Tunisia was ruled by a local colonial bureaucracy loyal to collaboration with the Nazi–Fascist alliance of Germany and Italy. It was then liberated by British and American forces, only to be returned at once to the care of much the same colonial bureaucracy as before. All this was painful, but it stimulated convergence between the nationalists and the masses of the population. This was the convergence which led to a demand for independence.

The French government's response was along familiar lines. Tunisia must remain part of 'greater France'; nothing, essentially, was to be allowed to change. Many now thought that only a stronger pressure could avail to shift the French from their positions. That would have to mean the application of a counter-violence. Partly in prison and partly not, the leaders of the Néo-Destour found this a hard choice. They hesitated and held back. Would not counter-violence inevitably fail against overwhelming French violence? Or, if it succeeded, would it not radicalise the whole nationalist movement and remove the leadership from the hands of the educated few: from those, in short, who saw the future of Tunisia as a nation-state controlled by the educated few?

Their hesitations made little difference. Nationalism had put down roots in wide sectors of the Tunisian people. Towards the end of 1952 small guerrilla bands began to appear in the hills west of the capital. Known as *fellaghas*, or

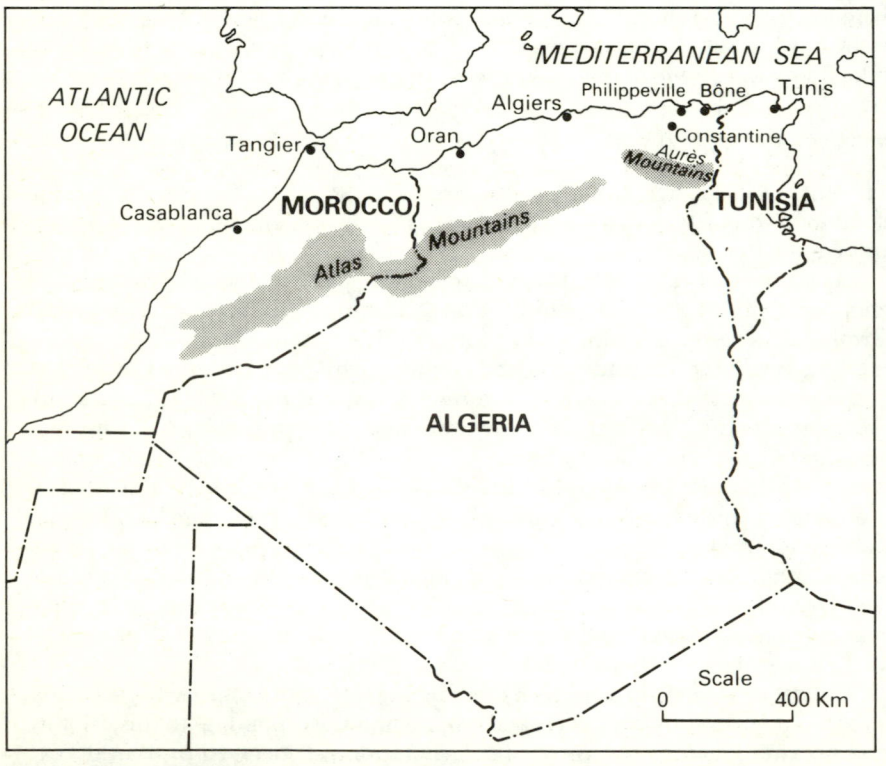

Map 7.1 *North Africa and the Algerian and Moroccan wars of independence.*

'peasants', these unexpected fighters were of diverse social origins, urban as well as rural. Many were peasants from the countryside, but others were urban workers, students, youthful nationalists impatient with the cautious manoeuvrings of the Néo-Destour politicians; and soon they were hundreds strong. By late in 1953 they had spread their insurrection to much of the country, and it was clear that they had popular support. Operating in small bands, ambushing French military transport, attacking police posts, taking advantage of hilly terrain, they obliged the French government to import an army of repression of some 70 000 troops.

Meanwhile, far away in another part of the old French empire, other forms of the same pressure were being applied. This was the period when France was fighting a major colonial war in Vietnam, but without success; and in May 1954 the army of the Vietminh won a decisive victory at Dien Bien-phu, signalling an overall French defeat which began to be ratified in negotiations for French withdrawal in June. And then, nearer home, the beginnings of a similar armed resistance were making their mark in Morocco: at first on a small scale, confined mostly to the towns, and gradually, towards the end of 1954 with a rising tide of clashes in which, between September 1954 and September 1955, sixty-six Europeans and 406 Moroccans lost their lives.

Under these multiple pressures, and with anti-colonial protest growing in France itself, Paris decided to cut its losses in Tunisia and agree to end its 'protectorate' there. The Néo-Destour was re-legalised and its leader, Habib Bourghiba, released from detention in France. The guerrillas in the hills were offered an amnesty if they would stop fighting and hand in their arms. With independence evidently on the way, the guerrillas agreed; by December 1954, some 2 000 had accepted amnesty and handed in their weapons. Local autonomy was granted to Tunisia in April 1955, and independence under Néo-Destourian control eleven months later.

Something of the same pattern of events occurred in Morocco. By 1955 an armed resistance of rank-and-file nationalists in Moroccan towns was joined by a revolt in the countryside. Late on 1 October of that year, marching by night, well-armed commandos of a new force calling itself the 'Army of Liberation of the Muslim Maghrib' burst from those same mountains of the Rif where Abd al-Krim had fought for independence thirty years earlier. Taking the colonial forces by surprise, this Army of Liberation pushed southward into the jagged hills of the Middle Atlas and soon threatened the plains below.

Who were these fighters? They were young nationalists, but evidently more than that. They were also revolutionaries in that they conceived the ends of nationalism as being the unity of the whole Maghrib, and its peoples' liberation from the divisive heritage of pre-colonial as well as colonial history. In the words of a veteran French historian, writing from a prolonged study and experience of North Africa:

> They were fighting both for the independence of Morocco, the first step towards which must be the restoration of the [French-deposed] Sultan Mohammed V, and for the independence of Algeria by giving their support to insurgents in the [western Algerian] region of Oran. In appealing to patriotism and religion, the [Army of Liberation] meant to

win over Moroccan officers and soldiers serving in the French army, and so obtain war-tempered fighters and, even more, arms.

They had considerable success. Faced with it, and with their existing troubles in Vietnam and Tunisia as well as in Algeria, where insurrection began on 1 November 1954, the French decided to cut their losses in Morocco as well. Reluctantly again, their government released Sultan Mohammed V from confinement in an island of the Indian Ocean and restored him to his throne. Early in 1956, France followed the logic of that restoration by conceding Moroccan independence. As in Tunisia, victory for nationalism was the fruit of stubborn political organisation, but it was guerrilla warfare that enabled the fruit to be plucked and held. The educated few had led, but the 'unknown men from below' had overtaken them. It remained for the aftermath of independence to reverse that order of leadership, and put the 'unknown men from below' back into their place.

But now came Algeria.

ALGERIA : THE YOUNG MEN 'CUT THE KNOT'

Algeria repeated the same pattern on a scale of violence and counter-violence that went far beyond anything that Tunisia and Morocco had had to undergo. Here the 'cycle of repression' and its corresponding 'cycle of rebellion' went year by year to ever greater destruction and defiance, horror and heroism, 'pacification' and resistance. Whole countrysides were wrecked. Miseries abounded; and in the end even the French Republic was shaken to its foundations, and France itself threatened with civil war.

Why was this? Essentially, Algeria in 1954 had the same situation as South Africa then and later. With racism as their weapon, a local European community (partly French in origin but entirely so in citizenship) held all effective power, dominating the French administration either directly in Algeria or indirectly through influence in Paris. Discrimination against the 'natives', Arab or Berber in language, was complete. Even elementary education had to be in French. This racism was less systematic than in South Africa, but the consequences were much the same. All but a handful of privileged Algerians were reduced to political, economic and cultural subjection.

Once again a counter-violence was going to be the only way forward. Yet for a long time after 1945 there was very much a question if counter-violence could be applied, or, if applied, could hope for any measure of success. For the harsh repressions of 1945 had left the nationalists in disarray. Broadly, they were as much divided on what to do next as their fellow-nationalists in Tunisia and Morocco. Their established leaders believed that they must continue to play the electoral game in relation to the French parliament in Paris and the local Algerian parliament launched after World War Two. But they could not be unaware of its futility, French 'electoral fraud in Algeria being a State institution', according to Charles-André Julien (well placed to know what he was talking about), and 'considered to be a legitimate means of defending French sovereignty'. Yet most of the established leaders disbelieved in the efficacy, and even in the possibility, of extra-parliamentary action.

Others, 'down the line', saw matters differently. Younger men, as yet perfectly 'unknown men', pressed for extra-parliamentary action on the grounds that parliamentary action would achieve nothing. They partly had their way, if only because it was impossible to stop them. In 1950 the leaders of the most effective and therefore most persecuted Algerian nationalist movement, the MTLD (*Mouvement pour le Triomphe des Libertés Démocratiques*) agreed to allow some of their younger adherents to form a secret 'action wing'. Known as the 'O.S.', *Organisation Secrète*, this had in fact already taken shape in embryo. A year or two earlier, it seems, a handful of young Algerians led by a World War Two veteran called Mohammed Ben Bella had slipped discreetly over the frontier into neighbouring Tunisia with the aim of working out a combined strategy for liberation, much along the lines that would afterwards lead to the 'Army of Liberation' in northern Morocco, and, secondly, of helping their Tunisian comrades to form an 'action wing' of their own. No doubt their influence may have had something to do with the later launching of guerrilla war in Tunisia, as we have seen, in 1952.

Weak though it was, the os was able to foreshadow the coming insurrection with small armed actions similar to those now taking place, on a larger scale, in the urban centres of Morocco. Soon the os had gained some 4 000 adherents while, at the same time, its activities and even its existence were increasingly rejected by the leaders of the MTLD. But as the os grew, so too did its indiscretions. Disaster ensued.

Betrayed to the police – and the whole Algerian experience was to be harassed by betrayals large and small – the central network of the os was destroyed in 1952 with the arrest of some 363 militants, including nearly all its leaders. The setback was enormous; but so, by now, was the bitterness that could absorb it. The bulk of os membership was not taken; new leaders emerged to carry on the work of preparation. Two years later, in March 1954, eleven of these formed a new 'action wing', known this time as CRUA, *Comité Révolutionnaire pour l'Unité et l'Action*; and the appearance of this new word, 'revolutionary', was another sign that the reformist leaders of Algerian nationalism, and the young activists of ex-os and CRUA, were now divided by a gulf both wide and deep.

Was CRUA really formed a little earlier than March 1954? It seems probable from a comparison of evidence but the truth, in any case, will have been that its founders had long believed that fighting would be needed. The latest repression pushed them further. Between April and July 1954 a secret meeting in Algiers took the fateful decision. The date for insurrection was fixed for 1 November of the same year.

So it was to be; and what was to grow into the most testing and terrible of all the great struggles for liberation in these years would end only seven and a half years later. Up through level by level of rising pain, destruction, and abandonment of all restraint, the cycle of repression would be met by the cycle of resistance in a ruthless competition for mastery or survival. When at last it was over, upwards of a million Algerians would have died.* French military losses were to total about 18 000, not all of them Frenchmen, while European civilian casualties are claimed to have totalled 2 788 and another 500 'disappeared'. This small war loss – rather less than the annual rate of those killed on

---

* As usual, casualty figures vary by source. See Horne (Guide to Sources), p. 538, for a résumé of casualties on both sides.

the roads of France – was outmatched on the moral and political side, for the good name of France emerged from this contest with wounds no less terrible for being self-inflicted.

The French of France found it hard to learn, whether they were generals, prime ministers, 'experts', or assorted specialists. Their common opinion at the outset, apart from sections of the actively leftwing, was that this great insurrection had, and could have, no wide popular support, but was merely the work of 'agitators', 'terrorists', and 'adventurers'. If these could be eliminated, a 'grateful' Muslim population would thank France for relieving it of fear and intimidation, and would flock to the arms of Marianne. Continually nourished by the undoubted fact that the French could always find a number of Algerian supporters, this opinion held firm through most of the war. It collapsed before the end, but only in the face of irresistible evidence to the contrary.

Mass support at the outset was diffuse and little organised but still very general. The young men of CRUA proved to be right in believing that they could count on the sympathy, and soon enough on the active participation, of wide urban strata at or near 'the bottom of the heap': as, for example, Algeria's 120 000 small shopkeepers and traders who daily felt the weight of settler racism. To these, it was soon found, were added a part of the Algerian commercial middle class, numbering some 11 000 families owning some 7 000 enterprises, for most of these likewise suffered from settler racism.

Support capable of being transformed into active participation came also from Algeria's urban working class. This was then very small, most skilled jobs being monopolised by Europeans. But alongside it, in the towns, was a large 'floating population' of those who were officially labelled, if they were labelled at all, as being 'unemployed'. These were youngish men, mostly, who had come in from the countryside in search of any kind of living they could find, 'legal' or otherwise, and whose roots were nowhere in particular. Numbering perhaps half a million, these 'unemployed' were to provide the French with instruments and collaborators, but, much more, the insurrection with recruits. They are hard to classify, being neither 'working class' nor 'peasant' but somewhere in between, but they were to be an important factor in the coming war, just as others of their kind would be in other such wars a little later on.

Yet the great vehicle of this insurrection, once it could be got to move, were the rural multitudes, 'the peasantry' in all its many groups and strata from relatively well-off to desperately poor, with the last far more numerous than any other sector of the population. For the bulk of these rural millions, colonialism had been a history of deepening dispossession and deprivation. For years they had suffered in a silence broken only by outbreaks of violent despair. Yet from as early as the 1920s they had sent many sons to find work in France, and these, flung into the lowest levels of French society, had learned bitter lessons and returned to teach what they had learned. It was largely through the influence of these migrant workers that the ideas of nationalism were gradually extended into the Algerian countryside. If the insurrection spoke now of renewal and revolution, it was the teachings of the migrant workers that made these themes both meaningful and real.

By 1954 it was clear that the great vehicle was ready to move. The Yugoslav historian Zdravko Pečar, our best external source on these aspects of the war, has summed up the evidence as the young men of CRUA found it at the time, and saw it afterwards confirmed:

> Led by no party or previously organised front of nationalist parties, the armed uprising of 1954 was the independent work of young patriots. The call to insurrection had been impatiently awaited by the mass of Algerians, and they at once gave an unshakeable support to the armed struggle. The beginning of the insurrection did indeed correspond with 'a further ripening of national consciousness'.

The older nationalist leaders, mostly men of the 'educated few', had hesitated or rejected insurrection. They had not foreseen this 'further ripening' among the mass of Algerians, or understood its process. That was why no party or 'front of parties' prepared the call to fight. So the young men, sure in their belief of winning wide support, 'cut the knot' and began without their veteran leaders. The inner split was already sharp, and it would continue so until the end. As Pečar, who knew many of them well, analysed the situation in 1954:

> The background lay really in a conflict of two generations, or two points of view and conceptions about how best to deal with French colonialism. (Unlike the older men), the younger generation no longer believed in any parliamentary solution. This was really a split between verbal nationalism, incapable of getting beyond words, and action for national liberation which demanded direct pressure to end the colonial system.

One notes again the accent on renewal as well as restoration, on revolution rather than reform: the 'dual accent' of all successful liberation struggles after 1945. For the older nationalists, the aim was to get rid of the French so as to make way for Algerian control of a society which should be, substantially, a continuation and extension of what existed; they were mostly men of middle-class values who wanted, naturally enough, a middle-class republic. But the young men wanted more, and something different. However confusedly, they looked to a republic which should serve the interests of the vast majority; they were not ready to fight for a republic of middle-class values and domination. Many might agree that colonialism would retreat only when the 'knife was at its throat', but that was only half the battle for those who drew the knife. The other half was to build a different society: a democracy of mass participation, not of bourgeois privilege. 'Our revolution', one of its protagonists said a little later, 'is not a means of displacing the present governing oligarchy by a new privileged caste which again will think itself above the law.'

For that purpose, clearly, a political base had to be found to accommodate many standpoints, individual or collective. A 'tight core' of tried leaders devoted to the dual objectives of decolonisation and revolution might prepare and begin and afterwards conduct the struggle. Indeed, there was evidently no other way in which the challenge could be met; and other liberation struggles would confirm the same necessity. But this tight core must be embedded and embodied in a broad fabric of multi-form support and participation. If no front of unity existed, it was vital to invent one. CRUA was the core, but CRUA was not enough.

The problem was resolved at a secret meeting in the Swiss city of Berne during July 1954. Meeting there in a small hotel whose proprietor, perhaps guessing they were open to that kind of blackmail, stung them for double payment which they could ill afford, Ben Bella and some others decided to form the Algerian Front of National Liberation (afterwards known universally by its French initials, FLN) and the Algerian Army of National Liberation (ALN). With insurrection coming, they further decided to set up a liaison and supply committee in Cairo where they now had firm friends, thanks to the Egyptian young officers' *coup* of 1952 and the emergence of Gamal-Abdel Nasser. Being already on good terms with Nasser and his colleagues, Ben Bella was placed in charge of this committee, whose task was to ensure external sources of supply and a means of making external propaganda. A little later, with Tunisian and Moroccan independence during 1956, links with external sources of support could be extended and multiplied; all these 'external links' were to be of great importance.

With these and other preparations, the die was cast. Its stamp upon events, when it duly came, was both hard and sustained.

INSURRECTION

The glinting gorges of the Aurès mountains of eastern Algeria were the stronghold chosen for the rising to begin. Issuing from there, on 1 November 1954, some 400 fighters with about 300 Italian rifles obtained several years earlier from armouries left around North Africa after World War Two, a few grenades, some pistols, passed at once to action.

They declared the insurrection not in the name of CRUA, which now disappeared as a name though not as a directing leadership, but in that of the FLN, appealing to all Algerian patriots of whatever social class or political preference. Their action burst on the country like a thunderclap whose warnings had been heard but whose roar was not expected. The French administration was taken by surprise, but so was its police and army, just as were the bulk of European settlers and all the existing political parties, including a (largely white) Algerian communist party, which, like the others, now hastened to condemn the insurrection as an irresponsible adventure which was bound to fail. Yet it rapidly grew clear that the insurrection had come to stay.

The enormous confrontations that followed may be summarised in several connected phases (see map on p. 72).

From November 1954 till the end of 1956 the insurrection spread slowly at first, but with a gathering momentum. Two opposing trends marked this initial phase. On their side, the insurrectionaries formed small fighting groups which operated from mountain bases in the eastern, central and western regions: in all those regions, that is, which lie to the north of the vast Saharan wastes which run on southward to the borders of Niger and Mali. Relying at this stage chiefly on the capture of arms and ammunition from police and army posts, these small units improved their strike-power, learned guerrilla tactics, and brought rural areas under their control or influence. They found that nearly everywhere they could count on peasant backing and could turn this into participation: levies of young volunteers, still mostly male at this stage, rallied to their ranks.

The French, for their part, began by expecting an early end to this revolt. I myself recall being assured by the prefect of the great maritime city of Oran, almost a year after the rising had begun, that it was 'practically over'. Even my own observations, superficial though these necessarily were, argued that he was wrong. Gradually, the French had to adjust to the fact that they were in for a long war, and were going to find it hard to win. But for the moment, in this initial phase, they did little more than bring in troops from France in the belief that they could suffocate the insurrection rather as one kills a fire by throwing a blanket over it.

The proof that more was going to be required came in August 1955, long before majority opinion in France had swallowed the fact. The ALN now showed that it had developed to the point where it could mount a combined offensive aimed at seizing control of a large piece of territory. This was in the region north of the eastern city of Constantine, and especially in the Colo 'peninsula' around the port of Philippeville. Having cut off this port from access by land, ALN units pushed the French out of adjacent areas. It was a smart defeat for the colonial forces, and it stung. From now onwards there set in that steady degradation which an admirable French patriot, Germaine Tillion, defined so well to General Parlange: 'the cycle of repression getting

Fig. 7.1 *Taken inside Algeria by the Yugoslav historian Pečar, during the long war for independence (1954–62), this shows guerrilla fighters of the 'first* wilaya' *or military district. They are typical, in appearance, of the men who fought in strong and well-equipped mobile forces developed by the Algerian army of liberation for tactical operation across wide areas. The man on the left seems to be a political commissar, for he carries a pistol instead of a rifle, and has a radio receiver to keep him up with the news.*

ever tougher, and the rebellion ever stronger, will ruin all your efforts at pacification'. Many on the French side saw and said that this was true, but their protests made no difference.

Massacres began again. Outraged by ALN success, French arms were turned against civilians. The official French figure of civilians killed at this time was 1 500; Algerian eye-witnesses have spoken of more than 15 000. Now, too, came the turn of 'dirty tricks'. Many assassinations began, on one side as on the other. The ALN lost Ben Bulaid, one of its leaders, by the explosion of a bomb placed in a radio-transmitting set 'planted' by a special French unit. Yussef Zigut, who had played a major part in the rising north of Constantine, appears to have died in much the same way.

As Tillion foretold, wild reprisals against civilian peasants or townspeople served only to strengthen the insurrection. By August 1956, having developed a civilian network of self-government in liberated or semi-liberated zones, the FLN had acquired weight and substance. It could count on some sixty-four organised sectors in the Kabyle mountains alone, and each of these, with comparable sectors elsewhere, supported its own fighting units. How many were these? Again the figures vary; but a reliable estimate suggests that from August 1956 until the middle of 1958 the ALN had some 15 000 armed and organised fighters, with a reserve of perhaps 60 000 men (and now, too, with women volunteers as well) who were ready to join as arms became available and more fighters were needed. The French, as it happens, put the active total higher, usually in this period at some 20 000 ALN fighters. Against them, by this time, the French had some 200 000 troops, mostly conscripts from France, spread around the country in a number of large garrisons and some 500 military posts. This was still the 'blanket technique' of stifling insurrection.

The military gains of the ALN were paralleled by gains for the FLN, its political embodiment. New political structures of self-rule began to take shape in ALN-controlled zones. Committees of peasants began to take over local government. Countless 'unknown men' – and, increasingly as the war went on, many 'unknown women' as well – emerged from this process of self-identification with national struggle. The 'ripening of political consciousness' among wide masses of people was carried further. This was the phase in which the Algerian nation, as Pečar, always a perceptive observer, noted at the time, was 'in full creation of itself': the phase, in short, when revolution began to gain on mere resistance.

Active participation in its self-defence now began to give this people, so long abused and beaten down in its own esteem and confidence, a new grip on the present and a vision of the future. So far as one may judge from copious evidence, this 'radicalisation' of the rising came less from any conscious programme sponsored by the FLN, even if a programme was now on the scene, as from the vivid and acutely democratic process of fighting and supporting the fight. Other liberation wars, as we shall see, were to produce the same effect.

A second phase had opened late in 1956. Bringing further successes for the FLN/ALN, it also meted out some sore defeats; and it ended with a prospect of Algerian disaster. It began with what became known as 'the battle of Algiers'. Here the governing idea was to attack the colonial power and its settler fortress in the greatest of Algerian cities, and to prove that the insurrection was more than a 'battle in the bush'. Another object was to relieve pressure on units in the hills. Having infiltrated fighting men and raised support among the Algerian population of Algiers, urban war was declared. The ensuing contest went on for weeks with growing French reprisals by bombing, street shooting, and the maltreatment and eventually systematic torture of prisoners. But the odds were on the French side. By September 1956 the Algerians had clearly lost this savage confrontation.

Was the 'battle of Algiers' a mistake? Opinions differed then, and have differed since. FLN leaders who denied it was a mistake held that it was well worth while. It proved to the French that urban Algerians were as much for independence as were rural Algerians. It brought great propagandist gains and corresponding political gains, for the 'battle of Algiers' undoubtedly thrust this war of independence on the attention of the outside world. Nothing could have been more instructive and dramatic than this spectacle, watched by the world's press, of a hungry and ill-armed or even unarmed city population pitting itself against some of the toughest regiments of the French army and their apparatus of repression.

Others disagreed. Ben Bella himself denounced the decision to fight in the city as a catastrophe, and he was far from being alone in this. It cost the lives of some of the FLN's most audacious militants; in the end, it seems, no fewer than 5 000 Algerians died in the battle. Still more serious, it deprived the whole insurrection of its internal leadership, at the top, at the very moment when that leadership was most required. Driven out of Algiers, this leadership fled the city and made its way across the Tunisian border. Established there in Tunis or neighbouring camps, it was soon bogged down in political in-fighting and personal intrigue; many losses were to come from this.

There was worse too. From this exodus of top leaders another destructive consequence followed. Command of the insurrection had been divided, operationally, into six regions or *wilayet*. So long as the top leadership remained 'inside', and therefore in fairly regular if not always easy contact with the *wilayet*, unity of action and policy could generally be achieved. Once this leadership was 'outside', each command tended more and more to do as it thought best without reference to the centre of command or even to neighbouring *wilayet*. This fission of authority and control was then found to have played into the still more divisive hands of an old habit and attitude of provincial 'regionalism' or 'clan-ism' well known in Algerian history. A hundred years earlier it had eventually frustrated the unifying achievements of Abd al-Kader. Now it bade fair to destroy the FLN and its army. The unifying politics of armed struggle began to decay into the military 'commandism' of this or that local chieftain. The damage was considerable, and French action now increased it.

A BITTER WAR OF LIBERATION

Divisiveness was still at an early stage. Even though established 'outside' in Tunisia, the top leadership could still have asserted its authority and unity if it could have stayed in touch with the 'inside' by regular couriers and supply columns. But now France's generals began to draw conclusions from their failures since 1954.

In September 1957 the French command embarked on a systematic attempt to cut off the 'outside' entirely from the 'inside'. To that end they built a continuous electrified fence of barbed wire, powered with a lethal 3 000 volts, along the northern sector of the Tunisian–Algerian frontier, though west of it by a distance varying between 70 and 100 kms. Between fence and frontier they sowed some 900 000 landmines and ordered their troops along the barrier to shoot at anyone who tried to cross. Meanwhile the 'outside' leadership suffered another loss when Ben Bella and other leaders were hijacked in a Moroccan plane taking them from Morocco to Tunisia, and stowed away in a French jail.

The fence proved a tough obstacle. Picked units and couriers got through it or crossed the frontier south of it, but units carrying supplies into Algeria had a very hard time. Onward from 1957, moreover, the French command developed new tactics. Paratroopers began to be committed by helicopter to anti-guerrilla operations in the bush. Borrowing on British tactics developed earlier in Malaya or, earlier still, in the Anglo-Boer war, the French undertook systematic efforts to isolate ALN units from their supporting population.

Fig. 7.2 *High-explosive and napalm bombing were much used by the French during the Algerian war, as by other colonial forces in other such wars, in order to destroy forest cover of value to liberation fighters. Here, in one of Pečar's unique photos of about 1958, we see guerrillas of the Algerian army of liberation on the move through bombed woodlands. Huge forest areas were blasted or napalmed in this way.*

Villagers were rounded up and driven into 'centres of concentration'. Soon enough, a million people had been wrenched from their homes.

Sorely hit, ALN units were driven back on small actions by small groups. Much liberated territory was lost. Supplies ran short. They still held the initiative, but only just, and now they had to face the darkest time of all. Charles de Gaulle had come back into power in France and was eager for an end to a war that was straining French unity, and French resources, to a point that could become intolerable. He sent out a new commander, General Maurice Challe, with orders to finish it off. Challe proved very effective. With more than half a million French troops at his disposal he went over to highly mobile warfare in the bush whereby 'search and destroy' commandos were backed by a 'general reserve': once an ALN unit or units could be cornered by 'search and destroy' commandos, the 'general reserve' was rushed into action with an overwhelming force. At the same time Challe built another electrified fence right down the Algerian–Tunisian frontier, and backed it with powerful patrols.

Bereft of their top leadership, harassed by appalling weather as the snows of winter came, and hunted unceasingly by Challe's multitudes of well-fed troops, the fighters of the ALN were now close to defeat. If they could still survive it was thanks only to the limitless self-sacrifice of the people upon whom they depended, as well as to their ruthlessness in killing those individuals who betrayed. All pity was gone by now, on either side; and many betrayed. Yet they were still a small minority, for, as one of the FLN leaders remarked to an English historian, 'the base of the pyramid always held firm'.

Pečar has recorded the memories of those who fought through these fearful months. Kabylia, for example, was one region among several selected for a 'saturation offensive'; it began in July 1959 and continued with little remission until March 1960. A Kabyle commander of the ALN, Colonel Mohand al-Hadj, has told the story from the Algerian side:

> The enemy used any and every means: killing, torturing, the burning down of property, beating people up so as to break their morale. For months people were forbidden even to go out of their houses. They could relieve their hunger only at the risk of death. If anyone went ten steps outside house or village they were at once shot down. And if the 'heroic' French soldiers showed fatigue or reluctance, at once their officers gave them some means of recreation so that they could recover themselves. For weren't they in a conquered country? Why should they hold back? Quickly then the population of a village would be gathered with the help of blows from rifle butts or kicks, the men would be divided from the women, and a target thus provided . . .
>
> Our national liberation army lived a difficult life. Enemy units searched all our woods, occupied every position of advantage . . . So that while we manoeuvred by day, at night we had to go in search of food. That was when the enemy installed his ambushes round villages. And if we still held out against the French, we can only thank the support our people gave us. Thanks to that, and above all to the families of our fighters who sacrificed themselves day by day to keep in contact with us,

we were able to get food and information on the enemy's whereabouts and intentions.

Another offensive of the same kind lasted for even longer, for no less than thirteen months, in the Colo 'peninsula' of Philippeville, one of the ALN's earliest liberated zones. Another local commander who endured it, Captain Abdelkader Laribi, recalled two years after independence that:

the French, living in the woods with us, were determined to stop us from making any move or action. At first we counter-attacked them, but after four months we were no longer capable of that. We hid our wounded in shelters, but the French brought whole battalions to burn the vegetation that hid our shelters . . . Towards the end we had nothing left to eat, and so we followed French columns and gathered the waste food they threw away. But then they realised what we were doing, and buried their waste food . . . For us there was nothing left but to eat grass, but then they drove us into places where there was no grass . . . For each of our rifles we had left only eight rounds, and a little more for our machine-guns . . . Their ambushes cost us dear, as did their marksmen in helicopters hovering over us . . . And then they began to burn down whole forests, leaving us only scattered hilltops. And finally they burned those too, surrounding them and shooting to kill everything that tried to save itself, whether animals or human beings.

Meanwhile, 'outside' in Tunisia and Morocco, the FLN leadership had transformed itself into the provisional government of an independent Algerian republic and begun to build a regular army. Under the command of Colonel Houari Boumédienne, this took shape as a tough and well-disciplined force. But between it and the fighters of the interior stood the electrified fences and their million or so landmines with French troops behind these. Heroic efforts were made to get through with supplies. Most failed, and an effort which partially succeeded shows why. In February 1960, while Challe's 'saturation offensives' were in full swing against every zone of ALN strength in the interior, a column under Ahmed ben Sherif fought its way through the fences from Tunisia, losing sixty dead in the process.

Exhausted and without food, the survivors marched straight into a French offensive sweep. They managed to evade this and continued into the district of Bône where, they believed, they would find peasants who would feed and shelter them. What they found, instead, were incinerated villages and shattered homes; all the inhabitants had been driven away into 'camps'. At last they came upon an ALN unit and knew that the insurrection still lived. Taken prisoner with their ammunition exhausted in the following October, ten months after crossing from Tunisia, the survivors were shot by the French, excepting only ben Sherif. He was brought before a military court and sentenced to death. Yet the war was now entering its last phase; execution of the sentence was delayed and then cancelled. Ben Sherif was the only one of all his company who survived, and even this by something of a miracle.

POLITICS DECIDE

The French now had to absorb the central lesson of successful liberation war: that military victory over liberation forces is still defeat unless it is accompanied by political victory. With 700 000 troops in the field by 1960, the French had fought the ALN to a standstill and commanded the battlefield. But 'the base of the pyramid' continued to hold firm: morally and politically, the vast majority of Algerians remained true to their independence struggle and its leadership. A million or more peasants in the bush might be in 'centres of concentration' and countless others browbeaten or exhausted; but now, as if to prove that none of this could count in the end, new and massive demonstrations of support for the FLN were somehow organised inside the cities.

De Gaulle had already reached the view, as his memoirs show, that the war would have to be ended by negotiation with the FLN, or rather with its provisional government in Tunis. In June 1959 he proposed a ceasefire, and an Algerian delegation came to France to discuss what he had to offer. This turned out to be very little: if the Algerians would stop fighting there could be talks about the future, possibly some form of federation in which the Algerians might enjoy local autonomy within the French system. Naturally they rejected this, and the war continued: bitterly, as we have seen, but without Algerian political defeat. Then, at the end of 1960, there came what Alistair Horne has rightly termed another turning point. Massively, the Algerians of Algiers demonstrated for independence. Two other turning points followed in April 1961. A revolt by European settlers in Algeria won the backing of French generals who attempted a *coup d'état*, which failed. Secondly, de Gaulle reopened negotiations with the Algerian government, and these, while indecisive, continued. Reacting to these negotiations, extremist settlers organised in a terrorist group called the OAS, *Organisation de l'Armée Secrète*, began a campaign of bombings in France as well as in Algeria. It was very bloody:

> In less than a year the OAS had killed 2 360 people in Algeria, and wounded another 5 418 according to the calculations of Vitalis Cross; in the Algiers zone alone their activities over the last six months of the war had claimed *three times as many civilian victims* as had the FLN from the beginning of 1956 onwards: i.e. including the Battle of Algiers.

None of these horrors achieved their purpose. While France itself was now menaced by the shadow of civil war, the Algerians stuck to their negotiating policy: nothing without independence. Finally, the French agreed to a ceasefire in March 1962 and independence in July. This agreement was put to a referendum in Algeria; and the result of this referendum, carried out in a country deeply ruined and on a soil drenched with blood, was perhaps the greatest Algerian success of all.

Upwards of a million Algerians had died. Upwards of two millions more were in 'centres of concentration'. Some 8 000 villages lay in ruins. Huge forests had gone up in flames. Small livestock had fallen in numbers from some seven million to perhaps three million; large livestock was practically annihilated. Yet on 1 July 1962, 5 993 754 Algerians voted for independence under the FLN, and 16 478 against it, while ten per cent, who were mostly European settlers, abstained. Well indeed might it be said that the 'base of the pyramid' had held through every test and trial. With an astonishing unity of response, no matter what internal conflicts existed or might lie ahead, the Algerians could say that they possessed their own country, and without conditions imposed from outside.

CHAPTER EIGHT

THE LAND AND FREEDOM ARMIES

Some eighty years ago a certain Colonel Meinertzhagen, very British for all his very German name, was much occupied in 'pacifying' the peoples of central Kenya. These peoples, it was discovered with annoyance and surprise, were averse to being taxed, 'controlled', dispossessed of land, and generally colonised. They went to war against that kind of thing, and, as the colonel put it in his diary, they had to be 'hammered' for doing so. Having hammered the Embu and the Nandi, the colonel got to know the country and consequently to like it, for central Kenya was a land of handsome ranging hills fertile with crops and forest, abounding with game, and splendid in its climate.

But he still thought that Kenya was 'a black man's country', and that white settlers had no right to usurp it. This was a time when the Kikuyu of these highlands were beginning to lose their land to white settlers, and Meinertzhagen liked the Kikuyu best of the African peoples whom he knew. He thought it wrong to take their land. 'They will be', he wrote in 1904, 'the most progressive under European guidance and therefore they will be more susceptible to subversive activities. They will be one of the first tribes to demand freedom from European influence and in the end cause a lot of trouble. And if white settlement really takes hold in this country, it is bound to do so at the expense of the Kikuyu, who had the best land, and I can foresee much trouble.'

He was right about that, though wrong in his guess as to when the trouble would start. Reporting to his diary the views of Britain's first high commissioner in this infant colony, he noted in 1902 that 'Eliot thinks there is a great future . . . for a huge white farming and stock area', and commented that:

> Perhaps that is correct, but sooner or later it must lead to a clash between black and white. I cannot see millions of educated Africans – as there will be in a hundred years' time – submitting tamely to white domination. After all, [Kenya] is an African country, and they will demand domination. Then the blood will be spilled, and I have little doubt about the eventual outcome.

These lonely prophecies came entirely true, but half a century earlier than Meinertzhagen had foretold; when they did come true, moreover, it was not through the action of educated men.

Even so, the ideas of nationalism first spread by men of some education, and by one or two of much education, were to be the motor of 'the trouble', the ideological engine of the contest so well foreseen by Meinertzhagen. These ideas took their time to develop into a programme of action and a form of mass resistance. More than fifty years were required, after the coming of the enormous provocation embodied in British nationalist invasion, before an African counter-nationalism could become effective. But when that happened, a new resistance could begin; at first by larger kinds of agitation and protest which derived from earlier but ineffective demonstrations of that nature: and then in 1954, when none of this availed, by armed struggle. For it was above all the nationalist programme, looking to an anti-colonial independence, which gave spur and shape to the Land and Freedom Armies and their 'Kenya Parliament' of what the British, invariably, called 'Mau Mau'.

THE RUN-UP TO REBELLION

The route of armed resistance was of course the route of last resort. Crooks or fantasists may 'reach for the gun' as a matter of preference; no one in their right mind has ever done so. The point may bear emphasising if only because, in the mistaken view of some writers, these armed resistances marked a break from different and alternative concerns with 'improvement': that is, with the long and varied effort of colonised peoples to absorb the colonisers' skills and knowledge peacefully. On the contrary, these resistances were always, at any rate in their initiating purpose if by no means always in their outcome, a 'continuation of improvement by other means'. They were intimately a part of African peoples' attempts, successful or not, to come to terms with the world from which the colonisers came. Raised only after peaceful routes to 'improvement' has all been closed, they were aimed at a reopening of peaceful routes.

It became the common coin of European denunciation, often enough, that anti-colonial insurrections were little but the helpless gestures of savages or 'backward children', an 'atavism' or 'return' to supposedly mindless ancestors, a blind denial of the blessings of colonial rule. The evidence shows otherwise. The evidence shows that even those insurrections which failed in bloody chaos had begun with one or other form of 'improvement' as their primary aim. Which is not to say – but need one really insist on this? – that the continent had no criminal or irresponsible outbreaks in these turbulent years. Quite certainly there were many of these, and sometimes for nothing but the sake of violence itself; but those are not the accidents we are concerned with here. They had as much to do with the prosecution of guerrilla warfare as a serious enterprise – that is, as a means of self-liberation, *above all* of 'improvement' – as bank robbery has to do with honest investment. Such outbreaks of anger or despair invariably proved that counter-violence, merely in itself, has no more virtue than any other form of violence, and that terrorism is always an admission of defeat.

Nor is it to say that serious enterprises of this kind are necessarily to be admired in any of their uses of violence, or that misuses did not occur. Acton's familiar dictum about power may be reasonably adapted to the effect that all war degrades, but colonial war can degrade absolutely. The history of colonial systems and their wars will scarcely disagree with that. But the truth has applied to the coloniser in the first place, and only afterwards, but then by no means always, to the colonised. On this, too, a balanced view of the evidence is scarcely open to question.

Violence against the peoples of Kenya began early and became chronic. Responses were of many kinds, ranging across the whole continuum from

'primary' resistance through 'secondary' insurrection to efforts at 'accommodation' or 'improvement', right on down to the rise and development of
modern nationalism, in a process that could well encapsulate the history of the
whole colonised continent. None of Kenya's peoples stayed outside that
process. But their responses obviously varied with their local circumstances.
Some resisted. Some 'accommodated' whenever opportunity offered. Others
did both.

The Kikuyu of the central highlands were among the latter. Their history
is complex. Briefly, they became the Kenyan people who most closely felt the
impact of colonisation on the white-settler model. They lived in fertile country
much desired and increasingly enclosed by immigrant British settlers who, of
course, needed African labour as well as African land. Kikuyu territory also
included Nairobi, which became the capital of colonial Kenya and the great
urban centre where the challenges of European technological and other forms
of cultural change were strongest. Just as Meinertzhagen had foreseen, the
Kikuyu duly proved to be the people most capable of becoming 'susceptible to
subversive activities': in other words, of understanding the mechanism of
colonisation and of reacting against it.

In principle, at least from early in the 1920s, this mechanism was supposed
to put the interests of the Africans first. Its doctrine held that the interests of
the majority of the country's inhabitants were paramount over those of
minorities: Europeans, that is, and Asians. But the doctrine remained a dead
letter. In practice, Kenya was ruled by the British Colonial Office in partnership with the immigrant settler community, and it was the interests of the
latter, above all in the 'white highlands' taken from Kikuyu and some others,
which were treated as paramount whenever any serious conflict ensued. From
the earliest years, accordingly, any African organisation which tried to organise Africans in the interest of Africans was likely to be thought subversive by
the Colonial Office, and outrageous by the settlers.

Political responses by the Kikuyu were on the scene at an early date. A
Kikuyu Association appeared in 1920 with modest 'self-help' aims. It was
followed in 1921 by the emergence of Harry Thuku's more consciously defensive Young Kikuyu Association, and then, in 1924, by a Kikuyu Central
Association (KCA); with the latter, early ideas of nationalism began to be
expressed. These were modernising ideas epitomised in the Kikuyu Independent Schools Association, formed in 1928 as a means of bypassing Christian
mission schools now beginning to be seen as tools of the colonial system. One
may note at this stage, for it will be important later on, that none of this was a
united Kikuyu response. Some Kikuyu found they could do better within the
system, whether as servants of the administration or as traders or even as
small farmers, tenants, or the like. But those who responded belonged to a
potential majority of dispossessed peasants and of wage-workers in Nairobi
and some other towns. Their influence and following continued to grow.

In 1939 the KCA seems to have had some 2 000 paid-up members, quite a
solid number for the time and place, and was evidently expanding fast. The
system already saw this as a threat. With the onset of World War Two as a
convenient justification, the KCA was duly banned in 1940; at the same time,
various measures suppressed or disarmed other forms of African organisation,
such as the trade unions then beginning to make an impact in the major East

African city-port of Mombasa. But in 1944, thanks partly to the consequences of World War Two, the leaders of African political opinion, including those of the still banned KCA, were able to form a new organisation. They called this the Kenya African Union (KAU), and began to think in terms of an all-Kenya nationalism. Its founding constitution declared that its aims were

> to unite the African people of Kenya; to prepare the way for the introduction of democracy in Kenya; to defend and promote the interests of the African people by organisation, educating and leading them in the struggle for better working conditions.

as well as to extend to all adults the right to vote and to be elected in political elections right up to the Kenya Legislative Council. While not demanding independence, KAU thus asked for reforms which should lead to majority rule and thereby make good, at last, the old doctrine of the paramountcy of interests of the majority of the inhabitants.

Although Africans numbered some six million at that time, and the European community only about 30 000 (of whom no more than a fifth were farming settlers and their families), the KAU demands were rejected out of hand. Like others of its kind, this European community came out of the world war with a strong will to stay on top. Given that the British colonial administration had become a more or less direct instrument of the European community, tensions inevitably grew. Peaceful change towards the kind of democratic aims pursued by KAU became ever more improbable. As in Algeria at exactly the same time, there were those who now argued that stronger forms of pressure would have to be applied.

In 1950, drawing this conclusion, the KCA leaders inside KAU began to build a clandestine movement, at first among Kikuyu wage-workers, unemployed and dispossessed farmers, but with the intention of spreading it to other Kenya communities. Their object at this stage was not to launch an insurrection, or so it appears, but to reinforce KAU with sufficient muscle to influence the colonial administration. To that end, but in an atmosphere of growing expectation of violence, these men worked at 'the base' of Kikuyu society. Obliged to aim at secrecy and strong discipline, they introduced the kind of simple oath of unity, loyalty, and non-betrayal that many people in their circumstances, including sections of the English working class long before them, had used to bind their members. Reasonable concessions to African interests and opinion could have quickly taken the sting out of all this. None was forthcoming. Instead, aware now of 'something moving under the surface', the administration grew nervous and the settlers furious. All the elements of violence and counter-violence were thus assembled.

On 31 May 1950, nineteen Africans were tried at Naivasha, in the heart of the 'white highlands', for administering oaths. Among these, it was charged, was an oath binding its takers to something called 'Mau Mau'. This special oath, an especially binding and therefore minatory oath, introduced a number of unpleasant and possibly traditional features; and, when these became known (as rapidly they did), they offered an encouragement to settler and colonial opinion generally to believe, as naturally it wished to believe, that 'Mau Mau' was no kind of political movement but an 'outbreak' of 'savage atavism'. The sillier sides of colonial opinion would still be clinging to that view many years after; but another view soon appeared in the light of the facts. As early as 1963 a scholar as prudent as Dr Lucy Mair, when reviewing a book about the Emergency by the late J. M. Kariuki (see Guide to Sources), could say that 'what [this book] abundantly demonstrates is that "hard core Mau Mau" were not some sinister kind of devil but ordinary people, sincere adherents of a cause now recognised to have been just. They swore loyalty to their leaders as many in their situation have; only the prejudice that has surrounded the whole history of Kenya could have invented the ludicrous word "oathing".'

With the movement of insurrection duly fortified by methods such as a second or 'warrior' oath, events in any case now hurried. Nobody knew what 'Mau Mau' meant, the term evidently appearing for the first time at the Naivasha Trial, but everyone knew that the 'something beneath the surface' was an anti-colonial conspiracy, and probably a serious one. Increasingly harried by white-settler demands for repression, the colonial authorities duly banned 'Mau Mau', whatever it might be, in August 1950. The ban proved ineffective. By a month later some 400 Africans were in prison for having administered the oath, and hundreds more were awaiting trial on comparable charges. We know now that very large numbers of Kikuyu cultivators, labourers, and Nairobi workers or unemployed were taking this oath of unity in favour of determined struggle; some neighbouring peoples were also beginning to take it. The elements had fused, and the fuse was alight. Early in 1952 sporadic outbreaks added their illumination.

One needs to remember the wider context. Anti-colonial movements had everywhere acquired strength. India had become independent five years earlier, and other Asian territories had moved in the same direction; in Africa the Gold Coast had won internal self-government a year earlier, and wide regions of Nigeria followed suit in this same year of 1952. Large sections of British political opinion were in tune with all this. The times seemed ripe for change.

But not to the whites in Kenya. With a majority of settlers howling for blood – and the words are no exaggeration – the colonial administration embarked on an outright trial of force, just as was about to happen in Algeria. On 20 October 1952 they declared a state of emergency. No emergency existed, but the excuse was there. Now, if ever, was the moment to smash African organisation and reduce African pressures for change to impotence and ruin. All those recognised as the shapers or leaders of African political demands, including the accepted spokesman of African nationalism, Jomo Kenyatta, were taken into prison or detention. Altogether some 200 African political leaders, trade unionists and businessmen, as well as the organisers of the independent schools' movement, were removed from the scene.

That was a beginning. In case it did not prove sufficient, new pass laws were introduced, police powers were extended, African or pro-African publications were suppressed, and some 100 000 'squatters' were evicted from white-owned farming land and, in case they were infected by 'Mau Mau', were sent into an already overcrowded Kikuyu 'reserve'. It was asking for trouble, and the trouble followed. With all their known leaders taken from them, peasants and workers who had sworn the oath of unity and struggle, and even many who had not sworn it, found themselves menaced by an increasing settler fury. If there had been no emergency before, there was certainly an emergency now. Two dominant beliefs appear to have emerged among these masses of frightened or angry people. One was that all hope of peaceful change was gone beyond recall. The other was that what could not be got by argument or appeal might still be got by force. This was when the 'biggest' oath began to spread widely, the so-called 'warrior oath', swearing war against the system.

Had an inner core of leaders nourished this intention from the outset? Did the new oath spread before or after the declaration of emergency? It matters little. Concessions could have kept the peace; with none forthcoming, but fresh repression in their place, events took their course. By early in 1953 large numbers of Kikuyu, Embu and Meru began to quit their homes or places of employment, and make their way discreetly into the high forests of the Aberdare mountains and the towering massif of Mount Kenya. The great rebellion was on its way.

FINDING A LEADERSHIP

This was a rebellion such as nobody in East Africa had seen before, whether in its force and drive, its manner of organisation and leadership, or its aims. In all these respects it made a bridge between the past and the future. Once launched, it grew with astonishing speed. No later than the middle of 1953, it appears, there were some 20 000 fighters available for action, and many had arms. The judgment on fifty years of British rule was extraordinarily harsh.

Its geography was small. Chiefly, the rebellion found its base in the foothills and bamboo-clad upper slopes of the great range of the Aberdare mountains; these rise into bitter cold at more than 3 000 metres and run for about 150 kms. from Thomson's Falls in the north almost to the outskirts of Nairobi in the south. A lesser base was made on the lower slopes of Mount Kenya, some sixty kms. to the east. With unimportant exceptions, the insurrection never got outside this 'cauldron' of central Kenya. Yet its intensity within the 'cauldron' was as severe as its geographical limits were small.

With some 15 000 fighters in the Aberdares and perhaps a third as many on or near Mount Kenya, the rebellion seized an overall initiative and held this for the first year or for most of it. From the middle of 1954, heavily reinforced from Britain, the colonial forces began to close on these mountain bases, isolate them from each other, and obstruct their communications with their chief sources of material and manpower supply in Nairobi. Again with heavier reinforcements, this isolating process was continued through 1955, when the rebellion began to disintegrate. In a final phase, ending effectively with the capture in October 1956 of the rebellion's chief commander, Dedan Kimathi, military defeat became complete; but at least indirectly it was not, as we shall see, political defeat.

From a military standpoint, four negative factors on the African side can be seen to have governed this course of events. These were, first, a weakness of overall command structures as between different bases. Secondly, the failure to draw in peoples outside the 'cauldron'. Thirdly, a complete lack of access to any outside help, and even, in any direct sense available to the fighting units, of any outside sympathy or support. Lastly, the fact that the Kikuyu, though providing the main force from first to last, were seriously divided between those who backed the rebellion and those who opposed it. The social and economic reasons for this must lie outside our inspection here; but they were always of great importance to what happened or could happen. The leaders of the rebellion proved unable to reduce this internal division, or even to prevent what became, effectively, a civil war. Their defeat, in the end, was in no small measure at the hands of Kikuyu 'loyalists' who remained on the British side.

Even so, the rebellion succeeded to a point that few had thought possible and the British, certainly, did not expect. Not only did the bulk of these 'forest fighters', as they became known, fight on for more than three years against the most determined effort to destroy them, but they also proved able, in doing this, to withstand the strain of very adverse conditions of food and ammunition supply, hostile weather, increasing isolation, and the lack of any previously experienced leadership.

A number of positive factors contributed to this stubborn resistance. The first of these, and for long decisive, lay in the wide support given to the insurrection by large numbers of Kikuyu in Nairobi, whether in the provision of fighting volunteers or in the organisation of clandestine supply networks. A

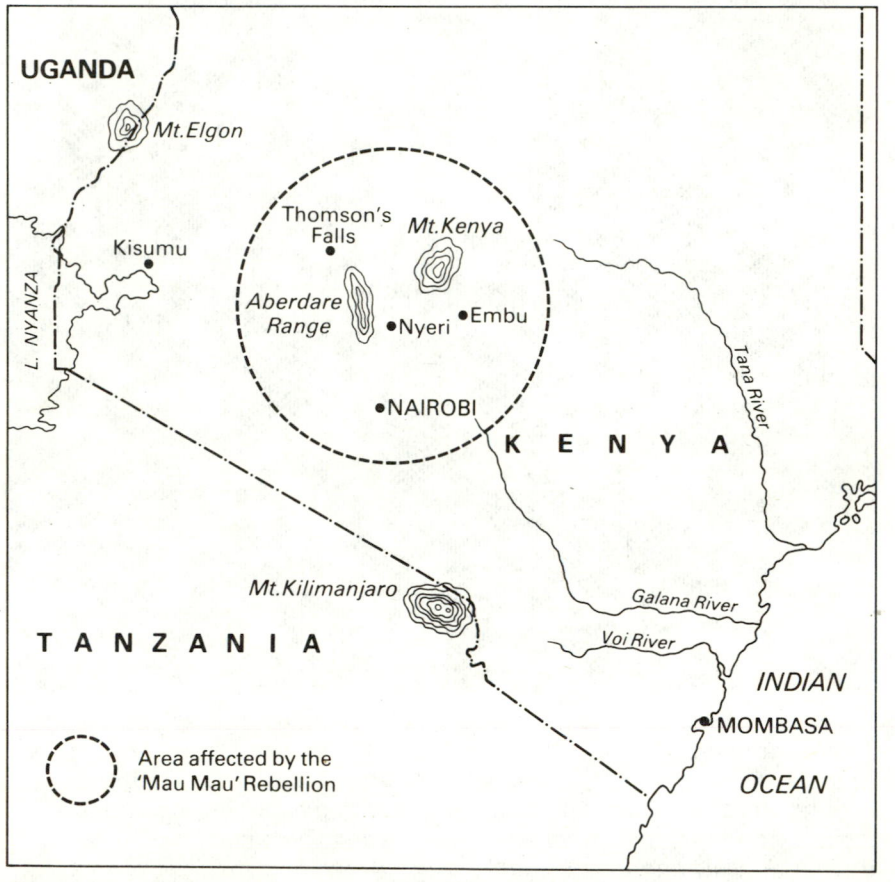

Map 8.1   *Kenya and the area of the 'Mau Mau' rebellion.*

second lay in the emergence of a number of skilful military leaders, especially in the Aberdares. A third was provided by the intelligent use of local custom and tradition in the formation and deployment of fighting units. And a fourth, again decisive for the first two and a half years, developed from a morale and consciousness that grew out of political objectives, and from the practice of fighting for these objectives.

From the start, and all the way through, these insurrectionaries had to find their own leadership; all those to whom they had previously looked for that were now in prison or detention, or, in any case, unwilling to support them.

Fig. 8.1 *Waruhiu Itote or 'General China', commander of the Kikuyu 'land and freedom army' on the slopes of Mount Kenya and captured by colonial forces in January 1954, in court before his judges. He agreed to help the police in an operation designed to bring about the surrender of the Mount Kenya fighters, but this in fact failed. The photograph is a dramatic indication of the extent to which Kenya Africans were divided for and against the insurrection.*

Some of those who now emerged and took the lead possessed an elementary military experience from British colonial service; most had none at all. Prominent among them were the 32-year old Dedan Kimathi, Stanley Mathenge, several literate men or primary-schoolteachers and notably Karari Njama, all of these being in the Aberdares; while, on Mount Kenya, there was Kimathi's nominee Waruhiu Itote, who took the name of 'General China'.

With initial supplies of arms and ammunition channelled from networks in Nairobi, these men set about raiding police posts and settler farms in search of more. Gradually they evolved a fighting organisation. This they based partly on Kikuyu traditional patterns, just as with the preliminary oathing of 1950–52. At the base of Kikuyu organisation was the *itura* or village locality; several *itura* formed an *mbari* or 'sub-clan'; and several *mbari* formed a *mugonya* or 'ridge community' such as Kikuyu settlement patterns had evolved as their largest unit of self-government. Though autonomous, all the 'ridge communities' thought of themselves as belonging to the same people: to the same traditional loyalty, as we may call it, or tribe as colonial usage preferred.

Kikuyu attitudes to leadership were similarly helpful. They were rootedly democratic. Traditionally, leadership of *itura, mbari* or *mugonya*, whether in peace or war, was not by ascription but by appointment: was not, that is, inherited by birth or rank but won by individual capacity and courage. The thousands of men and many women who flocked or fled up into the mountains during 1953 found it easy and natural, by all the accounts we have, to accept a fighting organisation based on these traditional community structures, and a leadership consisting of a number of councils, with a senior council at the top, commanded by leaders of general acceptance.

Speed of guerrilla movement, strong discipline, and a capacity for quick reaction were essential to seizing an initiative and holding it. Having begun with large camps, the leadership quickly found it better to reduce these to small and dispersed camps whose locations were frequently changed. Soon, in the Aberdares, there had emerged six 'Land and Freedom Armies', as they named themselves in witness to their objectives, with others of the same general type on Mount Kenya. Linked by couriers and to some extent capable of combined action, these 'armies' raided the settled areas below, sought new recruits and weapons, attacked government-nominated chiefs and their 'loyalist' followers (as they were called at the time), besieged police posts and small army posts, and ambushed the troops sent up to drive them from their forest bases.

THE STRUGGLE IN THE FORESTS

As all this unfolded on the military side, the rebellion developed its political profile. Denounced by the British authorities and settlers as a primitive reversion to 'tribalism', this profile suggested the contrary. Far from 'losing themselves in the past', the young men who led this rebellion possessed a modernising concept of what they were about. In August 1953 they formed a 'Kenya Defence Council' to unite their fighting groups and spread their rebellion. Proving ineffective, this was found over ambitious, not least because of the sore lack of literate men to keep records and use written communications. In February 1954, with the wind still in their sails, Kimathi and his fellow-leaders tried again; this time they formed themselves into a 'Kenya Parliament' with twelve elected members and the same task of reinforcing unity and developing objectives.

Grappling with its political problems, this 'forest parliament' has its place in history. Named to legitimate democratic procedures, its declared aims were to separate political power from military power – the 'legislature', as it were, from the 'executive' – as well as to insist on the all-Kenya vocation of the rebellion of the 'Land and Freedom Armies'. Efforts were made to contact and draw in other peoples besides the Kikuyu, Embu, and Meru already involved, and this indeed was essential to the further development of a strategic initiative. They failed through isolation by the colonial forces as well as through a far more general political isolation. All the same, in its perspectives if not in what now happened, the rebellion had begun to pass beyond the stage of mere protest or revolt, and to enter, however confusedly, the stage of revolution: to aim, that is, at building a new political society in Kenya.

Karari Njama's memoirs, recorded by Barnett a few years later, offer the best available means of understanding the process now in play, as well as its eventual frustration. Rare in being fully literate, Njama became the secretary of the 'Kenya Parliament', and was the closest to a political commissar that the 'Land and Freedom Armies' were able to achieve. His approach put the accent on democracy and equality:

> Some of us may seek privileges, but by the time we achieve our freedom [he said in a speech at the elections to the 'Parliament'] you will have learned to share a grain of maize or a bean amongst several people, feeling selfishness as an evil; and the hate of oppressing others (will) be so developed in you that you will not like to become another class of 'Black' Europeans ready to oppress and exploit others just like the system we are fighting against.

Isolation began to eat into morale and fighting capacity after the middle of 1954. Widening the rebellion had proved beyond the leaders' strength. Confined within the 'cauldron', the 'Land and Freedom Armies' began to make grave tactical errors. Perhaps it could not have been otherwise. Beginning with actions which often alienated other sections of the Kikuyu or their neighbours, Kimathi and his fellow-commanders had in any case no time or opportunity to develop a better way. In April 1954, now with some 25 000 troops and police in the field, and with growing support from 'loyal' Kikuyu while nearly all the rest of Kenya's peoples stood aside, the British embarked on strong and shrewd measures of counter-insurgency.

They had begun with big offensive sweeps aimed at depriving the forest groups of supplies, food and recruits. The forest fighters' mobility and tracking skills generally defeated these sweeps, though far from painlessly. Two other measures now did better. One was to round up and incarcerate great numbers of Kikuyu and other peasants and townspeople, eventually more than a million, in special camps or 'villages' under military guard and control: just as the British commanders' forerunners had done on a lesser scale in the Anglo-Boer war, and as French commanders were about to do in Algeria. 'The entire African population of Nairobi', Barnett records, 'were rounded up and driven into a huge field where 70 000 Kikuyu, Embu and Meru were sorted out and screened' over a period of weeks; in the end, 50 000 of these were sent into camps.

Such measures scarcely succeed, however, without an isolation of the fighting groups from the population still outside such camps. A second measure saw to that. Backed by numerous patrol-posts in its rear, a substantial trench lined with barbed wire and sown with landmines was now dug along eighty kms, so as to cut off Aberdare fighters from those on Mount Kenya. This was another forecast of what the French would shortly do in Algeria, and it had its effect. Isolation deepened. From now onwards, the 'Land and Freedom Armies' lost the initiative they had held, and, in fatal consequence, suffered in coherence and discipline as well; surrenders began. Hunger and loneliness came as companions to this isolation, and, with these, the degradations of colonial warfare. Terrorism became a method. Some units fell into banditry. Women among the fighting units began to be abused. Latent rivalries and personal quarrels, hitherto more or less contained, broke surface.

With this decay, worse followed. In the early phases the Kikuyu *mundo mogo*, oracle spokesmen or diviners, had helped to enforce discipline and morale; now they began to undermine what they had helped to build, relapsing into magical explanations of reality, claiming to command operations by reference to their prophecies, spreading belief in the efficacy of charms. Developing 'pseudo-guerrilla bands' on tried principles from experience elsewhere, British messages began to penetrate the forest with offers of clemency for those who would surrender. Many responded.

The 'Kenya Parliament' and its commanders still had authority, even so, and their units could still hit hard and often. Then with January 1955 there came 'Operation Hammer', this time with a division of fresh British troops and many auxiliaries deployed against the Aberdares for three weeks. The forest fighters seem as usual to have lost few killed, the official count being only 161; but their physical and moral condition was now desperate.

In this situation the 'joints' between traditional and modernising ideas and forms evidently continued to collapse. Quarrels became worse, and sometimes lethal. Superstition flourished. Discipline went by the board. Even the few literate men, such as Njama, found themselves distrusted by the illiterate. With their backs to the foodless bamboo forests, fighters and commanders fell increasingly into actions of despair. Many still held out, but comforting themselves now with the simple thought that the longer they could survive the better would become the chance of real change after the insurrection was over. The leader of a small group, Kachinga Wachanga, recalled afterwards of this grim time that:

> Myself and a few other fighters were able to live for a whole month without being noticed in a small clump of trees about 200 yards from a settler's house and 400 yards from a military camp. We got water from a tiny stream . . . and we raided settler farms at night for animals and wheat. After a raid we started off toward the forest, walking a long way before returning to our *mbuci*. The Government patrols sent out the next morning followed our tracks, but were misled by the fact that we returned to the forest walking backwards.

But too much was against survival. Not only did the Government now have 100 000 men in the field, but there was no longer any need to call on troops from Britain. More than three-quarters of this huge force were Africans drawn from eight or nine other Kenya peoples. These men served in the King's African Rifles and Kenya Regiment, backed up by four battalions from Britain; while another 30 000 Africans were formed in the so-called 'Home Guard', with 10 000 Africans in the regular police, another 8 000 in the police reserve, and 4 000 in 'tribal police' units. And the current of non-Kikuyù opinion was running ever more strongly against a largely Kikuyu rebellion, now increasingly regarded as a bid for Kikuyu hegemony over Kenya. Meanwhile the old Kikuyu leaders of Kenya nationalism were silent in understandable prudence or, more often, in prison. By the end of 1956 the rebellion was effectively finished, although it would still be several years before the last of the forest fighters were willing to give up.

BALANCE SHEET

When it was over, the cost was seen to be very great. Some 13 000 Africans died in this rebellion, very many as non-combatants. Few European civilians, on the other hand, had been killed. An interested propaganda liked to represent them as dying in dozens; the number of European civilians who had been killed was in fact thirty-two from first to last. Over 80 000 Africans were held in detention camps before the end, sometimes under conditions which became so brutal as to lead to parliamentary investigations in Britain and Kenya. Hundreds of thousands of peasants were uprooted from their homes. There was much material destruction. The Kikuyu community was riven to its roots.

It was not all in vain. Though sorely beaten in the end, the will of the 'Kenya Parliament' and its 'armies' nonetheless prevailed. No doubt colonial rule would have come to an end in any case during the coming years, but it is far from certain, without the 'Land and Freedom Armies', that it would have ended with the complete disarming of settler control. Most observers have thought that the insurrection brought the end of colonial rule much sooner than would have occurred otherwise; further, that it gave the leaders of Kenya nationalism a much stronger position than they could have won for themselves. For the enormous cost and disturbance of the rebellion, maintained for more than three years in the heart of white-settler country, irreversibly changed the internal balance of power between Africans and Europeans. In this respect it seems likely that four veteran leaders of KAU, and afterwards of the Kenya African National Union which would lead the way to independence, composed the forest fighters' true epitaph. Writing a few years later, they affirmed that

> Kenya owes a great debt of gratitude to them. Anyone familiar with the political scene here in 1952 [the year, it will be remembered, when the emergency was declared] cannot fail to see the close and direct link between the political changes of recent times and the shock of the Kenya Land and Freedom Army revolt to the British government and the settlers. Indeed, it would not be an exaggeration to say that

the political consequences of their sacrifice have been felt throughout East Africa.

Was this statement a mere reflex of Kikuyu patriotism? No: for only two of the men in question were Kikuyu, while one was Maasai and the fourth was Luo. But whatever judgment one may prefer, any future history of liberation struggles in colonial Africa seems likely to award the 'Land and Freedom Armies' a memorable place.

THE CONFUSION IN THE CONGO

Vast in its forests, plains and hills, the Congo colony of Belgium (Zaire today) became independent in 1960 with a population of some fifteen million. This population, though very small for all that land, was composed of many different cultures and languages, few of whom had ever known unity among themselves save what Belgium had imposed by force. Congolese nationalism was a very new idea.

Almost a tropical world on its own, this great colony had been governed by a rigid autocracy which allowed no practice of politics, before the very eve of independence, even to its Belgian settlers. Yet in January 1960, suddenly willing to withdraw its political and administrative power while evidently calculating that the Congolese would still have to rely on Belgian guidance, the Belgian government announced that it would concede independence six months later. If confusion was expected, disaster ensued. Certainly, nothing else was prepared.

No Congolese had reached the senior levels of administration or even, save for one or two, the middle levels; nor had any Congolese been able to acquire a university education or, still more usefully, travel the world as a politically informed observer. When formal independence came in June 1960, only one among a host of Congolese political groups, often though misleadingly called 'parties', was ready to act in all-Congolese nationalist terms. This was the *Mouvement National Congolais* (MNC) headed by Patrice Lumumba. Unique in this respect, Hoskyns concluded in 1965, the MNC 'aimed from the beginning at creating a national consciousness which would rise above tribal or regional interests'. This agrees with Lemarchand's conclusions of a year earlier, when he noted that Lumumba made 'repeated efforts to affirm the national vocation of his party', and to build a united Congolese nationalist movement. It was indeed, among serious students, a general judgment.

Lumumba and the MNC were destroyed soon after independence. Then every last hope of stability and unity was swept away on a torrent of dissidence, secession and betrayal. Succeeding Lumumba's government after Lumumba was murdered by Katanga (Shaba) secessionists early in 1961, the so-called 'central government' in Léopoldville (Kinshasa) was quite unable to bring the country under its control. Put into office by a combination of local intrigue, opportunism and external pressure, above all the pressure of the USA, these 'central ministers' were for the most part petty-bourgeois adventurers with no vision of a national cause. They were in any case quickly mastered by Washington's protégé, the army commander Mobutu.

Defeated in the narrow arena of Kinshasa politics, harassed and fearing for their lives, the surviving Lumumbist leaders took up their stand in the east-

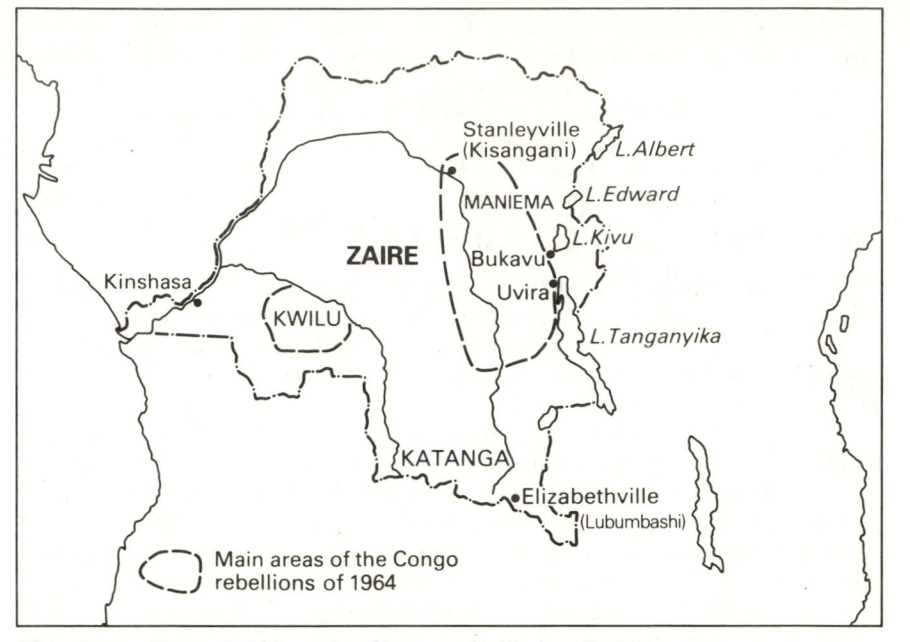

Map 9.1   *Central Africa; the Congo rebellions of 1964.*

central forest regions centred on the town of Stanleyville (Kisangani). There they set up a brief government of their own. But although these Lumumbists possessed a vision of a national cause and some of them had the will to fight for it, they lacked the influence and organisation to maintain their leadership in wide regions flung into confusion and disturbance. Old conflicts long suppressed by colonial rule broke surface. Huge provinces and their populations fell away from any effective administration. And all this occurred with an extraordinary and even frenzied violence which the history of the colonial Congo alone seems able to explain.

These peoples had suffered the piratical excesses of King Leopold of Belgium's 'Congo Free State' for some twenty years before the Belgian state took over the country as a colony of Belgium in 1908. There followed many years of colonial 'pacification', 'military promenades', the widespread imposition of forced labour, even on women and children, and the heavy hand of an authoritarian colonial system. Scarcely one of the country's larger peoples failed to embark on revolt, sometimes repeatedly, and there was barely a region which escaped the repressions of Belgium's colonial army, the *Force Publique*. When fresh upheavals erupted in 1960–61, especially in the secessionist Katanga (Shaba) of Tshombe and his partners, death and destruction became for a while the rule of daily life. Other secessions and upheavals added to the chaos.

So it went on till 1964, with Mobutu striving to extend the zone of Kinshasa's tottering authority. He had small success, for this was an authority that few would willingly accept, being widely seen as the more or less direct instrument of an external control. To the surviving Lumumbists and those

101

ready to follow them, the conclusion was evidently clear. The first independence of 1960 having failed, salvation could be found only in working for a second independence which, this time, should not be a fake. This could not be done by peaceful means, since none was to hand, while violence or the threat of violence was practically everywhere. Men would have to fight for it.

There followed the rebellions of 1964.

SOUMIALOT IN KIVU AND MANIÉMA

They add another and curious variant, or group of variants, to the history of insurrectionary warfare. Vaguely linked by a common sense of loyalty to the ideas of the murdered Lumumba and the MNC, as well as by a corresponding opposition to the 'central government' in Kinshasa, these rebellions were made in several regions under different leaders, and, so far as evidence can now show, without co-ordination between them. Such co-ordination as there had been in the first place, it appears, was only a shared intention to overthrow what remained of the 'central government's' authority and establish an independent all-Congo authority in its place.

Chiefly, the risings came in two enormous regions widely separated from each other: in the centre-east provinces round the Rift Valley lakes but spreading south into northerly Katanga and north-west into Maniéma; secondly, in the south-western region of the Kwilu. Much is known about them from documentary and recorded oral sources, although several of their leaders died before they could tell their side of the story, or else have preferred or been obliged to keep silence. What is clear, at least, is that no rebellions in modern history have been as strange, and often as grimly strange, as these.

It will be convenient to begin with the rebellions in the east.

What survived of the Lumumbist movement gathered itself together in October 1963, partly in exile in the neighbouring Congo (Brazzaville) republic, in an elusive body calling itself the *Conseil National de la Libération*. This council entrusted its representation in the eastern regions to a Lumumbist leader called Gaston Soumialot, then aged forty-one. It seems generally agreed that he was an honest and effective administrator, and a patriot. He needed the backing of an armed force, and formed one at Uvira in May 1964, the *Armée Populaire de Libération* (APL), consisting of a variety of volunteers with a variety of motives, but generally Lumumbist in spirit. Its avowed and principal opponent was the *Armée Nationale Congolaise* fashioned by Mobutu, partly from demoralised remnants of the old Belgian *Force Publique* and partly from conscripts, with no doubt a few volunteers as well.

A summary of what happened next is hard to make. Rather should one hold in mind the picture of small bodies of armed men moving across huge areas of very sparse population. They 'capture' or 'lose' whole provinces at a few strokes of success or failure. They set up 'authorities' which endure for days, or weeks, or at best for a few months, before being toppled by adversaries with whom, otherwise, they meet quite seldom. Little reaches the outside world save the din of distant strife and the muddled reports of newspapermen striving, usually in vain, to understand what is going on. But fortunately, thanks to Benoît Verhaegen and some others, oral testimony and documentary record were rapidly collected in the aftermath.

Soumialot's troops went first into action in the far eastern province of Kivu during April 1964, a little before they were organised in the APL. They seized the provincial capital of Bukavu easily, although as yet they had little but spears and matchets for an armament, and marched off to the south. By the end of May their movement had spread to Albertville, provincial capital of the northern districts of Katanga (Shaba), and here the rebellion continued until August 1964.

Meanwhile another wing of APL, Soumialot's army, pushed north-westward into the great forest region of Maniéma on the upper reaches of the Congo (Lualaba) river, where it swept all before it until being finally defeated, partly by a reorganised Congolese National Army and partly by a force of some 500 white mercenaries recruited from Europe and South Africa. The end here was signalled in November 1964 by the dropping of a force of Belgian and American paratroops on the town of Kisangani, partly to save European hostages but still more, as it appeared, to finish off the rebellion. Repression then completed its work, largely with the help of white mercenairies, and silence fell upon the scene. In 1980 the silence still continued.

What kind of rebellions were these? What did their leaders and partici-pants hope for?

The evidence is fairly good. Gaston Soumialot and those closest to him, notably Joseph Ramazani, aimed chiefly at helping to establish an indepen-dent Congolese state. They wanted to build zones of independence free of all those influences from Kinshasa which they condemned as corrupt, reaction-ary, or neo-colonialist. They regarded the leaders of the secessionist Katanga (Shaba), those who had murdered Lumumba after Mobutu had delivered Lumumba into their hands, in just the same light. 'I consider the Tshombe government (in Katanga) as an extension of the Adoula government (in Kinshasa)', Soumialot stated to a Belgian newspaper in July 1964: 'Assassins have taken over from assassins'.

They declared their overall loyalty to the *Conseil National de la Libération* and its president, Christophe Gbenye, and the zones they secured were seen as the base for liberation of the whole country. Beyond that they had little pro-gramme, and were obliged in any case to work from day to day, meeting their problems as they could.

Soumialot's speeches are interesting in this respect. Speaking to a Luba audience which had suffered dreadfully from secessionist violence in northern Katanga, Soumialot spoke in July 1964 (as his secretary noted at the time) in praise of

the nationalism that the people must preserve in order to overcome all the difficulties which handicap progress and emancipation. He traced the history of the Luba and appealed for unity among the peoples . . . He strongly condemned the abuses and mishandlings from which people had suffered during the last legislature [of the Kinshasa parliament]. He appealed to all those who had fled from the town [of Nyunza, where this meeting was] to come home and start work again. Then he explained the role of the APL [Army] and said it was above all in the service of the people.

Working in a region where Belgians had settled as farmers or managers or skilled workers, he stressed that there could be no question of being racist or anti-European. 'Ours is an ideological struggle', he told a Belgian reporter. 'No matter how our adversaries care to interpret that, we are not fighting against Europeans but against a corrupt fascist regime. We are not against individuals, not even against Adoula [then the Kinshasa prime minister] and his gang'. His concern, Soumialot explained, was to build a post-colonial state based on a sound economy. On this the Belgian reporter said that Chinese – and Chinese were regarded in those days as revolutionaries – were said to be active in his movement. Soumialot laughed, replying:

> It's lying propaganda. Walk around Albertville and you won't find a single one . . . Every African nationalist is automatically considered as a communist, whether he's left or right, Christian or not. Our arms, as it happens, are American and not Chinese – look for yourself . . . But I frankly emphasise that we are for a *positive* neutralism. We are for non-alignment. That's why Patrice Lumumba was killed: because he was for positive neutralism.

None of this could help Soumialot to disarm his enemies, whether at home or abroad. Both were convinced that 'positive neutralism' must spell the end of a Western monopoly of influence or control, and was therefore tantamount to 'communism'.

But Soumialot's immediate problems were not with his adversaries. The Congolese National Army fled, demoralised by the fury of the rising, by its own indiscipline and indiscriminate use of violence, and also by its fear of the superior magic of the rebels. Many Belgian settlers had followed the same route, or, unlike their fellows in secessionist Katanga, were in no condition to take a hand in affairs. The populations of the zones invested by Soumialot's army (APL) were for the most part firmly and even enthusiastically on the side of anyone who would protect them from the Congolese National Army and sundry bandits. They welcomed the APL as liberators. They also welcomed them as a force which could help them to share, with richer provinces, in the fruits of independence.

Soumialot's difficulties developed from another direction: from within the ranks of the insurrection itself. Known variously as *simba* (lions) or *jeunesses* (youth), these were volunteers from the young warrior age-grades, but also from the primary-school students, of the peoples of these regions. Great numbers flocked to Soumialot's banner, bringing courage and utopianism to the APL but also, coming out of their village background, a whole range of magical beliefs and customs. A strongly politicised core might well have absorbed such beliefs and customs and transformed them into positive or at least unharmful exercises; as we shall see, this transformation was already beginning to happen in the anti-Portuguese insurrections. But Soumialot had embarked on insurrection without the kind of revolutionary approach and programme which could have evolved a strongly politicised core. He had none to hand, or, at least, none that was in any way sufficient to the problem. He had begun a war of liberation with much goodwill, but without the means to ensure a revolutionary practice which could, in turn, evolve a revolutionary movement. It may be hard, even so, to say that this was his own fault.

Through the early part of the rising, however, the *simba* of the APL nonetheless appear to have retained some of the discipline of a politicised army. They were mostly followers, after all, of Lumumbist leaders who had long preached the need for a principled resistance to those who had ousted and killed Lumumba. They used their ritual of *simba* baptism as an intelligent means of uniting different ethnic loyalties, for every difference of origin, whether ethnic, social or professional, was supposed to be eliminated by that ritual. Beyond that, they listened to the advice of their corps of specially recruited 'doctors' and took the *dawa* that promised magical protection from the enemy's bullets. They went into battle with their spears and machets, firearms still being few, and duly scattered the troops of the Congolese National Army who ran away because they possessed no such *dawa*. Yet they also listened to their political leaders and followed the orders of their military chiefs. They accepted a fairly stiff discipline.

An observer sympathetic to their cause described one of their attacks, evidently typical of others. The *jeunesses* numbered about 300. They wore head-dresses of woven grass, while their commanders wore leopard skins; their arms were machets and spears. Yet

> it was not an attack made in confusion, but based on serious organisation and effective discipline. The guards of the (attacked) camp were neutralised and the rest followed without disturbance, except that they had the surprise of capturing a missionary. 'The revolution has begun', said the son of Marandura (commanding the operation). All the officers and their orderlies were from the region. Some had been workers at the (nearby missionary) college. They had received a clandestine training, and they exercised a real authority over their men.

That was at the beginning, back in April. The fighters had their training and their magic, and both worked. How well it worked is suggested by a pro-Mobutist Belgian observer. A battalion of the Congolese National Army was attacked by *jeunesses* near Kamanyola. Visiting the unit, General Mobutu wanted to show himself as a military leader. He took the place of a machine-gunner and began firing volleys:

> The tracer bullets flew at the group of rebels who jumped and shouted as they came. Now we could hear the famous cry of 'Mulele Maie!' ('Mulele saves us').
>
> A soldier says to the general: 'It's useless, the bullets can't touch them'.
>
> 'Idiot, it's because the range is too long'.
>
> But, turning round, the general sees looks of fear around him. If he doesn't now do something spectacular, these men will take to their heels. Anyone can guess that . . . So Mobutu orders a mortar to open up, and calls for the 75 mm. recoilless cannon to be brought into action. And this eventually restores morale.

For months, the discipline as well as the magic held firm among the young men of the APL. Unluckily arriving in Albertville on the day that the town was taken by the *jeunesses* of the APL, an African official of the central government recalled that

> We were encircled by a group of rebels including kids of twelve years old. They seized our baggage while affirming that they had not come to destroy and that there were no Chinese in their ranks. They looked in a pitiful state. So as not to break the rules of their '*Nyanga*' ('doctor') they were unwashed: a mass of rags and tatters blown by the wind. On their heads they wore a magical bit of foliage or a leopard-skin cap. Their foreheads were tattooed, and the marks filled with ashes.

With Mobutu's troops in flight, the risings spread: notably, north-westward into the Maniéma. Here their task, on Soumialot's orders, was 'to reorganise the territorial administration in agreement with the inhabitants of each of the liberated regions': eventually, to establish area government in Kisangani and join this to other liberated regions. But now the lack of a strongly politicised core, of a movement acquiring revolutionary substance, began to make itself felt, and ever more painfully. Instead of drawing the populations of these zones into an active participation in new structures of self-rule, the *jeunesses* did the reverse. Accepted as liberators, these *jeunesses* were seen increasingly with fear or dismay.

With more and more young men and primary pupils flocking to the APL, and meeting there with no political guidance and training, the magic began to get the upper hand of the discipline. Violence gained on persuasion, and soon there was no persuasion. Soon, too, the *jeunesses* were out of control of their commanders, deciding when or what they would attack, or not attack, and guided ever more directly by their 'doctors', or by any person claiming magical powers who happened to be around. These, after all, were the ardent children of peoples for whom the whole long colonial period had meant a repression of all initiative in common action, and for whom every modernising idea had come in the guise of repression: now, with colonial power removed, the 'old tradition' came back in strength.

By the concluding months of 1964 the tables were turned. Mobutu's army had somewhat recovered, and was in any case stiffened by white mercenaries who proved to be fairly worthless fighters but at least had the advantage of not believing in magic. Meanwhile the *jeunesses* had increasingly taken matters into their own hands. From acting as liberators from oppression, the bulk of the APL's now uncontrollable forces turned into oppressors on their own account. Their 'doctors' smelt out witches wherever some misfortune befell the *jeunesses*, and the hapless victims were beaten to death or burned alive. It appears beyond doubt that wide populations began to live in daily fear of this 'liberating' scourge, and to raise militias in their own defence.

Soumialot and some others, notably the APL commander Nicolas Olenga, made efforts to reverse disaster, but the odds against success were now too great. With their 'troops' scattered or massacred by mercenaries or Mobutu's 'remoralised' units, rebel power slipped and fell. Those who stayed true to the objectives of the risings fled across frontiers, mostly into Burundi, or took refuge in the mountains or bush of eastern Zaire. Some of them persisted there for years under the lead of one of Soumialot's co-workers, Laurent Kabila. Even in 1980 the end of this story was still unknown.

MULELE IN KWILU

A little earlier, and from preparations made in the previous year, another rebellion erupted in the Kwilu region far to the southwest. This was the rebellion whose major leader, symbol, and one may even say prophet, was Pierre Mulele, a strong Lumumbist then aged thirty-five. So widely did his reputation spread, magical or otherwise, that the far-away *jeunesses* of Soumialot, as well as his own followers, went into battle shouting his prestigious name.

Aimed essentially at the same objective as the other rebellions, the forging of a genuine independence by the liberation of wide territories which should eventually be joined together, the Kwilu rising nonetheless differed greatly from the others. That seems largely due to Mulele himself. He saw further than Soumialot, or, at least, he saw differently. His background helps to explain why. Very rare among Congolese in having achieved a secondary education, he had also thought his way to a radical position. Minister of education in Lumumba's brief government of 1960, he was among those who went to Stanleyville (Kisangani) after Lumumba's murder; there he became a minister in Antoine Gizenga's briefly surviving 'opposition government'.

For a while, somewhat later, Mulele represented Gizenga's 'government' on foreign missions, chiefly in Cairo, and in 1962 made a visit to China. As later became clear, there he absorbed some of the teachings of Mao Tsetung, especially on guerrilla warfare. Returning to Kinshasa, he was able to stay at liberty in the 'twilight period' of 1963, but came rapidly to the conclusion that armed struggle for a genuine independence was going to be required, being, in this, at one with the Lumumbist *Conseil National de la Libération*.

So much is clear from the sources, although Mulele himself wrote little that has survived. Perhaps he would have done so later, if he could have had the time. As it was, he afterwards stayed silent until his death. This came in 1968, three years after the rising was over and when, returning to the Congo (Zaire) upon Mobutu's promise of amnesty, a promise immediately broken, Mulele suffered the same murderous fate as Lumumba seven years earlier. One result is that while the documentation on the early months of Mulele's movement is fairly copious, it is far less satisfactory for the concluding months, and contains no commentary or explanation by Mulele himself, or indeed by any of his principal supporters.

Its outset was well prepared and well organised. Training camps were set up in July 1963, six months before the rising was to be launched; and the training was conducted with discretion. Analysing the movement afterwards from first-hand evidence, three well-placed observers noted that

> The transformation of a rebel into a convinced and determined partisan fighter must have required a training both systematic and progressive. Going through this training, the rebel went to and fro between his village and the camp (in the forest), staying for weeks at a time in each, receiving doctrinal and physical training in the camp, but

returning to his village to maintain his contacts . . . over a period of several months.

As to physical training, the rebels learned guerrilla warfare in different phases. They were taught to hold out against hunger, thirst, weariness, and rain; to move rapidly and repeatedly without noise or being seen. They were taught unarmed combat, how to kill, how to make Molotov cocktails (petrol-filled bottles). They were taught how to sabotage bridges, ferries, roads, and how to gather information.

Signalled by a series of well-organised guerrilla attacks on central-government police and army posts, and by ambush on central-government transport, the rebellion got under way in January 1964, some three months before Soumialot and his companions in the east went into action. Its partisans at the beginning were Mulele's own people, the Mbunda, soon joined by their more numerous neighbours, the Pende. Their operations were everywhere successful in the early stages, revealing good discipline and tactical leadership, while the central government's provincial administration was taken by surprise; and available units of Mobutu's Congolese National Army showed small resistance, or, as was to be the case in the east, fled before the superior magic of Mulele's name and reputation. These successes were repeated through much of 1964; but the rebellion failed to spread beyond its Mbunda-Pende periphery, and, in this isolation, was gradually mastered by its own weaknesses and by Mobutu's troops and white mercenaries.

The weaknesses were little apparent in the early stages. Rather to the contrary, for Mulele evidently possessed a far clearer grasp than the eastern leaders of the necessary conditions for success. He appears to have understood that the mobilisation of people on behalf of serious political change could succeed only in the measure that a sufficient number of people were drawn into active participation, transformed into militants, and endowed with the means of achieving a new political and moral consciousness. Here Mulele differed clearly from the leaders of the eastern rebellions. Where they fought simply for an independent state that would be cleansed, as they said, of 'corruption and neo-colonialism', Mulele aimed the Kwilu movement at far-reaching change. And where the eastern APL was modelled on the organisation of the Congolese National Army, according to Verhaegen, and had nothing new in its formal structure or mode of operation – until, that is, the *simba* took control of it – Mulele organised his men on a revolutionary plan.

How far Mulele's teachings were absorbed by the bulk of his volunteers may remain an open question. In the beginning, at least, things went well for him. Political instruction was given by picked militants who were appointed as political commissars, another innovation unknown to the eastern risings. These introduced their volunteers to the ideas of social revolution. They were fighting, the volunteers were told, to eliminate an evil and incompetent set of exploiters who were in the service of foreign powers. But that was not enough. They were also fighting to introduce a new social order. In this approach to a people's war, as one sees, the theme of 'dual revolution' was firmly sounded.

The Kinshasa government might give its orders as though these were in the name of the people but in fact, the teaching said, these orders were given only in the name of those who governed. 'And this means that the government protects only the possessions of those who govern.' In truth there were only 'two classes' of people in the Congo (Zaire):

> The rich, who have all the wealth in their hands. These are the *capitalists*. They profit from those who work, just like a mosquito that sucks your blood.
>
> The peasants, the workers, all those who toil. They have to work hard, but the rich take all the profit: that is, the *capitalists* take all the money and the wealth.
>
> All the wealth is really in foreign hands. So people can be divided into three kinds:
>
> 1 The foreigners or the *imperialists*: these steal all the country's wealth . . .
> 2 The people of the bad government. These help the foreigners or the imperialists to steal the country's wealth. They are the *reactionaries*. They live thanks to the help of the foreigners. They do not worry about all their brothers who die of poverty.
> 3 All the other people. These are the *poor*, the *peasants*, the *workers*. They are like dogs that hunt down game, but eat only the bones.

Struggle alone could change this state of affairs. There were, continued the lectures prepared for and given by political militants, two possible kinds of struggle:

> 1 To reduce sufferings. This is *reformist* struggle.
> 2 To change, to reorganise, the country. This is *revolutionary* struggle.

The first kind was favoured, said the lectures, by intellectuals or privileged town workers. They could make gains for themselves through trade unions, popular demonstrations, newspaper agitations; but 'village people' had no share in those gains. That kind of struggle, reformist struggle, usually failed, because those who led it were not clever enough to get the better of the 'imperialists', or stop the imperialists from stealing the country's wealth. At best, such struggle could only corrupt the reformists by gains that carried them over to the side of the imperialists. This being so, the second kind of struggle, revolutionary struggle, was necessary because, through this, 'the masses of the people' could make gains. Only the people themselves, through their own revolutionary action, could relieve their own sufferings.

Taught or at any rate told to young village volunteers and students from schools who joined the Mulelist movement in large numbers almost from the start, often with a strong idealism, these summary prescriptions were reinforced by a code of rules for behaviour and discipline. Here again we find the influence of Mulele's visit to China. Almost thought by thought his 'eight orders' for partisan behaviour repeat those devised by Mao Tsetung for China's revolutionary armies. Mulele asked his young fighters to

1 Respect all men, even bad men
2 Buy honestly from village people, and not by any theft
3 Give back what you have borrowed in a difficult moment, and without making difficulties

4 Pay willingly for whatever you may damage
5 Hit no one and insult no one
6 Do not destroy village crops, or trample on them
7 Respect women and do not take your pleasure with them as you like
8 Do not hurt those you capture in war. Do not confiscate or take their personal possessions such as rings, money, watches.

Much else was in this style. Mulele's partisans were enjoined never to quarrel among themselves; they were to volunteer for village labour; they were to teach and advise village people.

It would seem from the sources that Mulele's partisans did in fact behave like this in a significant number of cases: at any rate, in and soon after the beginning. But two conditions were evidently required if practical directives of this kind, and the theory of social change promoted by them, were to prevail and foster corresponding politics and morale. One was a capacity to resist for long enough to enable such a consciousness to gain ground throughout the movement: in other words, to train and form militants who would consistently enlarge Mulele's politicised core, and so ensure the expansion of a movement of liberation rather than one merely of reform or protest. This would have to mean fighting a protracted war, for no such training and formation could be accomplished within a few months. The second necessary condition was a leadership which remained firmly in line with the practice and theory of its revolutionary teachings. Neither condition was fulfilled.

Other factors help to explain the eventual failure. Like the Land and Freedom Armies in Kenya, these partisans were soon cut off from neighbouring regions, while at no point did they enjoy any significant access to external help. Peoples living round them failed to join them, or even sympathise with them; and Mulele and his militants were unable to break through this isolation, or even, increasingly, to rise above purely local concerns and objectives. More and more, the rebellion was reduced to regional and 'tribal' protest.

Much effort was spent on secondary, unnecessary or even plainly mistaken targets. Among these were a scatter of Catholic missions whose staffs, whether black or white, were indiscriminately driven out as a matter of priority, even though a politically advanced movement could have ignored or absorbed them. There was much wild violence which directly contradicted the sense of Mulele's 'eight orders'. Here and there the missionaries were rescued by Mobutu's troops trucked in along forest roads, but with a violence even greater than the violence practised by Mulele's *jeunesses*. Village people suffered appallingly, yet Mulele's *jeunesses* were for the most part unable to profit from Mobutu's army's excesses, too often matched by excesses of their own.

Even aside from such actions, bound in themselves to obstruct any useful spread of the movement outside its 'home bases', the fate of the rebellion was clearly going to turn on the use that was made of the considerable zones brought under the movement's control. These were where the modernising ideas of Mulele's teachings and objectives had to meet and defeat contrary ideas, including the ideas of the 'traditional' past. This was where the 'dual revolution' must take at least its early shape, and where the ideas of the future must get the better of the ideas of the past. Here, in short, was where the spokesmen of the ancestral shrines must learn another language, for otherwise they would drown the whole movement in confusion and defeat.

It failed to happen. Rapidly after the early months, the ideas of modernising revolution gave way to those of traditional belief and custom. The failure, it seems, was not so flagrant as in the east; but it was enough to guarantee defeat.

Like other Congolese peoples, the Pende and Mbunda had deeply resented colonial rule and fought against it. The last big Pende rising had occurred a generation earlier, in 1931, but was not forgotten; nor were the messianic beliefs which had accompanied or followed it. It had been defeated, but now the colonial power which had won in 1931 was gone, or, if not quite gone, was visibly weakened. A new situation had arisen. From this new situation, the Pende looked for large and immediate benefits. The Europeans would all be sent away, whether as officials, traders or missionaries. Power would return to the shrines of the ancestors, and the half-remembered but far better life of the pre-colonial past would be restored.

Yet the independence of 1960 brought what seemed to be the same old situation as before, even if black men (though not Pende or Mbunda) now shared authority with white men. The Pende quickly agreed with the Lumumbists: the first independence was obviously a fake. And then Mulele came to them, and they joined Mulele so that he should lead them to a second independence that would realise their expectations.

The equivocation proved fatal. Pende volunteers might receive a revolutionary teaching; but with them, and more powerful, came also the beliefs of their own rural culture. Theirs, increasingly, was a messianic fiction of a golden age when the ancestors should govern once more, the goods of the Europeans should pass automatically to the Africans, and power would once again reside in spiritual shrines. All this soon took precedence over 'big words' about capitalism, exploitation, class conflict and the rest. And, as it did so, corresponding beliefs in magic did the same.

While Mulele's *jeunesses* seem not to have introduced the 'initiation bath' imposed in the eastern rebellions as the ritual which marked the passage from 'one life to another', and guaranteed security so long as the 'doctors'' rules were obeyed, there was the same reliance on magical immunity. The fighters attacked as though they need fear no bullets, and, wherever the defenders held firm, the outcome was bloody massacre. Of an attack on the aerodrome at Idiofa, a Belgian newspaper reported in March 1964 that

> the garrison repelled the attack. But only those who were there can understand the horror that followed. Hundreds of confused men, their heads covered in parraqueet plumes, shouting while they threw handfuls of earth upon their bodies to protect them from bullets, brandishing their charms, firing off clouds of arrows: only to collapse under a hail of bullets from automatic weapons. At the beginning we buried them in groups, by dozens, in common graves.

Ideologically, as one sees, the *jeunesses* were not only at war with Kinshasa, but the past was also at war with the future; and it was the past that won. How far Mulele and his commanders strove against this reliance on magical beliefs, or tried to keep their political objectives on top of ancestral belief and custom, remains no more clear than it does in the case of the eastern rebellions: perhaps less clear, for the later documentation is inferior. After the rebellion was smashed, there was much discussion by various observers. It was said that Mulele had encouraged such beliefs and practices. He was said to have helped to spread belief in his own supernatural power; to have promised his partisans, that they would come back to earth after four months if they died in combat; or, alternatively, to have taught that only traitors died, since their magical immunity would otherwise protect them and turn the enemy's bullets to water.

It is hard to be sure, especially in the absence of Mulele's own testimony. Much seems to indicate that he did indeed possess a rational vision of a radically different future, and even that this was shared by some of those who followed him. Wild violence was practised against village people, yet Verhaegen quotes the opinion of an eye-witness who, although he had suffered from this violence, could still say afterwards that

> I suffered from them and lost people of my family. But in spite of the crimes of these rebels, my opinion is this: they were patriots and wanted to do good. There may have been opportunists among them, but I believe in the patriotism of the rebels.

But patriotism, in such perilous matters, is never enough. More is needed than to want to 'do good'; one needs to know how to do it. To the extent that this was an attempt at the development of people's war, it failed by reasons of its own nature, and was swept away on a tide of uncontrolled violence. The rising simmered on a while and then another silence reigned which was also, here as in the east, sorely often the silence of the dead.

COMPARABLE CASES ?

Such records, in any case, dismiss any simplistic view. These risings cannot realistically be seen as merely 'anti-colonial'. Beyond that, they clearly developed out of older conflicts and intentions, and in line with cultural conceptions belonging to a pre-colonial time. With the withdrawal of direct colonial power, the 'limbs' of societies and cultures such as these could come to life again, move and stretch, exercise a freedom long denied. Their risings would therefore seem to belong to a transitional period when abused peoples began to search once more for their own identities and come to grips with their own problems. What authority should now be accepted as beneficial? What should be 'restored', what 'renewed'?

Questions like these became acute in the Congo (Zaire) because authority had fallen to groups whose right to rule was denied by most of the peoples enclosed within 'the Congolese nation'. 'Our Congo', taught a Mulelist parable, 'is like the meat of an elephant':

> When an elephant is killed, many come to cut it up. Some steal and hide what they take, others steal and send the meat to their families. Our country is like a big elephant. Its boss is bad. Many thieves have come: from America, Belgium, Portugal, Holland, Germany. They have come to steal our riches and carry them away. Our wealth goes everywhere

because there is no-one to look after it. Our country is an elephant whose owner does not exist.

But how to put this right? Clearly, by finding the owner; and the owner is the people. The issue then turns on a host of contingent circumstances: geographical, historical, ideological. Does a leadership emerge that can really lead 'out of the past into the future'? If so, can this leadership prevail? Can the movement in question rise on one hand above the bedrock of its rural culture, above utopian or messianic hopes, above magic and corresponding superstition? Can it rise, on the other hand, above the temptations of an uncontrolled violence, petty quarrels, the paying off of old scores, local rivalries? Can it overcome the pre-colonial past, going beyond it to new cultural understanding, as well as holding out against and then defeating the colonial present?

We have looked at a few examples, and the answers clearly vary. Much was decided in each of them by the degree in which a modernising leadership could not only stay close to the movement of rebellion or liberation, but could also, in the process of staying close, transform its own culture, lose its élitism, become part and parcel of the movement as a whole. This happened in Algeria during the early and even middle stages of the war, but ceased to happen in the later stages. The Land and Freedom Armies in Kenya never possessed any modernising leadership save what they could produce out of their own ranks; and so it stands all the more to their credit that the regenerating ideas of modernisation, of social renewal, evidently held their ground until near the end.

From this standpoint the Congo rebellions appear ideologically and culturally less developed than the Land and Freedom rebellion in Kenya. Certainly in the east, less clearly but also in the south-west, they remained much more firmly within the cultures of the past, drawing their inspiration from a 'backward-looking salvation' rather than from the vision of a revolutionary future. Other rebellions using guerrilla warfare in this transitional period of approaching independence, or during a 'first independence' felt to be a fake, showed the same ambiguity of ideological content.

A great insurrection in Madagascar during 1947–48 aimed at independence from France in the absence of all the recognised leaders of Malagasy nationalism, whom the French had seized before they could vanish into the forest. So far as incomplete evidence can show, this was another insurrection which fell back on the past for its methods of organisation and its moral reassurances, and was crushed with a violence comparable to what was used in Kenya. Was this, therefore, another if late 'secondary resistance' aimed at restoring what colonial rule had taken away? Or was it another attempt at people's war: at the building of a different kind of post-colonial society? Students of these subtle and dramatic subjects will find plenty of problematical cases which beckon more research.

None is more interesting, perhaps, than the insurrection of the Bassa and afterwards the Bamiléké in Cameroun, both before and after France withdrew direct political and military control. Not only was it led by outstanding men such as the late Reuben Um Nyobé and Ernest Ouandié, who strove to implant the ideas of revolutionary change within societies still largely enclosed by traditional beliefs and pre-colonial perceptions of community interest: but these men stayed close to their movement until they were killed. Why then did their movement fail? Was it because colonial power and that of its local partners or agents proved too strong? Or did they fail to break from a purely local insurrection into something wider because the movement came too soon? What other factors may have counted? Can one, for situations so very diverse, even summarise the decisive factors of success or failure? It is admittedly difficult.

CHAPTER TEN

CONDITIONS OF SUCCESS OR FAILURE: A SUMMARY

History has shown that guerrilla warfare in the colonial or comparable context was always a form of people's warfare whenever it enjoyed success, being essentially defensive and political in its methods and liberating in its purposes. Whenever men fought without such methods and purposes, their fight was or else became the banditry of the politically bankrupt, the terrorism of the few who sought to intimidate the many whom they had failed to persuade, or did not even wish to persuade. Such disastrous adventures were known in Africa – as, for example, with the FNLA and UNITA in Angola* – just as they were known elsewhere: in Western Europe, for example, with the Italian 'Red Brigades' and the Irish 'Provos'. These proved once again that terrorism, the chosen weapon of the morally defeated and politically inept, is another and particularly odious enemy of liberation.

Yet people's war is always difficult, and even the most advanced movements have had to face defeat. What, in those movements, prevented their decay into militarism or terrorism, twin aspects of the same road to disaster? The answer evidently lies in the moral and political condition which governs military capacity to absorb and counter enemy action. However difficult its circumstances, a resistance movement wins by developing an ideology of liberation, or dies by failing to do that. In other words, a people's sympathy with a movement of resistance either develops into participation, or it withers and disappears.

The examples also insist that an ideology of liberation cannot be developed except in step with the potentials of a people's consciousness in any given and specific time and place. That is where the art of leadership has been decisive. Whenever leaders have 'gone too fast' for the feasible development of political consciousness, support has failed to develop into participation, and disintegration has followed. Whenever they have 'gone too slow', and failed to promote an appropriate understanding of the needs and possibilities of social liberation, the 'old tradition' has taken over and disaster has ensued. Two decisive factors of success can be discerned: or, in their absence, two decisive factors of defeat. One consists in an inner harmony between liberating objectives, policies, or methods, and the level or condition of a people's consciousness. The other is the use of that harmony as a basis for the further development of that consciousness.

There were conditions under which success remained impossible, no matter how closely leaders might stay in harmony with the aspirations of their people. That was the case with anti-colonial resistances made by peoples, in

* See next chapter.

earlier times, whose consciousness was still enclosed within the narrow loyalties of a pre-colonial age. In early twentieth century Kenya, for two examples among many, the Embu and the Nandi were picked off one by one by the British, often with the assistance of neighbours. The case was general. In a large sense, Africa was conquered for Europe by Africans.

But even within unavoidable failures, participation could still yield a certain development. Some of our examples have shown that. There were anti-colonial leaders who saw the fatal weakness of fragmented resistance, and tried to forge an ideology of unity that was wider than clan or region, and who, partially at least, secured a positive response. Such was the case with the Amir Abd al-Kader in Algeria, the Sayyid Mohammed in Somalia, the leaders of *maji maji* in Tanganyika, others elsewhere. They reacted against the national unity of their invaders by promoting a new concept of unity among the invaded.

That concept could only partially prevail: it had still to take firm root in popular consciousness. But wherever it could partially succeed, there came the beginnings of an ideology capable of liberation. The experience of colonial systems then nourished those beginnings, and these, eventually, could develop into the ideas of nationalism. This development was necessarily slow and erratic; it had to wait upon its time. Partly it came from the collapse of pre-colonial loyalties and structures of self-rule. Partly, then, it came from the emergence of new groupings or classes joined together in the consciousness of a common condition, no matter what might be their inner differences of ethnic or social origin. All these could find some common ground, and, in varying degrees of clarity, accept nationalism as a prime instrument by which, together, they could defend or advance their interests.

Yet nationalism, becoming successful, could mean one thing for one group or class of persons and a different thing for other groups or classes. It could be destructive and disintegrating as well as constructive and unifying. Some gained, but others lost; and those who lost could become many more in number than those who gained, or feel themselves to be so. New forms of intra-nationalist conflict accordingly appeared; and these were also forms of class conflict, more acute than any known before.

So the question of ideological development, of the meaning of an ideology of liberation, then became a new one. How could the ideology of anti-colonial nationalism be moved forward, further developed, into an ideology of post-colonial progress? To this a new reply began to emerge: an ideology of post-colonial progress must go beyond the removal of colonial controls and the writing in of 'black' where 'white' had previously been stated. Beyond all that it must resolve the resultant class conflict within the new nation state, and resolve it in favour of the many, not the few. This was why all the major insurrections of the late colonial or neo-colonial period took a dual form. They combined a struggle against colonial or para-colonial rule with a class struggle of the 'many dispossessed' against the 'privileged few'.

This seems to have been the case everywhere, and explains why all the major successes of this period were both the product and the producer of new perspectives within a new consciousness. The unity that brought success was the unity which could achieve participation. Men might embark on armed struggle with divided minds and allegiances, suspicion of neighbours, doubts about the value of combined effort. But the joining together in action against a common enemy could overcome this divided consciousness. It did not work easily and sometimes it did not work at all. Generally, though, the evidence seems to show that the practice of participation could evolve a new unity of consciousness, a new morality of common purpose in the service of a new society. Even while besieged by the squalors of war, men and women could feel themselves changed and enlarged: dragged from personal concerns, fortified in companionship, capable of confronting what before had seemed impossible. Or else, falling short, the failures could end only in disaster, and the move into a new consciousness was then reversed into a destructive caricature of the consciousness of the past.

The process was all the more striking in regions where armed struggle was developed by peoples enclosed within small-scale societies, remote clans, ethnic groups with little or no experience of the world outside their boundaries. Their problems of ideological development could be extremely severe. They lacked the kind of 'trans-cultural cement' or 'world view' long provided by Islam in various regions, or by the memory of having belonged to prestigious unities in the past. Their leaders had to find a way, in practice, of transforming local objectives into wider ones, of building a multi-ethnic consciousness of common aim and interest. This was always difficult. The Sayyid Mohammed could appeal with some success for unity among contentious Somali clans on the basis of Islam and *Somaalinimo*, 'Somali-ness': but what was to unite, for example, the many divided peoples and cultures of Guinea-Bissau or Mozambique?

No less difficult, as we have also seen, leaders had to find a way of carrying insurrectionary peoples out of old interpretations of reality, such as the notion that charms can render bullets harmless. The movements that were to succeed had to insist on tactics before divination, on weapons-training before amulets, on military analysis before magic. They had to persuade the spokesmen of ancestral shrines to see beyond local priorities and speak in broader terms, even in national terms.

And all this they had to do while fighting the colonial enemy in unrelenting danger, deprivation, loneliness, and at times the fearful onset of despair. These realities have been touched on earlier; it may be well to touch on them again. For any condensed history of these extraordinary confrontations risks overlooking the conditions under which they had to be accepted on the insurgent side. They were realities where strain and weariness, hunger and uncertainty, became a living presence, a drag upon the limbs, a weight upon the mind, a potent enemy among so many other enemies and one, besides, that was almost never absent. For months and even years men and women had to live as the hunters and the hunted, moving as the wild animals they grew to understand so well, sympathising even with the snakes, enduring every manner of physical and moral test, braving old beliefs and taboos, fending off the rumours and the intrigues that grow and burgeon under such conditions: often in small groups or even quite alone, sometimes battling for sanity as much as for bodily survival, and always with a host of daily troubles and distractions crowding across their vision of the wider problem, of the contest as a whole. 'All true manuals of guerrilla war', one of the foremost of their leaders, Amílcar Cabral, once remarked, 'have been written by people who have taken part.' Several reasons can explain why he said that. But the need for an experience of the governing conditions of such warfare was certainly among them.

The range of possible examples is wide, not least in regions where the development of a new consciousness of unity and progress was often very hard to promote. In these years of the 1950s to 1970s there were struggles that failed in the face of odds too great for them to overcome. There were others that failed to rise above the level of disaster, others again that started well but ended badly, and a few that fought their way to a remarkable achievement. But all of them, I think, whether by the negative proof of failure or the positive proof of success, may be seen to confirm the general truths set out above. And all of them, from one angle or another, build into the history of Africa's march for resurgence along this route of armed resistance.

We move now into recent years, and consider movements whose development of political and moral consciousness did not fail. They occurred in every major region of the continent, and revealed a maturity of practice and theory through which the actual meaning of their ideology of liberation became vividly clear. High on the list of these were the movements in the Portuguese colonies. We shall look at others of the same new type, but these three, in Angola, Guinea-Bissau and Mozambique, will be examined in some detail because, in many ways, they can be taken as a pattern for the others, and were, in any case, especially rich in their experience.

CHAPTER ELEVEN

BUILDING MOVEMENTS OF MATURITY

The peculiarities of the Portuguese system were many. They derived from Portuguese history; from the interaction of Portuguese colonisation with a wide span of African peoples; more narrowly, from the nature of the modern Portuguese state, but especially in its fascist form developed by the military and Salazarist dictatorship after 1926.

Histories of Portuguese colonialism have begun to explain all that. Here, to

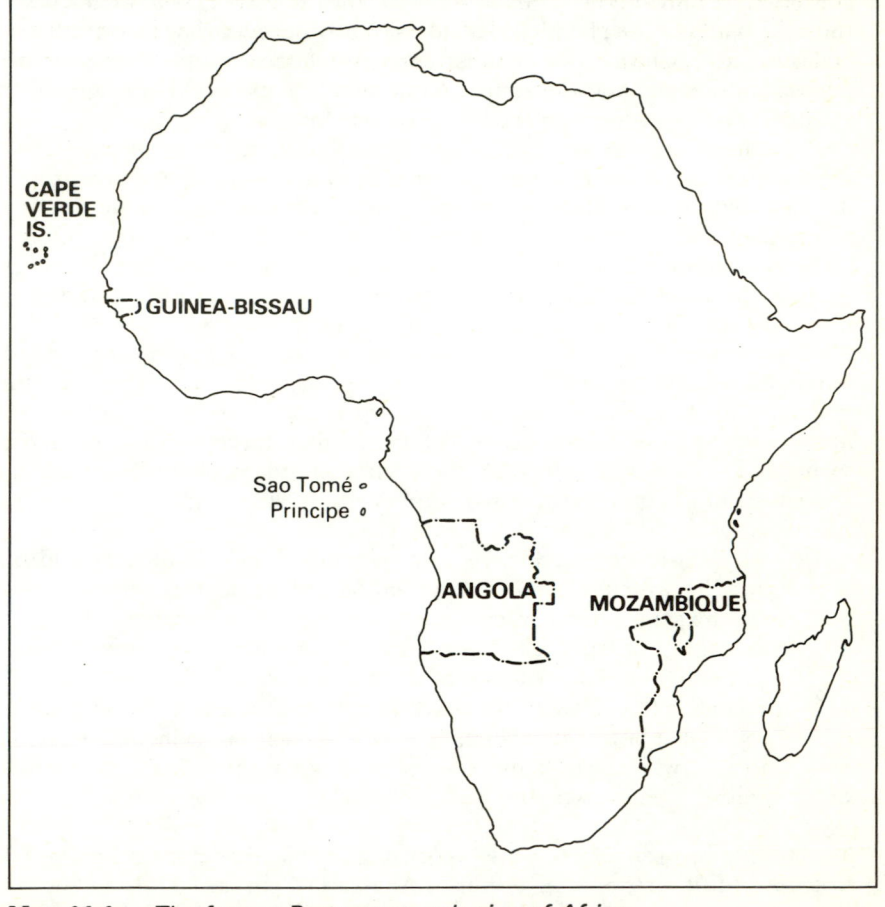

Map 11.1   *The former Portuguese colonies of Africa.*

119

borrow from Amílcar Cabral in 1965, there is 'no need to speak of those peculiarities at length'. One peculiarity above all defined the circumstances in which advanced movements of national liberation could take shape in these extremely backward colonies: so backward that literacy, to mention only this, was never achieved by more than one per cent of African populations. And this peculiarity, Cabral remarked, 'consists in a very simple fact. It is that Portuguese colonialism, or, if you prefer, the Portuguese economic infrastructure, cannot allow itself the luxury of practising a policy of neo-colonialism.' The British and French and others might withdraw their political power from many territories, being convinced that they could still retain a sufficient economic influence and advantage. But the Portuguese were sure that this could be no solution for them.

There were fairly large white-settler communities in Angola and Mozambique, and these had their characteristic influence on policy. But the real springs of intransigence were elsewhere. They arose, as Cabral said, from the weakness of the Portuguese economy. Industrially undeveloped, with upwards of half its population effectively illiterate, and governed by a stiffly conservative bureaucracy, this economy lacked the strength to follow where the British and French had led. Its rulers rightly believed that the withdrawal of Portuguese political power must entail the loss of Portuguese economic power, and Portugal, at the same time, would lose its 'world prestige'. They must hold on to everything they had, or else lose everything.

'And it is from this fact', Cabral went on to say, 'that we can understand Portugal's stubborn determination' to retain a full and outright domination of its colonised peoples. But 'if Portugal had an advanced economic development, then surely we should not be at war with Portugal today'. Only a reckless romanticism, in short, would engage in anti-colonial war when seriously useful concessions could be obtained by peaceful pressure. And these men were not romantics, reckless or otherwise.

The 'simple fact' had its profound consequences. For it meant that the nationalists faced a complete absence of any 'reformist option'. Given this system, and its incapacity to reform itself or be reformed by others, the nationalist movements had a choice of unrelenting starkness: to surrender, or to fight. The late Eduardo Mondlane, first president of the Mozambican movement of liberation (FRELIMO), explained in 1969 that:

> By 1961 two conclusions were obvious. First, Portugal would not admit the principle of self-determination and independence, or allow for any extension of democracy under her own rule . . . Secondly, moderate political action such as strikes, demonstrations and petitions, would result only in the destruction of those who took part in them. We were, therefore, left with two alternatives: to continue indefinitely living under a repressive imperial regime, or to find a means of using force against Portugal which would be effective enough to hurt Portugal without resulting in our own ruin.

The finding of an effective means of using force against Portugal proved far from easy. But insurrection began in Angola in February 1961, in Guinea-Bissau in January 1963, and in Mozambique in September 1964; and gradually, surviving many early setbacks, this armed resistance developed strength and scope. In choosing to fight and not surrender, these movements then discovered that their choice imposed a dynamic process of its own. It faced them with another choice. In order to win, and in any case to justify the sufferings of these wars, they must now destroy the Portuguese colonial system as a whole: or else, if they settled for less than that, the system would infallibly destroy them. Still there were some in the leadership who preferred to compromise; but it is characteristic of the equally stark nature of this 'second choice' that all these compromisers ended in impotent obscurity or in downright betrayal, the two most notable cases of betrayal being a vice-president of the Mozambican movement (FRELIMO), Simango, and a vice-president of the Angolan movement (MPLA), Chipenda.

Those who held firm till the end knew that compromise, in their situation, could only spell defeat. That is the central reason why these movements chose not only to fight but also to transform themselves from movements of reform into movements of revolution. For the need to destroy the colonial system led directly, and unavoidably, to the need to build a different one; and this, in the circumstances, had to mean a revolutionary programme. It was in these factors of choice that there lay the explanation of their aims and originality, and not in any exotic fancies about 'foreign influence'.

The results were extraordinary on any reckoning. Their efforts resulted not only in the destruction of the Portuguese colonial system but the Portuguese dictatorship as well. These resistances were instrumental in sweeping away a Portuguese state which no quantity of Portuguese protest had been able to shift in nearly half a century. Here was a case where the despised 'periphery' decided the fate of the supposedly advanced 'centre'.

ADVANTAGES

How was it done? The chief elements of decision and a brief outline of events may be sketched here.

The movements that count were three: *Movimento Popular de Liberataçāo de Angola* (MPLA), *Frente de Libertação de Moçambique* (FRELIMO), and *Partido Africano de Independencia de Guiné e Cabo Verde* (PAIGC). These were movements of nationalism which developed into movements of national liberation: into movements, that is, aiming at the reconstruction of their countries on the basis of a mass participation of their peoples and an untrammelled independence. Other movements present at the time were incapable of such development, and remained merely regionalist, 'tribalist', or faked by colonial power; all of these, by the logic of their nature, ended in futility or betrayal.

Each of the movements of national liberation had to begin from a position of extreme numerical weakness. Each faced enormous obstacles, but each had some advantages. It was in causing the second to overcome the first that each grew strong enough to survive and win.

The first advantage lay in the clarity of mind and courage of their leaders. Why were those pioneering men and women of such quality? Leaving aside the ticklish problem of the role of leaders at decisive times of history, perhaps a simple answer may be sufficient. It is that only men and women of a rare

121

clarity of mind could see a route through the confusions of that time, and only those who possessed unusual courage were ready to lead along that route wherever it would go.

It cannot be said that they knew where it would go when they began, even if they were sure of the general direction and destination. That indeed is what they themselves said at the time and later. They chose to fight, and having chosen they found that their choice involved them in making other choices. And their practice led in due course to theory, because, as Samora Machel has recalled:

> Ideas come from practice. When we set out, all those years ago, we wanted to liberate our people, and we found that people have to liberate themselves if the thing is to be real. We found that people could not liberate themselves unless they were active participants in the process of liberation. And so, little by little, we applied a revolutionary practice – in the wartime zones that we controlled and protected from colonial power – which enabled this indispensable participation, this mass participation, to begin and grow and develop itself.

So that 'it was in the process of struggle', as he emphasised on another occasion, 'that we synthesised the lessons of each experience, forging our ideology, constructing the theoretical instruments of our struggle'. What we find, in short, is precisely the emergence in practice of that inner harmony with a people's level of consciousness, and the basis for ideological development which this harmony can provide, that we have noted as forming decisive factors of success. On this basis, progressively, these leaderships and their movements proved able to raise their level of political and moral consciousness, and thereby build their ideology of liberation.

Having made their essential first choices, to fight and to win, these movements then found that they could count on a second advantage: that each Portuguese colony had at least one friendly African neighbour upon whom its liberation movement could call for external shelter and assistance in supply from outside. In the case of Guinea-Bissau this friendly neighbour was (ex-French) Guinea, independent under the leadership of Sékou Touré in 1958, and to a lesser extent Senegal, independent in 1960. In the case of Angola, the first friendly neighbour was Congo-Brazzaville (now the People's Republic of Congo), independent in 1960, and then Zambia (ex-Northern Rhodesia), independent in 1964. FRELIMO in Mozambique could likewise count on Tanzania, independent in 1961, and also on Zambia.

Through these friendly neighbours – and in spite of hostile neighbours such as Zaire and Malawi – help could also come from more distant friends. Foremost among these, in early years, were several other African countries, notably Algeria (independent in 1962); and then, as the movements proved their value and effectiveness, decisive military help (in arms and ammunition, and the training of soldiers) became available from the USSR, Cuba, and several other countries with communist regimes, as well as erratically and partially from China. The motives of these aiding countries is beyond the scope of this book, but we may at least note that the major Western powers and some smaller ones were from first to last in strong and active support of the Salazarist dictatorship and its colonial system.

Solid advantages were still worth little without a mass support that was capable of being transformed into a mass participation. But here there was a gain to be drawn from the very harshness of their situation. For the Portuguese system had long become so repressive as to have convinced wide populations that anyone who could remove it must be worthy of support. The evidence in this respect shows that the initial problem was not to persuade peasant populations (or, for the most part, urban populations) that the system should be driven out, but to persuade them that this could possibly be done. The system was strong, ruthless, and had been in power for a long time: what could village people do against it?

Overcoming this scepticism was a prolonged affair. Less so in towns and cities where the direct and daily experience of racist discrimination, whether in wage-levels, living conditions, job opportunities or the rest, was always a spur to resistance; but very difficult everywhere else. Much patient political work was required, and then, clinching the argument, the commitment of early fighting groups who proved that the system could be attacked with success. Thereafter the problem changed. It became one of transforming a purely guerrilla war into an armed resistance fought on guerrilla lines but centrally organised, commanded, and disciplined.

This supposed a raising of the level of political consciousness from local, clan, regional levels to levels never achieved before: to levels, that is, which could accept a national loyalty. Volunteers from one clan or region must now be prepared to accept orders to fight in other regions for other peoples who, quite possibly, had previously been hostile or indifferent. They must go where they were ordered, and fight when they were told, taking commands from men and women outside their own clans or lineages. They would continue to use guerrilla-type tactics, but the units in which they fought and the plans by which they operated would no longer be of that type; they would be the units and plans of a regular but highly mobile army. This is why the term 'guerrilla warfare' rapidly became a misnomer with the successful insurrections. Although guerrilla-type units remained to the end, in the form of local defence militias, the bulk of the fighting forces were no longer guerrillas or partisans, but regular soldiers. Wherever this transformation could not be made, as largely in the Congo rebellions, then insurrections failed.

A capacity for success required stages of development. In 1964 the PAIGC in Guinea-Bissau began to develop out of a guerrilla-type insurrection into mobile and disciplined warfare. To that end volunteers were asked for. Two thousand responded to this appeal for men to serve in mobile units who would go where they were told and fight when they were ordered; of these, nine hundred were selected. Even so, this new little 'army' suffered at first a high desertion rate: not because deserters wished to withdraw from the anti-colonial struggle, but because they refused the discipline that was demanded of them. Yet the gains to be won from mobile warfare by compact units soon became evident; the desertion rate fell and then disappeared. By 1967 the army of the PAIGC no longer needed quotation marks; it had become a force that deserved the name. The formative process was little different in the case of FRELIMO in Mozambique or MPLA in Angola.

With growing mobile forces under tough discipline and commanders now with much experience, the strategy of people's war* could steadily unfold. The three chief advantages – clarity and courage of leadership, access to outside aid, and an ever-developing transformation of popular support into popular participation – could begin to overcome the corresponding obstacles.

OBSTACLES

The first of these obstacles, linked to the problems of transformation, lay in the nature of these populations. Most of them were rural peoples with no experience of the outside world; their loyalties were to their own traditions and ancestral shrines. Their interpretations of reality sprang from local beliefs and customs, and were the fruit of ancestral teachings and religions. We have seen the effect of these in the case of the Congo rebellions. Here in the Portuguese colonies it could be no different. Support or sympathy moved into active participation; volunteers for fighting units came forward; commanders emerged from among their ranks; actions against the colonial enemy were undertaken: but much of this, to begin with, was done from the groundwork of clan or local loyalty, and within the cultures of a purely local history.

The problems thus posed were serious and central; and it was only in solving them that these movements were able to avoid disasters such as overtook the Congo rebellions at almost the same time. Essentially, these were problems of cultural development: not technological, but ideological. Village volunteers never had much difficulty in learning to handle, fire, and even repair rifles and light automatics: the difficulty came in accepting secular explanations of reality in place of religious explanations. It was one thing to learn how to ambush the enemy, quite another that witches could not hurt you. This was the learning, together with the raising of political and moral consciousness of unity and understanding, which imposed the need for protracted war.

That was also imposed by the enemy's military power. Taken by surprise at the outset, the Portuguese commanders soon realised they were facing a major test. They built up very large forces. Men and money were poured into their wars on a scale which, by 1970, was considerably larger, on any comparison of population and resources of wealth, than the largest American commitment in Vietnam; and Portugal was now spending nearly half its annual budget in an effort to crush the movements and their armies.

Rising Portuguese military expenditure gives a rapid insight into the rising scale of these colonial wars, as the table opposite, drawn from official sources, will show.

The figures for 1973 were allocations; actual expenditure almost certainly exceeded them. They must be read, of course, in relation to relative sizes of the territories and populations: Guinea-Bissau, for example, being only a small fraction of the size of Angola or Mozambique, and having a population of little over half a million compared with some five millions in Angola and perhaps twelve millions in Mozambique. I have included the figures for Cape Verde and São Tomé, because, although no hostilities were in progress in the islands,

* See Part 3, Section 1.

Portuguese Military Budgets
(million escudos)

Territory and Year	Army	Air Force	Navy	Totals
ANGOLA				
1967	533.0	180.0	69.0	782.0
1970	1356.2	271.7	119.0	1746.9
1973	1595.6	311.0	130.7	2037.3
MOZAMBIQUE				
1967	609.4	166.0	63.0	838.4
1970	886.1	261.4	198.5	1346.0
1973	1831.1	267.0	106.6	2204.7
GUINEA-BISSAU				
1967	30.1	32.3	26.1	88.4
1970	39.6	59.3	65.0	163.9
1973	48.0	58.6	90.2	196.8
CAPE VERDE				
1967	15.0	1.4	3.3	19.7
1970	22.3	2.6	12.2	37.1
1973	24.6	2.7	15.2	42.5
SÃO TOMÉ AND PRINCIPE				
1967	7.4	0.8	2.3	10.5
1970	10.1	2.3	2.9	15.3
1973	9.1	2.2	3.7	15.0

Source: *Diário do Governo*, Series I, 1967–73, quoted by *U.N. General Assembly*: *A/9023* (Part IV) 8 October 1973.

their colonial defence against possible or expected hostilities added to the costs of maintaining the whole system.

Portuguese troop contingents, whether in army or air force, grew steadily from 1962 until 1974. They were comparatively very large by 1970, the 'middle year' in the above table. With conscription extended to all possible age groups (between, effectively, the ages of 18 and 40), the total strength of the Portuguese armed forces by 1971 was given officially as being 218 000 men. Of these, 130 000 were admitted to be fighting in Africa; but unofficial and probably more reliable sources – for the Lisbon regime had an interest in understating the strain of the wars – put the actual figure of fighting personnel in Africa as being considerably higher. A reasonable guess at the total of full-time liberation fighters in the three territories at the same time might rest on a probable total of fifteen thousand. In fighting manpower, the liberation armies were generally outnumbered in the order of about ten to one.

The colonial armies depended on large and continuous aid from Portugal's allies in the North Atlantic Treaty Organisation, but this never failed until the end. The overall size of this aid would be hard to estimate, since much was done in secret; but it was certainly on a generous scale. Its various forms were diplomatic, political, financial, and military; and something needs to be said on the last of these, for it gave the Portuguese armed forces a destructive capacity out of all proportion to the means they possessed at the outset. Thus a UN report to the General Assembly of October 1973 listed seventeen types of fighting aircraft, mostly of recent design, in service with the Portuguese air force in Africa. These included ten US types, four French types, one Italian, one West German, and one Spanish type: light bombers, fighter-bombers (much used for 'shooting up' villages and forest camps and hospitals), helicopters (again much used for commando raids), transports and trainers.

To these forms of military aid, others such as napalm were added without stint. As soon as the Portuguese commander wished to use herbicides and defoliants, these were duly made available, as the official figures for purchases made by Portugal in the USA duly show:

| | Herbicides not elsewhere classified | | Herbicidal preparations | |
	Lbs.	U.S. dollars	Lbs.	U.S. dollars
1969	22 050	57 330	23 590	22 210
1970	33 200	17 125	229 320	28 205
1971	109 297	202 195	—	—
1972*	18 203	9 664	239 268	234 696

* Jan–June 1972.

U.N. Gen. Ass. A/9023, 8 October 1973 (Part IV), p. 19, quoting U.S. Dept of Commerce Foreign Trade Journal, 410.

Naval shipping, sophisticated bomb-aiming sights, a wide armoury of infantry weapons, and special training facilities whenever required: all these came equally to hand from Portugal's allies.

Formally, of course, this military aid was supposed to be used for the purposes of the defence of the North Atlantic region and its peripheral land masses, and therefore not in Africa. The condition was easily evaded. Thus the West German Defence Ministry, when selling forty fighter-bombers to the Portuguese dictatorship, most of which were at once committed to the colonial wars in Africa, explained that:

> The sale took place on the basis of the principle of mutual aid between NATO partners. The delivery is subject to a clause agreed on between the Government of the Federal Republic (of Germany) and the Portuguese Government which states that the planes are to be used exclusively in Portugal for defence purposes within the framework of the North Atlantic Pact.

Upon which the Portuguese Government added no less blandly that

> The transaction was agreed within the spirit of the North Atlantic Pact. It was agreed that the planes would be used only for defensive purposes within Portuguese territory. Portugese territory extends to Africa – Angola, Mozambique and Portuguese Guinea.

Were not the African territories called 'provinces of Portugal'? The problem of continuous military supply was solved. There were those who said, afterwards when the colonial regime had been defeated, that it had lacked for means; nothing, as we see, could be further from the truth. The Portuguese lacked neither for manpower nor for weaponry; what defeated them in the end were the courage, skill, and determination of the liberation movements.

Yet the weight of Portuguese military pressure was huge and continually growing, and for a long time the Portuguese commanders, as well as their suppliers in the West, were convinced that it must prevail. In fact, however, this overwhelming superiority of military strength was always qualified by two elements of weakness, neither of them being concerned with military supply.

The first of these elements of weakness lay in the primitive political culture of the Portuguese commanders. They were never able to shake themselves free of their fascist and racist prejudices which remained, one may even say, the 'counterpart' of the 'witchcraft explanations' of reality which weakened the liberation movements at the outset, but from which the liberation movements were able to shake themselves free. Thus the Portuguese commanders began with the assumption that they were facing a few 'communist agitators' who, thanks entirely to outside help, had somehow managed to secure the backing of a 'mob of savages'; and they continued almost till the end to believe or at least to act upon such fantasies. Very typical of these commanders – Bettencourt Rodrigues, da Luz Cunha, Silvério Marques, and others – was Kaulza de Arriaga, commander-in-chief in Mozambique after 1970 and a candidate for the presidency of Portugal.

In 1966–67 General de Arriaga was teaching a military staff course in Portugal. Naturally enough, he turned his attention to what he called 'the wars of subversion' in Africa. His lectures were afterwards published, or, at least, put into restricted circulation. Here, in these *Lessons of Strategy in Courses for the High Command,* we read that:

> Subversion is a war above all of intelligence. One needs to have superior intelligence to carry on subversion; not everyone is capable of doing it. Now Blacks are not highly intelligent: on the contrary, of all the peoples in the world they are the least intelligent.

In 1970 General de Arriaga left the staff college and went to command the troops in Mozambique, and proceeded to apply his own lessons. Mounting a major offensive, code-named 'Gordian Knot', he proposed to crush FRELIMO's fighting units beyond all chance of their recovery. Having launched that offensive, he retired for a few days' rest to the island of Mozambique, and from there he telephoned his wife that his victory was imminent.* But 'Gordian

* Private, but reliable, phone-listening source.

Knot' was a disaster for the Portuguese. Out-thought and out-fought by Samora Machel and his army, it signalled a final Portuguese defeat.

This weakness was accompanied by another: that the colonial regime had to fight three wars in different countries at the same time. It derived from the liberation movements' capacity to prepare and develop these wars, and to conduct them on a long-term basis. The crucial point was not that each started at the same time as the others, for they started at different times, but that they reached their full development at more or less the same time. This imposed not only a dispersal of effort, but an effective ban on cutting losses. By 1968 the Portuguese were effectively beaten by the PAIGC in Guinea-Bissau, the best they could then hope for being a protracted defence of shrinking areas of colonial control. But to abandon Guinea-Bissau meant, in turn, a vast encouragement to the ripening movements in Angola and Mozambique. The same General de Arriaga explained this in the same course of lectures. He said there that:

> Naturally, as our troops are dying in Guiné (Guinea-Bissau), and as we are spending a lot of money there, I do not take losses into account, and don't consider that such an amount is spent only on defending Guiné. Actually, if that were so, I should find it [i.e., continuing the colonial war in Guiné rather than pulling out] unacceptable: but a man who dies in Guiné is indirectly defending Angola and Mozambique.

These countervailing factors of weakness in the Portuguese position – the incapacity of their generals to wage political warfare, and their need to disperse their effort in three territories – counted for much in the long run: just as, had the 'run' not been protracted, they must have mattered little.

Meanwhile another chief obstacle to success faced the liberation movements. There were limits to the unity they could inspire among their populations. This was least felt in Guinea-Bissau, a compact territory where the political influence and education of the PAIGC, maturing very soon, was able to reach all the ethnic groups and where colonial-nominated or -supported chiefs could only be effective – against the PAIGC – in respect of the small Fula minority and a part of a similarly small Mandinka minority. Otherwise the PAIGC was able to extend its influence everywhere, and even among urban groups in the occupied capital, Bissau, who depended on the Portuguese and the colonial war for their livelihood.

In Angola and Mozambique the obstacles to unity were greater, whether for reasons of history or geography. Each of these vast territories had groups who sided with the colonial power or withdrew into neutrality, especially when these groups were far removed from the zones of liberation war. Especially in Angola, the Portuguese were able to find African allies. UPA/FNLA, for example, had sprung from a regionalist movement of protest among the Kongo ethnicity of north-western Angola, its prime object being the 'restoration' of the ancient Kongo kingdom of those parts. UNITA, eventually drawing support from the large Ovimbundu grouping, began in 1965 as a breakaway from UPA/FNLA. Both proved totally ineffective against the Portuguese, and both turned their weapons against the MPLA, a prelude to their outright alliance with the army of South Africa. No dissidence or betrayal on any such scale occurred in Mozambique, where the colonial power proved unable to promote any significant puppet movement. Apart from such trends, there were of course instances of individual betrayal, and some of these proved very costly to the liberation movements.

Such were the chief elements in play. They help to indicate the nature of the colonial challenge, but can do little more than sketch the damage and destruction which the colonial wars brought in their train. These were enormous; and it is also against their brutal presence that the capacity and quality of the liberation armies must be measured. Altogether, given the scope and duration of these wars, their nature, development, and consequences, and their influence on liberation wars elsewhere, the guerrilla movements here provide examples that will long draw close attention. They provide the study of this type of warfare, in its widest sense, with a remarkable range of mature experience.

Before pressing further into that experience, a brief summary of events will be useful.

ANGOLA

Nearly as large as Western Europe, the colony of Angola had known no insurrections for some thirty years when a new surge of protest, impelled partly by the successes of nationalism elsewhere, broke suddenly upon the scene. Late in 1960 a rising of peasant cultivators and plantation workers – 'contract' workers from other districts for the most part – exploded in the cash-crop region northeast of the capital city of Luanda. Rapidly put down, this affair seems to have had little political content or influence, though further research may modify that view. Months later, in February 1961, the city of Luanda was shaken by a consciously nationalist rising, the work of MPLA militants, whose immediate aim was to rescue MPLA political prisoners from confinement and from deportation or even death. This, too, was rapidly mastered by the colonial forces, but was to be the rising from whose origins the long struggle for independence would now develop.

A third and larger rising followed in March 1961 when plantation workers in the north, at least partly led by UPA militants infiltrated from neighbouring Zaire, turned on European civilians and murdered some 200 of them, as well as an unknown number of literate Africans. Confusedly directed and inspired by a violent racism, this was more an outburst of long-repressed anger than a political movement entering an armed struggle, while the UPA spokesmen who helped to set it in motion were Kongo nationalist and separatist rather than adherents of an all-Angolan nationalism. Yet the insurrection spread impressively through the northernmost districts, and it was not until the following October, after the arrival of substantial reinforcements from Portugal, that the colonial forces were able to master it. Bereft of any effective leadership, what then remained became thereafter a mere instrument of its Zaire protector, General Mobutu, while its operations, in so far as it ever embarked on any (now under the name of FNLA), were chiefly aimed at destroying the MPLA.

If Angolan national development had any future in 1961, this could lie only with the MPLA. Yet little of the MPLA had survived. Portuguese settlers, police and troops responded to the February and March risings with a very general massacre of all Angolans suspected of nationalist ideas, and the total number thus indiscriminately killed may have surpassed 20 000 persons. Those nationalists who escaped gathered at first in Kinshasa, capital of Zaire, where they found that the Zaire authorities and the Kinshasa-based UPA were combined against them. Reinforced by the arrival of their major figure, Agostinho Neto, who had escaped from detention in Portugal, the little group which had survived nonetheless rebuilt an organisation. In 1963 they took refuge across the Congo river in Brazzaville, capital of the ex-French Congo republic (now the People's Republic of Congo).

Here they continued to build their organisation, and embarked on guerrilla warfare in the nearby Angolan enclave of Cabinda (separated from the rest of Angola by a tongue of Zaire territory and the estuary of the Congo river). Cabinda could at least provide them with a training ground. This proved useful, and in 1965, a year after Zambia's independence, they were able to secure a Zambian base for operations in eastern Angola. These were

Map 11.2 *Angola.*

initiated in 1966, and soon led to the establishment of a wide zone of presence and influence in those distant eastern districts.

In these sparsely populated plains they continued to fight a guerrilla war with considerable success until the general Portuguese collapse in 1974. But apart from the difficulty of this terrain, caused chiefly by its lack of population and hence its lack of local food supplies and other support facilities, the MPLA had to face a major handicap. The bulk of the Angolan population lived far away in the centre and west of the country, and it was there that the MPLA had to look for wide support. Determined efforts were made to forge supply and liaison links with these regions, but with little success, chiefly because the hostility of Mobutu's Zaire denied them any access to the north and west by way of the Zaire frontier.

Even so, a column of 72 fighters was successfully infiltrated, secretly, across western Zaire and the Zaire frontier with northern Angola, in January 1967; these were able to reach a zone of MPLA rural support in the Dembos forests, not far from Luanda, where survivors of the 1961 rising still held out. In the following June a second column, this time of 153 fighters and political workers (including a women's detachment), was sent the same way, but was ambushed by FNLA and Portuguese forces; only 22 managed to survive this disaster and

Fig. 11.1 *Guerrilla fighters of the* MPLA *began their armed struggle in the open plains of eastern Angola during 1966, and developed a war of rapid movement by small groups, backed by the majority of the rural people of that region. They concentrated on ambush and harassment, and relied heavily on light machine-guns, landmines, and bazookas (one here, of Chinese origin, on the left). One of their commanders, on a tour of inspection, is seen here on the right. The author took this photograph in May 1970 about 110 kms west of the Zambian frontier.*

reach the Dembos. No further attempts of this kind were made, but a third column of reinforcements was despatched from eastern Angola, only to be wiped out after completing rather more than two-thirds of an enormous march.

So it came about that the MPLA reached 1974 without a strong fighting presence in the centre and the west, as well as with rivals for power in the shape of the FNLA (former UPA) and UNITA. Yet it rapidly became clear that most of the highly populated districts along the Atlantic seaboard were strongly MPLA, and the movement, now transferred to this western base, found firm political ground beneath its feet. This it set about extending until, by September 1975, MPLA forces were in effective control of twelve of Angola's sixteen districts.

Plainly defeated, the FNLA and UNITA leadership now went into open alliance against the nationalist movement with the support not only of Mobutu's Zaire but also of the South African government. In October, evidently with covert American encouragement, the South African army invaded Angola from bases in Namibia and pushed armoured columns far up the coast and into the central districts. Having no sufficient military strength of its own to defeat this invasion, the MPLA called for help from its old ally, revolutionary Cuba, strong links with which dated from 1966. But it delayed doing this until Angola was proclaimed a sovereign republic under MPLA leadership on 11 November 1975. The Cubans therefore arrived at 'five minutes to midnight'. They turned the tide of invasion, together with a quickly mobilised Angolan army, and the last South African troops withdrew across the Namibian frontier at the end of March 1976. Meanwhile a similar invasion from Zaire had reached the outskirts of Luanda in October 1975, but was driven back across the frontier by January 1976. More than fifteen years after the initial rising in Luanda, a victorious MPLA could at last approach the task of reconstructing this badly battered country.

MOZAMBIQUE

The Mozambican national movement took shape in face of many of the same problems as those which confronted the Angolan movement, but in somewhat different circumstances. One may note four chief phases.

Small nationalist groupings crystallised among exiles and migrant workers in Rhodesia, Nyasaland (independent as Malawi in 1964), and Tanganyika (independent in 1961). In 1962 these came more or less uneasily together as FRELIMO, the Front of Mozambican Liberation, formed in Dar es Salaam in 1962 under the leadership of Eduardo Mondlane. Attempts were made to forge links with prospective supporters or sympathisers in various parts of Mozambique, and met with some success.

A second phase opened in 1963 when the leaders of the movement, though still divided on ultimate aims, came to the conclusion that they must answer colonial violence with a counter-violence, and prepare for guerrilla war. By this time the existence of FRELIMO was known as far as the southern capital, Lourenço Marques (Maputo); and volunteers began to make their way to Dar es Salaam. Small groups of these were sent to Algeria for military training. Returning, they were then sent in well-organised units across the Tanzanian frontier into northern Mozambique in September 1964, and war on the colonial system was declared. Safe external bases were meanwhile provided by the Tanzanian government.

These early units found support in the northern districts of Cabo Delgado, where peasant cultivators had already begun to organise themselves in co-operatives of their own, though with much difficulty; and also in the neighbouring northern district of Niassa. Elsewhere the Portuguese were able for a while to remain in firm control, but clandestine networks of FRELIMO support were slowly extended across the country.

This situation persisted with little real advance until 1968, when a third phase opened with a political crisis inside FRELIMO. Two political trends were now at work. One of them was for compromise with the colonial system. Led by the vice-president, Uriah Simango, and supported by some of the older

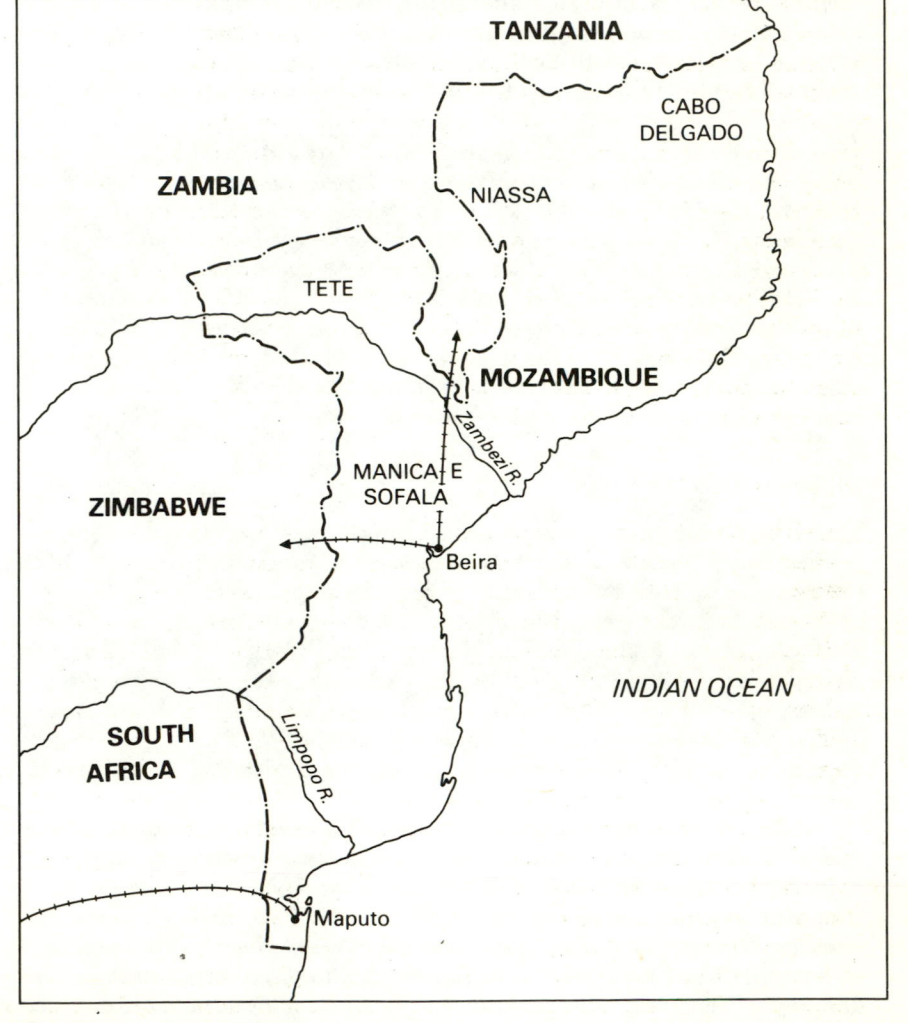

Map 11.3   *Mozambique.*

leaders in the Cabo Delgado district, men for the most part who looked for individual gains from compromise, this trend saw the armed struggle as a bargaining weapon. Their essential position was much the same as that of FNLA and UNITA in Angola. They were ready to bring the war to an end, provided that they could have some share in power and privilege within a system which the Portuguese would continue to dominate.

The second trend believed that compromise could only bring defeat and disaster, and that FRELIMO, if it were to justify the hopes it had raised and the aims it had proclaimed, must fight for and win an unconditional independence, however difficult that might be. Led by the president, Eduardo Mondlane, and supported by the bulk of the political leadership and all the young men now leading the guerrilla war, this second trend was in a large majority. Matters came to a head, after much intrigue and manoeuvre, in July 1968. A congress of leading militants met in the woods of Niassa district and gave overwhelming assent to a programme of all-out struggle for independence, as the author, who was present, can testify.

But a number of dissidents led by a Cabo Delgado elder, Lazar Nkavan-

Fig. 11.2 *The Mozambique front of liberation, FRELIMO, developed all-out 'people's war' after decisions taken at a week-long congress during July 1968, held in the woodlands of Niassa province. This in fact was the congress which prepared FRELIMO's victory of 1974–75. Here, in a photograph taken by the author, we see the FRELIMO leader and military commander (now President), Samora Machel, in discussion with a group of delegates to this crucial congress. Only after the right political decisions were taken, in FRELIMO's belief, could the military struggle go on to success.*

dame, held out against this. They now came out openly for a separation of Cabo Delgado from the rest of Mozambique, and, as Nkavandame put it at the time, for Cabo Delgado to become 'another Biafra'.* An open clash followed. In February 1969 Mondlane was murdered by means of a parcel bomb delivered through African agents of the Portuguese dictatorship. Under growing popular opposition in Cabo Delgado, Nkavandame then defected to the Portuguese, while Simango withdrew from the struggle before taking the same road. Now under the firm lead of Samora Machel, hitherto FRELIMO's army commander, the majority closed ranks and embarked on an intensification both of FRELIMO's political work inside liberated areas of Cabo Delgado and Niassa, and of FRELIMO's war for independence.

Thus unified and reinforced, FRELIMO entered on its fourth and finally victorious phase, going from one success to another and out-fighting every colonial attempt to crush its forces or destroy its liberated zones. In skilful operations, very tenaciously carried through, FRELIMO units pressed down through Tete district into the 'waist' of Mozambique, composed of Manica and Sofala districts, while at the same time intensifying military pressure in the northern districts of Cabo Delgado and Niassa. By April 1974, when the officers' *coup* in Lisbon overthrew the Salazarist dictatorship on the twin slogans of 'Decolonisation and Democratisation', FRELIMO's forward units were poised to cross the Savi river into southernmost Mozambique.

In this situation the immediate post-*coup* government in Lisbon, striving to rescue some chance of a 'neo-colonial' outcome to defeat, asked for a ceasefire; negotiations, it suggested, could then begin. FRELIMO replied that any negotiations could be concerned only with the technicalities of Portuguese colonial withdrawal; otherwise the war would continue. To this Lisbon had to agree, and an independent Mozambique emerged in the middle of 1975, more than a decade after the first small fighting units had begun their war of liberation.

GUINEA-BISSAU AND CAPE VERDE

Committed from the start to a conjoint liberation from colonial rule of the two related territories of Guiné (Guinea-Bissau) and Cabo Verde (Cape Verde), the PAIGC was obliged to operate in a very small territory which gave little room for manoeuvre, and with a very small population which, moreover, was very backward from a technological standpoint. Thanks to a remarkably clearsighted and united leadership under Amílcar Cabral, the movement was able to turn these sources of weakness into sources of strength; but, here again, carrying it out proved extremely difficult.

PAIGC development, from its clandestine formation in 1956, may be seen to have passed through three chief phases.

Little could be done, up to September 1959, beyond winning adherents in

---

* This was put forward by Nkavandame at a confrontation between himself and Mondlane, under Tanzanian chairmanship, in the southern Tanzanian town of Mtwara early in August 1968. It will be recalled that secessionists in eastern Nigeria were at that time fighting for an independent 'Biafra' against the Nigerian federal government and its forces, and that the government of Tanzania had recognised this secession. But at Mtwara the Tanzanians supported Mondlane against Nkavandame.

the only sizeable town of the mainland territory, Bissau, or in several of the small towns of the Cape Verde archipelago, notably Praia and Mindelo, and to develop forms of peaceful though illegal demonstration in support of social or economic concessions by the colonial regime. In this initial phase there remained a small hope, partly nourished by the spectacle of British concessions in the Gold Coast (Ghana) and some movement towards French concessions in French West Africa, that peaceful pressure might obtain results. In the event, however, peaceful agitation brought only a greater repression, crowned in August 1959 by the shooting down of Bissau dockers who were demonstrating for a rise in wages, with the loss of fifty demonstrators killed and many others wounded. Cabral and his companions at once decided to bring all such demonstrations to an end, seeing that these could only bring mortal losses for no return; they accordingly set about preparing for insurrectionary warfare based on their 90 per cent of rural people.

To that end the leadership moved its base from Bissau, where police repression raged, to the neighbouring capital of Conakry in (ex-French) Guinea, independent a year earlier, and began to train militants in the political work which, Cabral insisted, must be a necessary prelude to any effective insurrection. Responding to clandestine PAIGC appeals, many young volunteers from Bissau and other towns made their way through the forest to the Guinea frontier, and thence to Conakry, where they were put through a course of practical political training by Cabral himself.

They were then sent back across the frontier to win peasant confidence and peasant support, and, gradually, to begin transforming support into participation in the various tasks that lay ahead. At the same time Cabral was able to send a few volunteers for military training in Algeria, and afterwards elsewhere, mostly to the Soviet Union and East Germany, but also to Cuba.

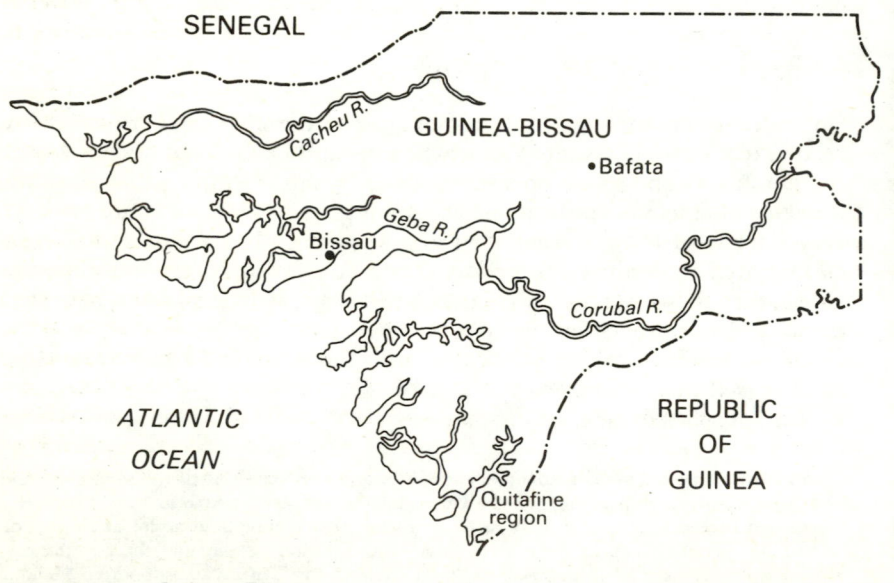

Map 11.4   *Guinea-Bissau.*

Adopting a policy of non-alignment comparable with that of the MPLA and FRELIMO, PAIGC leaders also travelled in Western Europe and the USA, and tried to secure aid and a political hearing. In this they entirely failed among the governments, except in Sweden, but won a growing volume of support from unofficial organisations and anti-colonial movements. Like its companion movements, PAIGC also won recognition and support from the Organisation of African Unity after its foundation in 1963.

A second phase opened in January 1963 when armed struggle began against the colonial system in Guinea-Bissau – no such struggle was feasible in the distant islands of the Cape Verdes – with encouraging initial success. Having carried through an effective political preparation among rural people, the PAIGC reaped an immediate harvest. This was sorely diminished late in 1963 by indiscipline, a severe outbreak of witch-hunting and reversions to traditional modes of thought and explanation, and other such phenomena. But Cabral and his companions, unlike Mulele and Soumialot in the Congo a year later, were able to master these invitations to disaster.

A congress of leading militants, held in February 1964, firmly put the movement and its insurrection back on the right lines, and the politics of national liberation were introduced and developed in every field of action. Zones of PAIGC control and reconstruction were held and extended, and the structures of a new post-colonial state began to be built. A full-time mobile army originating in 1964 was enlarged and improved in its training, discipline, and tactical effectiveness. Such was the success of its operations, backed as these came to be by well-organised liberated zones protected by peasant militias, that an army of some 30 000 Portuguese troops was steadily reduced to defeat. Having thus seized a strategic initiative, a PAIGC army of perhaps 4 000 men (later increased to about 6 000) had effectively won the war on the mainland by 1968. This was the point at which the Portuguese would probably have cut their losses, here in Guinea-Bissau, had they not feared adverse consequences in Angola and Mozambique. The war accordingly continued, but with a continued PAIGC superiority in the initiative.

In January 1973 the outstanding PAIGC leader, Amílcar Cabral, was murdered in Conakry by African agents of the colonial regime, and a third phase opened. Partly in a reaction to this murder, the PAIGC went over to an offensive designed to reduce the enemy's strongest points and force him back on his 'fortress' of Bissau. To that end they brought heavy mortars and light artillery into new forms of action. In March 1973, they were also able to begin using a Soviet-supplied ground-to-air missile (known as SAM-7), which rapidly neutralised a hitherto invulnerable Portuguese air force. By September of that year the PAIGC were strong enough to be able to declare an independent state based on a general election held in liberated zones (about two-thirds of the country) during 1972. In April 1974 there came the young officers' *coup* in Lisbon, and the war was effectively over. Fighting ceased in May 1974, spontaneous withdrawals of Portuguese garrisons began in August, and the last of Portugal's armed forces had left the country within a few weeks of the declaration of national independence in September.

Meanwhile, from July 1974, PAIGC militants in the Cape Verde islands were able to come into the open and develop a political campaign for Cape Verdean independence. These militants were joined in August by PAIGC leaders of Cape Verdean origin who had fought through the war on the mainland. It became manifest to all that the PAIGC had overwhelming support in the islands as well as on the mainland. A general election duly proved this in June 1975, and Cape Verdean independence under PAIGC leadership followed at once.

CHAPTER TWELVE

ON THE WIDER SCENE

Many factors explained the success of these anti-colonial wars in the Portuguese empire; and we have looked at the more important ones. Yet in all three confrontations a single and most decisive factor stood clearly out. Each of the movements was able to develop a political and social maturity, and therefore unity, that could lay foundations for a new culture: indigenous and national, but also secular and modern. Each was able to enlarge local and ancestral loyalties, often as deeply felt as they were divisive, into a unifying vision both of the present and the future.

More insistently and successfully than others before them, each combined a struggle against the colonial present with a struggle against all those aspects of the pre-colonial past which could no longer prove constructive. They were able to carry through a 'cultural revolution', as Samora Machel has explained, which 'began in the very moment when we fired our first shot': a continuing process of cultural change which 'rejects past values that are negative but survive as a deadweight, in ideas that are traditionalist, tribalist, regionalist, racist.'

Each movement's strength therefore came and had to come from struggle 'at and from the grass roots' of society, and then, with further practice, in a resultant theory of social change. Certainly, these were movements for which insurrection was the continuation of politics by other means. But the term 'politics', in this connexion, is misleadingly reductive. The politics in question was undoubtedly 'there': egalitarian, anti-élitist, insistently democratic in its implications, because success could come from no other kind of politics. But what was being 'continued' by the liberation wars, what was being developed by their practice, was evidently more than 'politics'. Rather was it the political and moral consciousness of all who were involved or influenced, each person's attitude to his or her collective, each person's sense of self-identity and self-respect. Some lost heart and others fell by the wayside. But the secret of the success of these movements, very evidently, is that most did not.

With these movements and their development across the years, accordingly, there may be said to have opened a new phase in the history of Africa's confrontation with the world of the twentieth century. Directly or indirectly influenced by them, other movements of the same type developed from the onset of the 1970s. These were movements facing an intransigence which reproduced that of the fascist Portuguese. In one way or another, and in differing degrees of maturity, each met its problems with a practice, and eventually a theory, that belonged to the same trend of democratic reconstruction as that displayed by PAIGC, FRELIMO, and MPLA. They had, besides, much the same inner process of development. To adapt the comment of a shrewd

Canadian observer, these were all movements which, in their early phases, combined 'a conventional nationalist movement frustrated of any easy transition to power, with a revolutionary movement struggling to be born'. The Eritrean movement is a good example of John Saul's comment.

ERITREA

Eritrea is a wide band of coastal plains and inland hills at the southern end of the Red Sea. Colonised by Italy between 1885 and 1941, Eritrea was brought under British military administration after fascist Italy's defeat in Africa, and remained under British caretaker rule until 1952. These seven decades of foreign invasion and domination were the period during which the various clans and ethnic groups of Eritrea began to evolve a sense of common identity, and then of nationalism, in much the same way as other colonised peoples: by reaction, that is, against the European nationalism which had dispossessed them.

Expressed for a long time by a minority of privileged persons who sought above all to ensure their own command of any future Eritrean entity that might emerge, this nationalism was weak, hesitant, and divided. What therefore should be done with Eritrea when, in 1952, the time came for Britain to withdraw according to the decision of the United Nations, Eritrea's formal 'trustee'? The relevant powers agreed that Eritrea should be joined to the neighbouring Ethiopian empire, but as a federated state retaining its own identity and local autonomy of rule.

Yet the masters of the Ethiopian empire formed some sixty years earlier by the Emperor Menelik were not content with an indirect control of Eritrea, such as federated status would give them. They wanted a direct control. Nothing stood in their way of achieving this except an immature and divided Eritrean nationalism. Sweeping this aside in 1962, the Ethiopian imperial government annexed Eritrea, destroyed all its autonomous attributes, and installed an outright administration of direct colonial rule, even going so far as to ban the use in schools of important Eritrean languages, Tigrinya and Arabic. This unilateral act of annexation was ineffectively opposed at the time; under Ethiopian pressure and corruption, the Eritrean assembly even approved of it. But the effect on Eritrean nationalism was then discovered to be immediate and profound.

Eritrean resistance to Ethiopian supremacy had been expressed in the later years of the federal period between 1952–62: partly by popular protest in the form of strikes and local protests, but chiefly, at the level of politics, by the members of a new middle class which had begun to emerge within the federated state. Yet now, from one year to the next, this resistance grew rapidly in strength and assertiveness. The Eritreans took to arms. Led initially by a loose coalition of nationalists, known as the Eritrean Liberation Movement (ELM), armed resistance began even while the ink was still drying on the imperial decrees of annexation. And it continued on a rising scale.

For a long while, however, this resistance continued with small success and with gross internal conflicts. Led 'from the top', and often by persons in exile who were in rivalry with one another, the ELM soon fell apart under the strains of armed struggle. Richard Sherman has remarked that the ELM was strongly nationalistic and favouring Eritrean independence, [but] was at the same time a loose coalition in which friction regarding ways and means created schisms in the organisational structure. It was during this [early] period that the seeds of [later] Eritrean organisational competition were sown. While today's unity issues [i.e. those of 1979–80] superficially regard ideology as the major stumbling block, personality conflicts must be superimposed onto the picture to understand it in its entirety.

Yet ideological points, issues of practice theory, were also at the root of early trouble, and they long persisted. Essentially, they defined a conflict of ideas and interests between an emergent middle class on the one hand and a 'grass roots' movement based on peasants and urban workers on the other hand; but this essential conflict, as Sherman tells us, was confused and sometimes contradicted by personal and other subjective disputes.

Here the parallel with FRELIMO in Mozambique, up to 1968, is in some ways close. In contrast with FRELIMO, however, the majority leadership in Eritrea at that time was reformist, not revolutionary; and the tensions, moreover, could not be contained within a single organisation. In 1970, after much internal violence and confusion, groups of fighters within the Eritrean Liberation Front (ELF), the successor of ELM, broke away and formed the Eritrean People's Liberation Front (EPLF). With their choice of name, they emphasised that they intended their new organisation to be the instrument of radical change.

As the EPLF developed in experience and effectiveness, clashes occurred with the ELF, and in 1972 a full-scale civil war between the two movements duly followed. This played directly into the hands of the Ethiopian colonial administration, and might have given the Ethiopian imperial government its opportunity for a 'neo-colonial' solution if only, of course, the Ethiopian regime had possessed the necessary economic and cultural strength. But it possessed no such thing: fearing to give a little in case it lost all, it gave nothing, and, in giving nothing, was encouraged by the spectacle of Eritrean disunity.

Sporadic fighting between the ELF and EPLF continued until 1974 when the dethronement of the Ethiopian emperor Haile Selassie, and the advent of a new regime, appeared to open fresh possibilities for Eritrean nationalism. The civil war was brought tardily to an end and attempts were made, vainly as it proved, to reach at least an operational unity. Yet the two chief components of Eritrean nationalism – there were lesser components on the scene, but they were not decisive – were closer than it could appear from the poor relations which persisted between them. Under the pressures of fighting an anti-colonial war – soon resumed and indeed intensified by Ethiopian efforts to crush resistance – both 'wings' developed towards movements of wide participation. By 1977, however, it appeared evident that the practice and theory of the EPLF had advanced considerably beyond those of the ELF, largely because this practice and theory emerged from an effective mobilisation of the inhabitants of liberated zones, not only for their self-defence but also for their self-government. These EPLF zones were now large, and solidly self-governed.

In 1978 the forces of the EPLF felt strong enough to depart from a guerrilla strategy and to attack many Eritrean towns occupied by the Ethiopian army. The decision looked sound at the time. It was followed by many successes; and

141

the Ethiopian army proved to be sorely demoralised. But it turned out badly. Now under the control of a strong military leader, Mengistu Hailé Mariam, the Ethiopian regime secured the active support of the USSR in arms, transport, bombing aircraft, and even military command. Acting as a great power riding roughshod over revolutionary issues in Eritrea, the USSR moved in and reversed the tide of Ethiopian defeat. Soviet-nourished Ethiopian units were able to retake the towns they had lost some months earlier, and 1979 saw the EPLF thrown back on a guerrilla strategy after many serious losses. The ELF, by this time, appeared to be in dissolution.

It was not the end of the story. Though hard hit, the EPLF was soon in firm control of wide rural areas and proved capable by 1980 of counter-attacking Ethiopian units and transport colums on a widening and effective scale; its political élan, meanwhile, had evidently not diminished. The EPLF had indeed emerged as a full-fledged movement of national liberation. Eritrean nationalism had acquired a correspondingly distinctive reality and profile. Whatever might happen next, it stood firmly on the scene.

ZIMBABWE

While these events were unfolding in the Horn of Africa, far to the south another great confrontation of these years was entering a new stage. The white-minority regime of South Africa, as powerful in its economic structures as it was extremist in its racism, had been forced to come to grips with the tides of liberation at home and on its borders. Long in the making, but lately developed to a new drive and pressure by the victories of FRELIMO in Mozambique and of the MPLA in Angola, these tides of liberation could no longer be contained by white South Africa's partners in Rhodesia and its administrative forces in Namibia.

Even within the South African police-state itself, 1976 brought an African challenge of a new scale and quality in the form of an anti-apartheid rising in the million-and-a-half strong 'township' of Soweto (short for South-Western Townships) and in other urban centres. For this was not only a massive and determined resistance to local forms of racist administration: this was also, as it appeared, at least the opening phase of another development towards the application of the practice and theory of national liberation.

Writing at a time when all these developments are far from clear, at least in Namibia and South Africa, one can offer no more than a provisional analysis. Of African political development in all three countries, and hence of its concept of armed struggle, guerrilla warfare, and the aims and consequences of these, one may briefly but safely assert that it followed the same pattern as we have noted elsewhere. With great variations of emphasis reflecting as many variations of circumstance, this nationalism moved from the politics of reformist compromise towards the politics of structural change: and hence from the armed struggle of limited aims towards the armed struggle of people's war. It moved along this line of development in no simple or direct way, but with many retreats, evasions, and disasters.

Many reasons for this complexity could be discerned. African nationalism in Rhodesia (known as Southern Rhodesia until 1964, when, with Northern Rhodesia's independence as Zambia, the 'Southern' was dropped from the name) had developed within the political ambience of British colonial rule. This was understandable in so far as the country, formally at least, was a British Colony whose constitutional destiny was supposed to lie in the hands of the British Parliament. Yet the reality was different. The British Parliament had in fact surrendered all effective power to a local white minority in 1923; since then, the country had been ruled by this minority with no reference to London. It had duly formed a state which was closely modelled, in all its essential laws and attitudes, on the state of South Africa, which, itself, had become independent of Britain under the rule of a local white minority (or rather of two white minorities) in 1910.

Developing in the late 1940s, African nationalism had seen its position and prospects in much the same perspectives as those of nationalists in the neighbouring territories of Northern Rhodesia (Zambia) and Nyasaland (Malawi). Yet these were colonies which really did remain under London's control, and where no decisive power had been surrendered to white minorities. Their nationalists could and did press for political concessions to the point where they became able to take over the colonial states, and emerge at the head of new nation-states. No such development was possible in Rhodesia. In 1961, true enough, a new Rhodesian constitution provided for eventual majority rule – that is, African majority rule – at some unstated but certainly distant time in the future. But while the African nationalists of Rhodesia then continued to press for more concessions on the same pattern, the white minority closed its ranks and voted for a government of white-minority extremists. In 1965, this government 'unilaterally' declared Rhodesia to be independent of Britain, and, by the same token, a sovereign state.

Thereafter the effective colonial opponent was no longer Britain, even if Britain remained formally responsible, but a white minority whose power rested, now, on the racist regime of South Africa. Rhodesia's laws and regulations were brought rapidly and ruthlessly into line with a fully racist conception modelled on the apartheid pattern of South Africa, even if differing in local variations. So the choice now, for African nationalists, was the same as that which had faced the nationalist movements in the Portuguese colonies. This choice was to fight or to submit.

But here, too, the choice of fighting imposed a second choice, just as in the Portuguese colonies. To have any success, fighting would have to draw on the active participation of the majority of Africans, for it was this majority which must provide the fighters and the means with which those fighters could succeed. This meant that the nationalists, if they were to have any success, must develop a practice and theory of anti-colonial liberation such as would emerge from the interests of the majority. They must fight, that is, no longer for control of an existing nation-state, structured as this was in harmony with the interests of the white minority (and any black hangers-on it could recruit); they must fight for the construction of an entirely different type of state. They must, in short, turn their backs on reform and embark on revolution.

The whole drama of African nationalism in Rhodesia was encapsulated in its attempt to achieve this necessary development of practice and theory; and this was to prove extremely difficult both before and after its success of 1980.

Forms of armed struggle were envisaged even late in the 1940s, and certainly before the white minority's declaration of independence in 1965.

They were thought of as a form of pressure for concessions within the British colonial ambience, and, as a nationalist afterwards recalled, for 'the purpose of carrying out acts of sabotage which were considered relevant to bring forth fear and despondency to the settlers of Rhodesia in order to influence the British Government and the settlers'. They were to be acts of counter-violence, in other words, which would give the legal nationalists a bargaining counter. They were launched, moreover, without the least attempt at the necessary preparation of African opinion. Not surprisingly, they came to nothing.

After 1965 it became clear that no such bargaining counter could serve any useful purpose: it merely provoked the racist regime into stiffer repressions. These sent leading nationalists into prison, detention in distant rural areas, or exile abroad. Critically, too, all this happened at a time when the nationalist forces were even less united than before; soon, they were sorely divided. With disunited leaders in prison or in exile, the development of a movement of effective struggle became ever more difficult. Many inside the country still hoped for concessions on the British colonial pattern, for that was the 'tradition' of their thinking on the subject of independence. Not a few outside the country still shared the same hope, even if they now spoke the language of resistance. Save among rare individuals, it seems that there was no serious attempt to think through the actual problems of the situation that had now emerged. Disputes raged.

Sporadic attempts continued to wage a limited guerrilla war. Militants of the two foreign-based wings of Zimbabwe nationalism, the Zimbabwe African National Union (ZANU) and Zimbabwe African People's Union (ZAPU) were sent for training in Ghana, the USSR and some other countries, and, upon their return, were infiltrated across the frontier of Zambia into Zimbabwe (Rhodesia). But this was done, once again, without a political preparation of the people upon whom they were to rely inside the country. On the contrary, it was assumed that African villagers in Zimbabwe would spontaneoulsy welcome these fighters and give them aid and shelter. Some did; many, inevitably, did not. The operations failed once more. It had been hoped that the white minority's declaration of a racist independence would have developed a fighting consciousness among the African masses. This, to some extent, it clearly did; strikes and demonstrations in Bulawayo, a principal urban centre, and in other places showed as much. But the white minority's security measures proved too strong for infiltrated fighters to be able to survive. Clearly, there could be no success without a much more intensive and determined campaign of illegal political work.

Yet the lesson was evidently hard to learn. In 1967 a force of some seventy highly-trained men, this time provided by the South African African National Congress as well as by ZAPU, went in from Zambia with orders to split into three groups. The ZAPU men were to establish themselves in northerly and southerly parts of Rhodesia, while the South African contingent was to march across the country, avoiding action with colonial forces, and cross the Limpopo river into South Africa. It was a brave enterprise which ended in tough battles to the death, for evasion in Rhodesia proved too difficult; but it failed as surely as others before it.

The underlying strategy had in fact moved from one extreme to another. Initially, as we have seen, there had been the concept of developing some kind of counter-violence as a means of providing political leaders with a bargaining-counter in their pressure for concessions. Now there was substituted another concept, that of full-scale guerrilla war by small groups of highly trained fighters who would, it was hoped, attract volunteers. But this jumped a vital stage in the process of successful insurrection. It supposed that military action would lead to political support, whereas, in every known example of success, the process was the other way round. It ignored the essential maxim of all such struggles conducted so as to succeed: that a people must liberate itself, since no one else can do it for them, or, to repeat the words of a veteran of the Vietnamese liberation wars, 'what has to be achieved is that people themselves discover the need for armed struggle. As for guns, those you can always find.'

This was likewise the period which saw member-states of the Organisation of African Unity falling into the same 'militarist' error. They proposed to establish a 'liberation army' which should go to war, for instance, with the still persisting armies of fascist Portugal. Even if that could have been achieved, and with success, it would have robbed the colonised people of the Portuguese territories of their right and opportunity to liberate themselves and, in so doing, to find out how to rebuild their own societies.

A new phase opened in 1972 as FRELIMO extended its operations in the Tete district of western Mozambique and, having crossed the Zambezi in force, opened new zones of contestation down the eastern border of Rhodesia. ZANU units infiltrated from Zambia combined with FRELIMO units in this border region to fight both Rhodesian and Portuguese units, and then moved into Rhodesia where they were able to begin a deep penetration. Successful guerrilla warfare forced concessions by the white-minority government in 1976 but these were nullified by white-minority resistance to any meaningful change. A prolonged conference in Geneva then provided the prelude to the holding of a general election while the war continued, and the emergence of a government under the nominal control of Bishop Abel Muzorewa; the practical control of the white minority (led by Ian Smith) and its South African patrons remained effectively the same as before.

Yet it was a control which could not long survive, for it now became increasingly clear that the Muzorewa–Smith combination could neither end the war nor win it. In this situation a variety of external pressures, notably those of the five 'frontline states' (Angola, Botswana, Mozambique, Tanzania, Zambia), and others in the Commonwealth, initiated a new drive for negotiated change. A conference in Lusaka succeeded in persuading the British government to the same effect; and another conference, this time in London towards the end of 1979, led to a general election under conditions of ceasefire. The whole people could now vote. They gave their support overwhelmingly to the ZANU wing of the Patriotic Front led by Robert Mugabe, while the ZAPU wing led by Joshua Nkomo carried most of the remaining seats available to non-white voters. With this, at last, an independent Zimbabwe became possible, and was duly proclaimed in April 1980.

IN THE DEEP SOUTH

The record in Namibia was to some extent parallel with that in Rhodesia, but there were great differences of circumstance. Namibia, since German eviction in 1915, had become to all intents and purposes a direct colony of South Africa. Its diverse populations were small and scattered across a large territory, and their development of a coherent nationalism had to evolve in relative isolation from the rest of the continent. Even so, reaction to white nationalism – in this case the nationalism, principally, of an Afrikaner settler community reinforced by other whites – was essentially the same as elsewhere. Backed by African support at the United Nations, this nationalism was able to make some progress: to the point, indeed, where South Africa's 'right' to continue occupation of Namibia came seriously in question, and where the International Court of Justice, in 1971, could advise the Security Council of the UN that this occupation was illegal, and that South Africa must withdraw.

Pressure derived from this and other such decisions was reinforced by guerrilla operations undertaken by the majority nationalist organisation, the South West African People's Organisation (SWAPO), as well as by the growing protest of African mineworkers and others inside the territory. Guerrilla operations begun on a very small scale in 1966 became larger and more effective; so did strikes and demonstrations in urban centres such as Windhoek. Aiming at an 'internal solution' on Rhodesian lines, the South African regime moved in 1974 to effect a plan of political devolution which would leave Pretoria in overall control. Under African pressure, this was challenged by major Western powers, but with no resolution. The year 1980 had to open with few good omens for an early or a peaceful independence.

It had long been obvious, in any case, that none of these anti-colonial campaigns, whether in relation to Rhodesia or Namibia or the post-colonial reconstruction of Angola and Mozambique, much less to any question about the future of Botswana, Lesotho, or Swaziland, could be divorced from the factor of South African intervention. This factor was of increasing importance. Back in the 1960s, powerful in its industrial, commercial, and military supremacy, the strength of the South African regime had seemed irresistible. Faced with the rise of African nationalism outside its borders, Pretoria had evolved policies of political absorption. It would accept 'black governments' with the aim of drawing all of them, as far north as the Congo Basin, into some kind of Southern African 'common market' which South Africa would manifestly dominate. And for a while, further strengthened by Western European and American support for some such scheme, this policy of absorption had every promise of success. The post-independence regimes of Malawi and Madagascar accepted it; so did the Portuguese dictatorship, then under severe strains of war, in relation to Angola and Mozambique. Meanwhile, inside South Africa, the 1960s saw the ruthless crushing of all manifestations of African political protest and organisation.

But 1974 brought the collapse of colonial rule in Angola and Mozambique, and the emergence in 1975 of strongly independent and radical regimes in those territories. This significantly changed the balance of influence, and even the balance of power, throughout the southern half of the continent. Taken by surprise, Pretoria was obliged to accept the change in Mozambique with as good a grace as it could. Recovering, it refused to accept the change in Angola and, with the aid of UNITA and FNLA, invaded that country with powerful armoured columns in October 1975. The invasion failed, and the change had to be accepted until further counter-action could be developed. This began soon after with the launching from Namibian bases of a programme of military 'destabilisation'. South African ground raids and aerial bombing of targets in southernmost Angola were accompanied by the infiltration of sabotage teams, and, in 1977, by an attempt to 'seat' the UNITA leadership in southern Angola at least for long enough to 'legitimate' the proclamation of a secessionist 'republic of southern Angola'. This failed in face of MPLA military defence assisted by Cuban forces; but from 1977, and on a rising rhythm of aggression, South Africa continued its aggressions in Angola.

Much the same policy was adopted, and again from 1977, towards the newly-formed republic of Mozambique, but here the war was indirect, being conducted by South African-nourished Rhodesian forces, or by South African aerial bombing masked as Rhodesian. Meanwhile the Rhodesian regime, capped now by a 'black and white' government, came ever more heavily under South African influence and protection. It was now seen, at least by 1978, that the old policy of sub-continental hegemony had been reconsidered and re-applied. Pretoria would ensure its control of Zimbabwe/Rhodesia, close in on Zambia by securing the ruin or control of its rail links with the outside world, while at the same time keeping up military pressure on Angola and Mozambique with the aim of wrecking the regimes of FRELIMO and MPLA. If further military invasions were necessary, they would be made. For whatever the outside world might say about such invasions, Pretoria appeared confident by now that the outside world would do nothing to prevent or challenge them. In this, and no doubt rightly, Pretoria counted on the major equivocation inside Western policy. On the one hand, major Western powers were obliged to pay attention to African pressures for change. On the other hand, Western interests in South Africa were of such a nature, not least in respect of Western reliance on South African gold production, as to make any serious pressure against the South African system much less than likely. In this situation the prospect of 1979 was for continued South African military agression.

Would the situation inside South Africa modify this prospect? The 1960s had seen the violent repression of all effective African protest inside South Africa. But here, too, the 1970s brought a change. Massive strikes by African urban workers had to be contained by the concession of wage-rises on a scale never seen since 1910. This in turn encouraged other forms of protest. Barred from any organised party-political action, groups of students turned to new forms of protest. There came the rise of a 'black consciousness' movement among African students in universities or colleges now strictly segregated on racist and even 'tribalist' lines. Though quickly repressed with the banning from public life, imprisonment, or even killing of its leaders, this 'black consciousness' movement did more than a little to resuscitate protest in the tradition of the African National Congress and other movements crushed during the 1960s. However indirectly, its influence helped to promote a revival of confidence in the possibility of change and the efficacy of protest.

Then, in 1975, came the collapse of Portuguese rule in Mozambique, and, more or less directly following from that, the great Soweto rising and other campaigns of active defiance of *apartheid*, beginning in May 1976 and continuing for many months. It was now seen that a huge 'township' such as Soweto – having more than a million black inhabitants 'controlled' by some fourteen police stations – could effectively defy the whole might of the *apartheid* state. Soon after, Soweto militants who had fled abroad with the aim of securing an appropriate military training for guerrilla war began to infiltrate back into South Africa. Trained in Angola or elsewhere by means of exile organisations of the African National Congress of South Africa, these young men began to score their first small successes in 1978. Police stations in Soweto were attacked by guerrillas who were now able to escape detection thanks to the shelter of a surrounding population. A wider armed struggle seemed to lie ahead.

How far that wider struggle would or could develop remained to be seen; and 1980 saw the initiation of additionally tough police and military measures to prevent it. Meanwhile, north of the Limpopo, the prospect of 1979 was profoundly modified by the emergence of an African-ruled Zimbabwe. With that, the South African plan for sub-continental hegemony once more received a major setback. The pressure came off Zambia, while the Angolan regime, though repeatedly attacked by South African forces in the far south, showed great solidity of response and was clearly in no way shaken.

Little more could usefully be said at the beginning of the 1980s. The liberation struggles had scored one success after another on the periphery of the South African system, removing Angola and Mozambique from its control, then removing Rhodesia and sharply challenging that control in Namibia, as well as promoting the opportunity for renewed African protest in South Africa itself. Now the 'front-line of liberation' came hard against the racist regime itself. And that regime, whatever 'cosmetic' concessions it might make towards a lessening of *apartheid* rigidity, had clearly shown that it was determined to make none of substance, and appeared firmly to believe that the Western powers, if with verbal public protests, would nonetheless remain its friends and effective allies.

CHAPTER THIRTEEN

A TENTATIVE TYPOLOGY

Africa knew other wars of various resistance in this most recent period, and each would be worth examination. The people of the Western Sahara took to arms against Moroccan and Mauritanian claims to their hitherto Spanish-occupied territory, and, as POLISARIO, found a strong ally in Algeria. A long and complex conflict developed in Chad. Dissidence continued in vast areas of Zaire. Amin's dictatorship in Uganda was overthrown by a Ugandan resistance fortified decisively by Tanzania. Ethiopia was the scene of other than

Fig. 13.1 *Sahroui units of the army of the* POLISARIO *independence movement in the Western Sahara proved able, late in the 1970s, to master the art of guerrilla warfare in completely open terrain. This photograph shows a handful of* POLISARIO *fighters escorting a column of Moroccan and Mauritanian prisoners of war. With Algerian support, the Sahroui were able to induce Mauritania to withdraw from the war and recognise Sahroui claims. But the forces of King Hassan of Morocco continued to invade this former Spanish colony, and fighting continued.*

Eritrean challenges by various national groups, notably Somali and Oromo. And still the list is not complete.

But I hope that the analysis of certain major struggles, as attempted in this brief history, can help to elucidate the nature of each of these upheavals, some of them by movements of an advanced political development, others by movements of little more than outraged protest against misgovernment or foreign interference. At the same time it needs to be remembered that history will not fit into neat patterns, and that historians who draw such patterns live usually to regret it. Nothing in this book, I trust, will be taken as proposing a doctrine or dogma of people's war. Circumstances alter cases. What I have sought to do is to examine a number of dominant and, as it may well appear, decisive trends; to measure these trends against factors of success or failure; and to set them against a wider history.

Along the continuum of popular responses by armed struggle, three chief phases of consciousness can be observed in the record, each with its corresponding range of aims and objectives, and, of course, its own peculiarities. They may be called the phases of *restoration*, of *transition*, and of *innovating change*.

In the phase of restoration, people joined together in resistance to a usurpation of accepted right, and in defence of a revival of that right. Their ideology told them that an established order had been infringed or sorely threatened, and that they must act to restore it. More or less emphatically, this ideology spoke often in the name of an ancestral time of peace and justice, of a 'golden age', or, at least, of a past period more desirable than the present.

The records of those who thus resisted, on the rare occasions that these records have survived, tell of folk heroes who defended the poor and despoiled the rich, who succoured the weak and defied the strong, and whose names and deeds live in popular memory as an underground river of self-respect, flowing beneath and beyond the monuments of official history. In official history, *per contra*, such persons tend to live as thieves and vagabonds. They are to be heard of in all continents and from the most ancient times that we can reach.

In Egypt of the Pharoahs, for example, central power broke down in periods of contention and confusion. Then, say the official histories in temple hieroglyphics or other written records, in this case around 2200 BC, 'the bowman is ready and the wrongdoer is everywhere', and a man 'who goes out to plough carries his shield, while thieves sit in the bushes until the benighted traveller passes by and his load is plundered'. There are many bandits; 'thieves grow rich'. But the official texts hint at another side to the story, for 'he who had nothing is now a man of wealth, and the poor man is full of joy', while 'every town says, Let us suppress the powerful amongst us', and 'the children of princes are dashed against the walls'.

Such examples must be inherent to all social formations in which wealth and power have accumulated among the few, and a sense of injustice and dispossession among the many. When the Sultan of Morocco's troops invaded Songhay, the 'core people' of that old empire gathered behind Askia Nuh and sought to restore their state and social order. But other peoples, tributary and subject to the Songhay, fought a different war: for them, the goal of restoration was not the Songhay empire but the ancestral order they had known before subjection. Or else they fought confusedly, rejecting the new power as well as the old, but without any clear conception of their goal. Or else, moving from that phase of transition to a phase of innovating change, they fought for the establishment of a different order, or at least for one conceived as being different; and from the ruins of old empires there came new kingdoms, new states, new constellations of power.

The three phases seem to have occurred in every major historical period. There is much to suggest, for example, that the nineteenth century in Africa, even before the colonial period, was in many ways a period of transition and a prelude to the search for innovating change. We cannot review the evidence here, but it points insistently to a widespread crisis of the socio-economic structures formed by previous centuries of development. Kingships became despotic, seeking greater control of trade or tribute; there were characteristic reactions in popular resistance. New states arose under new types of power; there was here and there a drive for reform, for modernisation, for new patterns of self-organisation. Sometimes this drive was in terms of extending a traditional ideology; and new shrines or gods legitimated new powers. In the Niger Delta, Alagoa tells us, the Nembe acquired Ama-Tẹmẹ-Suo, a 'national deity' called to preside over a union of four city-states in a time of expanding Nembe trade. Sometimes the drive for modernisation corresponded to a more or less severe break with tradition, and new states, as with the Zulu, imposed reorganisation.

Colonial invasion cut short the search for innovating change along indigenous lines, and introduced a new series of phases. The period began with primary resistances to invasion which sought, very emphatically, the restoration of pre-invasion law and order. But primary resistance could also become an occasion for attempts at innovating change, at least in a limited sense. Abd al-Kader mobilised many clans to resist French invasion. Most of them, by such evidence as we have, resisted in order to restore; but Abd al-Kader himself had the vision of a different Algeria, united as never before and organised in new ways. Broadly, however, primary resistances were in defence of restoration.

Then came what have been called secondary resistances to a colonial power which had usurped the established order, and displaced it by a colonial order. Some of these secondary resistances sought to restore, but others were transitional. Increasingly, as the colonial years went by, they were transitional in that while they sought for restoration, they were obliged to do this in a situation in which the breakdown of traditional structures had reached a point where these had little relevance to uprooted peasants, migrant workers, or 'deruralised' masses in urban peripheries.

This was the situation, notably during the Great Depression of the 1930s, and still more during the Second World War with its more intensive exploitation, in which popular resistance flowed into movements seeking to remove an Evil strongly felt but hard to grasp: into anti-witchcraft movements, into millennial movements, into visions of a Day of Judgment when God should dethrone this Evil. It was also the situation in which Africans repeatedly sought to take and use the spiritual power of the dispossessors, and make Christianity serve the dispossessed. It was the time of prophets and sects, and, as matters evolved, a time when the leaders of sects began to be displaced by the leaders of new forms of protest: by combinations of wage-workers, by anti-tax movements, by strikes and the like. The story of these transitional resistances is extraordinarily rich and various.

Out of the phase of transition there developed a phase of innovating change, or of the search for innovating change. This, too, could be neither simple nor unitary in form. As we have seen, a duality of theme characterised all popular resistance during the late colonial period and its immediate aftermath in a 'neo-colonial' period: whenever, that is, this resistance was more than a mere outburst of anger or revenge. There was still the aim of restoration, of removal of an intrusive control in favour of a lost independence. But there was also, now, the aim of renewal, of innovating change aimed at reconstructing a given community, at reorganising its inner relations of power and production, at giving it a modern ground on which to confront the modern world. We have looked at examples, and have marked their various outcomes.

Yet it seems, too, that the theme of innovating change gained steadily on that of restoration. This was perceptible even where the language of ideology might be archaic, or when its precedents and parables reached far back into the past. Those who led the Land and Freedom Armies often used the symbols of the past as a means of justifying their vision of the future. When they turned to the colonial power in their messages, they looked for arguments out of history: sometimes, shrewdly, out of English history. They recalled England's Magna Carta of 1215, the charter that so signally renewed the old law of 'just revolt against an unjust king'. Their 'Charter of Dedan Kimathi' said to the British:

> Do you remember what your grandfathers did during the reign of King Richard II? The people opened prisons, tore down the houses of the rich, and killed many who were their enemies. They burned the houses of lawyers and tax-collectors, and King's officers who had wronged them. . . . Soon after the King made them free for ever, and since that time Britons are ever free and are strongly ruling the world.

It might be inaccurate history; it was very accurate as a statement of the Land and Freedom case. King John had agreed in Magna Carta that any future royal failure to redress grievances and govern justly should empower the barons, 'and the community of the whole land', to join in violent counter-action to 'distress and harass (the King) by all the ways in which they are able'. It was precisely what the Land and Freedom armies were doing to the colonial system. The fact remained that they were not distressing and harassing the colonial system in order to restore the past, but, at least in their initial ideas, in order to establish a new and post-colonial system.

The ideology of innovating change grew in strength and appeal until it appeared to become a dominant trend. What, for example, did the future hold for peoples not yet free in Southern Africa? That question, affirmed the veteran leader of South Africa's African National Congress, Oliver Tambo, in April 1979, 'had been answered again practically by the realisation of popular power (*poder popular*) in Angola and Mozambique, and the process of social transformation which that popular power has started in those two countries'. In vast areas of the continent the consequences of colonial systems had gone far to proletarianise both rural and urban multitudes. Any movement of reconstruction capable of confronting their problems would have to be in harmony with their living reality, with their actual needs and aspirations.

Cabral had defined this necessary equivalence as early as the middle 1960s when arguing that the central aim of any movement of national liberation, rather than of merely national protest, would have to enable its people to regain command of their own history: 'to liberate, that is, the means and development of their own productive forces'. And because any such process of liberation 'calls for a profound mutation in the condition of those productive forces, we see that the phenomenon of national liberation is necessarily one of revolution'. This being so, the ideology of nationalism within this concept could move beyond the bourgeois limits borrowed from Europe, and, reflecting its mass-class basis, could open the road to wider unities. The reform of borrowed models was abandoned; instead, there came the search for indigenous models and, as the wars went on, their slow and difficult emergence.

PART THREE

ON STRATEGY AND TACTICS

E ka n'lidura di lagarto
que na tudjibu canoa passa

It's not the angry stare of a crocodile
that can stop your canoe from crossing

Guinea-Bissau: peasant saying

It was in the process of struggle that
we synthesised the lessons of each experience,
forging our ideology, constructing the
theoretical instruments of our struggle

Samora Machel, 1978

CHAPTER FOURTEEN

THE STRATEGY OF PEOPLE'S WAR

Propagandists on one side or the other have exercised their craft on countless occasions in trying to show that the decisive concepts of guerrilla warfare in a mature and modernising form, the warfare here called 'people's war', came into Africa from outside the continent, and, indeed, could not have come from an African thought and practice. It is an attitude compounded of ignorance and paternalism, but a refusal to follow it need not lead to overlooking a worldwide experience. A review of that experience would be out of place, but some brief reference may be useful as a means of drawing comparisons.

It seems that the first thoroughgoing analysis of the requirements of people's war under conditions specifically colonial or semi-colonial, and in circumstances of a large or very large majority of rural people, was made by Mao Tsetung, the Chinese revolutionary leader when, in 1936, he delivered a series of lectures entitled *Strategic Problems of China's Revolutionary War*. They were lessons drawn from more than ten years of an intensive and very varied conduct of political and military guerrilla war under severely testing conditions, ranging from the clearing of China's first liberated zones through long marches and manoeuvres to the establishment of a strong base in northern Shensi in 1935. They have much to say of general relevance, but their principal interest, given Mao Tsetung's characteristic insistence on the study of reality (at least in those days), lies within the context of Chinese history. At the same time, in reference to a familiar view that Africans have 'invented nothing', we may at least note an interesting comment of Mao Tsetung's to some visitors in 1971. 'You came to ask me', said Mao Tsetung on that occasion, 'to talk about people's warfare of liberation. And yet in your recent history there is Abd al-Krim al-Kattabi, one of the principal sources from whom I learned the meaning of people's warfare of liberation.'

Notable guides and manuals came out of other struggles under colonial or semi-colonial conditions. Prominent among them is another series of lectures, *People's War, People's Army*, by the Vietnamese revolutionary commander, V. N. Giap, an analysis of his people's anti-colonial struggles between 1945 and 1954. Here, once again, the strict inspection of a local reality yields principles of general relevance. Under different conditions the same holds good for the writings of another historic commander of people's war, Josip Broz-Tito of Yugoslavia. Like others of his quality, Tito in his writings or speeches invariably proceeds from practice to theory, and his general principles, in so far as he states any, are those that arise from the analysis of a specific time and place. Other cases, large or small, follow the same pattern: as, for one example among many, William Pomeroy's account of the Huk guerrilla struggles in the Philippines, again the work of a participant.

Did African leaders of this type of warfare, from Ahmed ben Bella at one end of the continent to Samora Machel at the other, set out with any detailed knowledge of such predecessors? It seems clear that they did not, or by little more than name and reputation. Cabral said as much in 1971; others have agreed with him. Yet Cabral and his companions undoubtedly developed a practice and theory that were close to the essential ideas and approaches of, for example, the Vietnamese liberation struggle. A case of copying, or of independent development? The answer, one finds, is independent development; there is copious evidence. Then how was that possible? An interesting comment on this particular question was offered by Samora Machel, in 1978, when speaking of the reasons for FRELIMO's having adopted 'Marxism-Leninism as a basic guide'. He said:

> Ideas come from practice. When we set out, all those years ago, we wanted to liberate our people, and we found that people have to liberate themselves if the thing is to be real. We found that people could not liberate themselves unless they were active participants in the process of liberation. And so, little by little, we applied a revolutionary practice – in the wartime zones that we controlled and protected from colonial power – which enabled this indispensible participation, this mass participation – political and social, cultural and military – to begin and grow and develop itself.
>
> We acquired a lot of experience. We learned much. We made mistakes and saw how to correct them. We made successes and saw how to improve on them. In doing this, we evolved a theory out of our practice: and then we found that this theory of ours, evolving out of our practice, had already acquired a theorisation under different circumstances, elsewhere, in different times and places. This theory or theorisation is Marxism-Leninism.

How far this label is meaningful, however influential were Lenin's practice and theory fifty years earlier under conditions that were enormously different, will remain a matter for debate. A notion familiar in some communist as well as non-communist writings that FRELIMO (for example) adopted the theory and then applied it in practice, is evidently wide of the truth. The truth, on the contrary, is that FRELIMO's theory derived and had to derive from a specific practice under specific conditions, and that the classics of Marxism, having almost nothing to say about such conditions, could provide no practical analysis. They could and did provide a general guide to action, which is precisely what Marx and Lenin had intended. But a general guide to action is not an analysis of a given society: it is only a means to the practice from which an analysis, and hence a theory, may emerge.

Originality was required. No one from outside could come and say to these leaders: this is how we did it in County X or Y, and so this is how you do it here; or, if any did so come (and I seem to recall that several tried) they had to be rapidly set right upon the point. That being so, these Africans made their own original contributions to the practical and theoretical solution of problems arising from characteristic twentieth century situations, notably the situations arising within and from imperialism. If outside opinions, sometimes very learned ones, have failed to see this originality, the reason can only be that colonial paternalism has had a long reach and deep roots.

Another conclusion follows. Meaningful discussion of these campaigns can arrive at general principles, but only so long as this is done from the examination of specific cases. I therefore propose to discuss strategy and tactics strictly in specific cases, and, largely because they are singularly well documented, in those of the movements in the Portuguese colonies. The leaders of those movements never in fact claimed any 'prize for excellence', and there is no reason to claim it for them. Yet, as noted earlier, their experience and success offer an unusually firm ground of approach.

AN IDEOLOGY OF LIBERATION

On wars in general there are plenty of well-nourished conclusions. Those who win military campaigns of whatever kind, the books say, are those who seize and hold the long-term initiative. This means the power to impose on one's opponent the key decisions which dictate the ways in which the contest takes shape, develops over time, and moves from one phase to the next. The embodiment of this power is called the *strategic initiative*; it can be seized and held, in other words, only by the application of an appropriate strategy.

Strategy is therefore that kind of planning which aims at enabling a commander to 'keep on top' of the commander on the other side, to anticipate the other's moves so as to counteract or deflect them, and, especially in guerrilla warfare, to lessen one's own weaknesses by concentrating on the weaknesses of the enemy. Strategy takes shape in tactics: that is, in a more or less large and always continuous series of detailed operations designed to serve an adopted strategy.

We have looked briefly at the conditions under which the guerrilla movements in the Portuguese colonies were obliged to fight their wars. They found that a successful strategy, a development of their own resources so as to enable them to seize and hold the strategic initiative, had to depend on two processes. The first of these was action to transform mass support – sympathy or goodwill – into mass participation that was voluntary, active, and therefore developmental in its effects on individual consciousness and collective effort. With mass participation they could win their wars in spite of all their material weaknesses; without it, they were bound to lose. But this imposed a second requirement: the process of a protracted war. Transforming support into participation among wide rural masses could not be done rapidly. On the contrary, it had to be a slow and painstaking work of gradual advance towards unity of thought and action among individuals and ethnic groups of widely varying ideas and attitudes.

These real requirements of success – a transformation of consciousness, and time to achieve it – dictated an ideology of liberation. This ideology could not spring from any kind of previously formed intellectual theory: it had to develop from real needs and interests. 'Always bear in mind', Cabral taught his militants, 'that the people are not fighting for ideas, for the things in anyone's head. They are fighting to win material benefits, to live better and in peace, to see their lives go forward, to guarantee the future for their children.' The 'big ideas' concerning liberation, nationalism, independence

must therefore develop out of the 'small ideas' concerned with local grievances, local protests, local aspirations: in the Portuguese context, these were
taxation, forced labour, abusive treatment, and the rest. A successful ideology
of liberation, in short, had to develop from the living reality of living people,
and not from any theoretical concept of what others might think good for those
people. Intellectuals might be useful, but only in the measure that they were
able to 'rethink' themselves into this reality of living people. Intellectuals
would otherwise be useless, or worse.

This ideology of liberation was the approach, analysis, and action by which
the people of Guinea-Bissau (for example) could develop an understanding of
their 'general situation' out of their 'particular situation', could as gradually
find ways of solving its problems, and, in so doing, could eventually prepare
that 'mutation of their productive forces' which, in turn, would signify 'the
development of their own history'. To achieve any of this, as the saying of
Guinea-Bissau put it, *povo na manda na su cabeça*: 'people must do it for themselves'; or, as Samora Machel in Mozambique was to say: 'People have to
liberate themselves if the thing is to be real'.

And hence the insistence on a crucial dimension of cultural development,
repeatedly stated in the experience of all these movements. For this development, this 'resumption of the making of history', had to mean what it implied:
purposive change, selective transformation, cultural reconception: not in some
kind of intellectual 'return to the source' by more or less alienated persons, but
at 'the base' among masses of people, mostly village people, who had no need
to 'return to the source' of their cultures because the source was the very
ground upon which, culturally, they stood. One of Cabral's internal seminars
for militants, in this case in 1969, had much to say on this point.

'A lot of people', he said on that occasion, 'think that to defend Africa's
culture, to resist culturally in Africa, we have to defend the negative things in
our culture. But this is not what we think.' A system to replace the colonial
system could not usefully be a reversion to pre-colonial times, even if that were
possible. On the contrary:

> Our cultural resistance consists in the following: while we scrap colonial
> culture and the negative aspects of our own culture, whether in our
> character or in our environment, we have to create a new culture, also
> based on our own traditions but respecting everything that the world
> today has conquered for the service of mankind.

All this being so, the aim of liberation war – and we have seen this in other
cases – was not only to remove the colonial system but also, and even more, to
develop a capacity to master the real problems of living people. The power
worth having could in no sufficient sense come out of 'the barrel of a gun',
however much the colonial enemy might (and did) impose the need to use a
gun: this power, primarily and finally, would always derive from the development of a new consciousness and a new culture. So that while this ideology of
liberation can be defined in terms of the theory evolved from practice, its real
meaning has to be sought in the practice itself.

This practice, in turn, imposed its needs. These were evidently four in
number. One was for an initial leadership which had grasped at any rate the

outlines of the real problem: that the struggle must be conducted in such a way that people, increasingly, 'do it for themselves'; and which, having grasped that objective, was capable of promoting it. The second need was for a movement of militants in whom the same understanding was evolved. The third was for a detailed programme consistent with real needs and interests. And the fourth, developing in line with the others, was for the building of an appropriate organisation of society. If these needs could be met, at least sufficiently to enable a continuous if gradual development of all four, then the PAIGC (for example) could cease to be a movement of anti-colonial protest, a movement of merely nationalist reaction against foreign rule. It could become something different and more significant. It could develop into a movement of national liberation.

Meeting these needs proved more difficult than fighting the colonial enemy. Huge problems of cultural disunity and indiscipline had to be overcome. Especially serious for the PAIGC in 1963, these problems were gradually mastered in 1964. At this point, by 1964, the PAIGC (in the real example I am using here) had achieved a solid leadership and a growing movement of militants; it also had a detailed programme of objectives. It knew where it was going, but it had still to develop the means of getting there. It lacked the fourth requirement: the pattern of a new organisation of society.

This would have to emerge from the experience of an ever wider number of rural people who were able to practise the ideology of liberation, and through practice achieve their self-transformation into citizens. This in turn meant the establishment of zones free of enemy control and, normally, from enemy incursions.

This, in its turn, meant the building of mobile units of a regular army combined with more or less static local militias. Moves to that end were initiated by the PAIGC leadership early in 1964; we will look at their results, in tactical organisation and operational method, in a moment. Meanwhile, what strategy should govern this fighting? Cabral defined it later, but 1964 saw its early application:

> In order to dominate a given zone, the enemy is obliged to disperse his forces. In dispersing his forces, he weakens himself and we can defeat him. Then, in order to defend himself against us, he has to concentrate his forces. When he does that, however, we can occupy the zones that he leaves free and work in them politically so as to hinder his return there.

That is how the war was won. Having moved out of the purely guerrilla phase into the phase of mobile warfare, the PAIGC applied itself to manoeuvring an always far superior colonial force into a fixed dispersal. Falling into this trap, the colonial commanders duly scattered their numerically huge forces into many fixed garrisons and fortified camps: in Guinea-Bissau, according to General Bettencourt Rodrigues, eventually into no fewer than 225 of these.* Next, the PAIGC set about clearing Portuguese control out of large areas, either by eliminating certain fixed garrisons or else by besieging others and

---

* Late in 1973. Of this total, the general says, 72 were held only with Portuguese troops, 82 with Portuguese troops and African militias, and 71 only with African militias. Most of the last category vanished of their own volition early in 1974. See Guide to Sources, p. 197.

161

preventing movement of their troops. These liberated zones were thereafter steadily enlarged.

After 1967, reacting against a strategy which had cost them the initiative, Portugal's commanders began to develop new forms of offensive action, chiefly by helicoptered commando raids combined with bombing and occasional ground offensives. But they were too late: by this time the forces of the PAIGC, and the political solidity of large liberated zones, had become strong enough to ensure that raids and occasional offensive sweeps could do no more than damage these zones. Generally, the zones were kept free from enemy action or, when attacked, their populations were sheltered by rearguard action and evasion.

What, in essence, were these liberated zones?

LIBERATED ZONES

They were little more, at the outset, than an idea; and often a wrong one.

Opening their campaign in January 1963, and taking the Portuguese commanders more or less completely by surprise, the PAIGC was able to clear considerable forest areas of enemy control. These were held by groups of guerrillas under local commanders; and, as the situation evolved, each of these commanders formed his own 'forest base' more or less distantly from neighbouring commanders and their units. Given the low level of political unity and understanding which still prevailed, trouble followed almost at once. In the words of one of the PAIGC senior militants who saved the situation from disaster, but speaking many years later:

> At that point, many fighters began to exploit their new authority for personal reasons. They began to reject the overall authority for unity of our party (the PAIGC), and to abuse the people, especially the women, in the zones they controlled. Above all, they began to group themselves on a tribal basis, to build an autonomy on tribal affiliation and religious belief (that is, loyalty to local shrines and diviners), and to give priority in recruitment and in the handing out of arms to members of their own tribes and families, or through their tribal chief if they had any.

What had developed, in short, was an armed resistance but not a movement of liberation. As in the Congo rebellions a little later, recourse was had to 'old customs and beliefs about witchcraft', charms and divination; so discipline faltered, military 'commandism' took over, and something like a reign of terror began in some of the guerrilla-held zones. An outraged leadership then found 'that abominable crimes were being committed in our name, and that people had begun to flee from some of our liberated zones'.

All this was reversed with drastic measures early in 1964. At their congress of February 1964, held in the southern zone of Quitáfine, Cabral and his leading companions were able to disarm and remove all commanders guilty of crimes or serious indiscipline, and to lay foundations for coherent military and political organisation. From now onwards the PAIGC had firm foundations; and now too, from about the middle of 1964, its political workers and fighters could begin the establishment of genuine liberated zones. These were quickly cleared of enemy control in coastal and forest regions of the south, and progressively in other regions.

What were they actually fighting for at this point?

Not, primarily, to complete the destruction of enemy control in Guinea-Bissau, but to continue and deepen the work of transforming support into participation in the zones now under their control. Further destruction of enemy control would march in step with the further spread of participation. The first would be useless without the second, because, without the second, there might be destruction of the enemy but there would be no liberation.

I am not suggesting, of course, that any such step-by-step pattern of parallel development – further spread of participation: further destruction of enemy control – worked out neatly or infallibly. All wars, including these wars, have contained a large element of confusion and muddle. But such was the underlying intention, the general plan of action.

What happened inside these zones?

Transforming support or sympathy into active and voluntary participation by rural multitudes implied, essentially, the building of new political and social institutions of self-government. To return to those of the pre-colonial past, even if possible, would have invited disunity and worse, as the failings of 1963 had abundantly shown. And since no others existed, because the Portuguese had governed by simple dictatorship, it was necessary to devise new ones. Within the institutional void thus caused by the eviction of Portuguese dictatorship from these zones, the PAIGC had to install a democracy. This was achieved in three stages: first, the promotion of representative committees of local self-government; secondly, the development of an elective assembly-delegate structure as practice improved; and thirdly, again with further practice, the devolution to these committees of increasing powers and duties.

Success in building these structures varied with time and place. Where zones could be protected from enemy action through long periods, political work was able to develop the foundations of a new democracy and a new state. I draw the following observations from a four weeks' tour of personal investigation in some of the southern liberated areas of Guinea-Bissau at the end of 1972, where some of the zones had been free of enemy control, save for occasional incursions, since 1965. Here it was evident that PAIGC success had become very general:

> The secret of success has lain in clearing liberated areas and then, inside them, building new structures of everyday life. Politically, these structures have consisted at the base – and the base is everything in this context – of a dense network of village committees which, as they have become increasingly elective and representative in nature, have repeatedly taken over fresh responsibilities. On the Como group of islands or half-islands, for example, there is a total of fifteen such committees; at various meetings I was able to identify members of thirteen of them. In another sector I was present at a meeting of representatives of seventeen of the sector's committees.
>
> At one level or another, these committees are concerned with every aspect of public life in their localities. They look to the full-time workers

of the PAIGC for leadership, but are encouraged to take over as much responsibility as they are able. New activities are continually being added to their work. The latest in importance, initiated since 1970, is the formation of a network of village courts; each of these tribunals consists of a judge (or, as we should say in England, a justice or lay magistrate) and two assessors appointed by their respective village committee. They hear all cases, and apply local customary law to all but the most serious ones, such as homicide or grievous bodily assault, and the latter they send to a military court under PAIGC control. Minor offences which they deal with, such as trading with the enemy, are punished by fines in kind

Fig. 14.1 *A scene during the general elections for the People's National Assembly of Guinea-Bissau, held in liberated territory during 1972 as part of the* PAIGC *plan to declare an independent state (duly done in September 1973). The* PAIGC *laid great stress on the participation of women in all the work of liberation, and here is a woman of Cubucaré speaking her mind. The author took this picture, in October 1972, in the forest zone north-east of Como Island.*

(usually rice) or assignment to porterage services for the PAIGC. More serious offences can be punished by local imprisonment.

So it is that the force which promotes the powers and functions of these basic institutions of a new democracy, displacing the old traditions of self-rule as well as the dictatorship of the Portuguese, lies both in PAIGC leadership and in the opportunities which that leadership has opened for rural people. One sees this especially in education and public health. The PAIGC began to found primary schools in liberated areas as early as 1964, planting them in places where, with very rare exceptions, no schools had ever existed under colonial rule. Today [this was 1972] they have 156 such schools with about 250 teachers, as well as one secondary school and a nursery school in the shelter of the neighbouring Republic of Guinea. The total of pupils was 8 574, of whom 2 155 were girls, another significant departure. As well as these, some 7 000 adults in liberated zones were also attending classes in elementary literacy and arithmetic; in these zones before the liberation war, one may note, non-literacy was almost 100 per cent.

In this field of education, as in other fields, Cabral laid down the guidelines for PAIGC action in his 40-page directive of 1965, the famous *Palávras Geráis* or 'Watchwords', a severe, concise but all-embracing guide to action and behaviour: 'Demand from responsible party members that they dedicate themselves seriously to study; that they interest themselves in the things and problems of our daily life and struggle in their fundamental and essential aspects, and not simply in their appearances. . . . Learn from life, learn from people, learn from books, learn from the experience of others, never stop learning'. There are many who find it hard to live up to such demands, and many, no doubt, altogether fail. Yet the demands are still made.

Public health is a third field for widening participation in new opportunities within these zones. In the area of Como, for instance, the village communities (in a total population of perhaps 3 000) disposed of no health facilities before the Portuguese were finally driven out of this area in 1965. Today there is a central clinic and several mobile ones. The central clinic has four beds for in-patients and thirteen nurses, eight of whom are women. Their main task is to treat out-patients who come from the villages round about. I picked up the register when I was there, and counted the names of 672 out-patients, including a handful of in-patients, for the month of October and four-fifths of November [1972].

In October 1972 the PAIGC had 125 small clinics, nine small hospitals, and three larger hospitals that were staffed by fully-trained doctors (at least two of whom are Cuban volunteers) inside the liberated zones of Guinea-Bissau, as well as three clinics and one surgical hospital in (neighbouring) Guinea and Senegal. Altogether these had 488 beds, of which rather fewer than 300 were inside the country. The total of nurses so far trained in Europe (mostly in the USSR) was 90, with 169 others trained by the PAIGC inside the country. Eight PAIGC doctors have completed their training in the USSR or elsewhere in Europe; and as well as the Cuban doctors, there are three Yugoslavs in the main surgical centre in neighbouring Guinea. It is still very little, but it is a great deal more than it was before.

In general, by 1972, nothing happened or could happen in these liberated zones without the active participation of their local people; and this was true down to small details, such as the organisation of canoe transport (in a country criss-crossed by rivers and long arms of the sea) or the handing out of personal permits for peasants to visit relatives in enemy-held towns or fortified villages. Here, I noted at the time,

> One sees in vivid everyday detail the difference between support and participation, and the many ways in which these rural people, through their active involvement, have begun to change not only their social habits and practices but also, and perhaps still more, their ideas about the present and the future.

Working to extend this practice of participation from a local level to a national level, the PAIGC promoted a general election for a representative national assembly. Preceded by a campaign of political explanation extending over several months, this took place late in 1972 by universal suffrage of all persons over the age of 18 and by secret ballot. Promoted in all the liberated zones, this campaign and its successful culmination were seen by the PAIGC as providing a democratic basis for an elected assembly which would declare the country's independence (as it duly did in September 1973); which would initiate a constitutional separation of powers between legislature and executive; but which would also serve as another means of widening mass participation.

And so, gradually, there evolved a new understanding of the means and purposes of liberation – of self-determination, of self-government, of self-respect – and of the practice they required. There came that harmony of consciousness between leaders and masses of rural people which could open the way to political and economic advance. Living and working in these liberated zones, or fighting to defend and extend them, people learned new social and cultural values and were continually influenced to accept them. Speaking to an American audience in 1970, Cabral put it this way:

> The leaders of the liberation movement, drawn generally from the 'petty bourgeoisie' (intellectuals, clerks) or the urban working classes (workers, drivers, wage-earners in general), have to live day by day with various peasant groups in the heart of rural populations. They come to know the people better. They discover, at the grass roots, the richness of the people's cultural values (whether philosophic or political, artistic, social or moral). They acquire a clearer understanding of the economic realities of their country, as well as of the problems, sufferings and hopes of the masses of its people.
>
> Not without a certain astonishment, these leaders realise the richness of spirit, capacity for reasoned discussion and clear exposition of ideas, and facility for understanding and assimilating concepts, displayed by groups who yesterday were forgotten or despised, and who were considered incompetent (in any of these matters) by the coloniser and even by some nationals.

The leaders thus enrich their culture. They develop as persons. They free themselves from complexes. They reinforce their capacity to serve the movement by serving the people.

This was one aspect of a two-way convergence between leaders and those they lead. But the second aspect was no less important to an effective ideology of liberation and its politics. Cabral continued:

On their side, the working masses, and in particular the peasants, who are usually illiterate and have never moved outside the boundaries of their village or region, come into contact with neighbouring or other groups. With this contact (in the conditions of the liberated zones and their development), they lose the complexes which constrained them in their relations with other ethnic and social groups. They realise their crucial role in the whole struggle. They break the bonds of their village universe, and integrate progressively with their country and with the world.

They acquire an infinite amount of new knowledge, useful for their immediate and future action within the framework of the struggle. They strengthen their political awareness by assimilating the principles of national and social revolution postulated by the struggle. They thereby become more able to play the decisive role of providing the principal force behind the liberation movement.

None of this, moreover, could be an optional convergence between leaders and the masses who followed. Unless it happened, and was progressively developed, the struggle would collapse and fail. And for the most obvious and concrete reason: only this convergence could convince the rural multitudes that they were fighting for their own interests, struggling for their own advancement, sacrificing for their own future. 'Orders from above', merely handed down by self-appointed leaders, would not be followed.

But the practice of the liberated zones, when it was carried out with success as it generally was here, proved insistently to the peasants that the struggle was theirs or it was no one's; and that this struggle could succeed only in the measure that they took it to their hearts and made it their own. Developing widely after 1964 in Guinea-Bissau, this practice of mass participation – in PAIGC parlance, 'mobilisation' – gave the PAIGC a firm hold on the strategic initiative in the political field: the guarantee in all such struggles that a strategic initiative can be similarly held in the military field, and that the war, in consequence, will be won. It was the movement's primary and decisive success, and it left the colonial commanders far behind.

Cabral summed it up like this:

The armed liberation struggle requires the mobilisation and organisation of a significant majority of the population; political and moral unity of the various social classes; efficient use of modern arms and of other means of making war; the progressive liquidation of the remnants of tribal mentality; and the rejection of social and religious rules and taboos which inhibit development of the struggle (gerontocracies, nepotisms, the social inferiority of women, rites or practices which are incompatible with the rational and national character of the struggle, etc.).

The armed liberation struggle therefore implies a veritable forced march along the road of cultural progress.

For consider these features inherent in an armed liberation struggle: the practice of democracy, of criticism and self-criticism; the increasing responsibility of populations for the government of their own lives; literacy work; the creation of schools and health services; the training of militants (cadres) from peasant and worker backgrounds; and many other achievements.

When we consider these features, we see that the armed liberation struggle is not only a product of culture but is also a *determinant* of culture. And this, without doubt, is a people's prime recompense for the effort and sacrifice demanded by war.

Without this qualitative leap into new understandings and new approaches, 'then the effort and sacrifices accepted during the struggle will have been in vain. The struggle will have failed. . . .'

The Portuguese commanders, for their part, evolved other means to make the insurrections fail.

COUNTER-INSURGENCY *VERSUS* POLITICAL WARFARE

They relied on methods of force. True enough, General Spínola in Guinea-Bissau made a brief attempt at political warfare against the PAIGC with a programme of social concessions, chiefly in the educational field. But it was very limited in scope, and came in any case too late for any chance of success. A number of Portuguese political advisers apparently recommended a similar attempt in Angola; if so, their advice was ignored. Generally, the Portuguese commanders were unable to think in political terms, while their government, almost to the end, left political warfare entirely to the liberation movements which, of course, used it as their principal weapon.

For a choice of methods of force the Portuguese commanders turned to the experience of others, chiefly the British in Malaya after World War Two and the Americans, somewhat later, in Vietnam. Unhappily for them, the circumstances were different in the Portuguese colonies. The British had succeeded in Malaya, largely because the guerrillas they faced were mostly Chinese, and these Chinese guerrillas had failed to win over any substantial number of Malayan peasants. It was therefore possible for the British to isolate the guerrillas from the peasants, deny the guerrillas any easy access to food, shelter, and information, and then, with suitably trained 'search and destroy' units, drive the guerrillas to defeat. In Vietnam the Americans failed with a corresponding strategy, largely because the Viet Liberation Front could not be isolated from its peasant base; and the Americans then fell back on heavy bombing, forest and crop defoliation, and other such techniques. These did enormous damage, but the fighting units of the Viet Liberation Front proved able to survive; and survival, in these circumstances, has invariably meant success.

The Portuguese commanders, as it came about, could neither isolate their enemy nor bomb him into silence. There was no situation in which these movements lacked a peasant base; nor did the Portuguese air force, however reinforced, achieve a bombing capacity in any way comparable with the American air force. But they tried hard. Inducing starvation was their first method. An Angolan commander of the MPLA, Jaime Morais-'Monty', has reviewed this method in one of the few books to have come out of these wars:

> The oldest way of defeating guerrillas is to spread hunger. To do this the anti-guerrilla forces launch large operations carefully designed to achieve good results. If the guerrillas depend essentially on food from urban zones, as in the Philippines or Malaya, the operation may succeed. But if the guerrillas can supply themselves, at least in basic foods, other methods may be used: such as defoliants, or, as with the Portuguese, the launching of a 'maize war': that is, the organisation of groups which destroy the fields of the nationalists.

The general reply to such methods was to insist that guerrilla units should cultivate their own crops and defend them. This was occasionally very difficult, as in parts of eastern Angola where MPLA units had to exist on poor or infertile soils. Elsewhere, in easier terrain, it succeeded.

In any case, promoting hunger could not be enough. As the British had shown in Malaya, it was also necessary to go out and destroy guerrilla units on the ground. Such operations in the Portuguese usage had a threefold slogan to direct them, 'Find, Fix, and Attack': in other words, track down guerrilla units, keep them fixed where they were when found, and then eliminate them. This, Monty continues, required certain conditions:

> 1 a spirit of initiative and aggression;
> 2 good shooting at short range;
> 3 sound knowledge of terrain.
>
> But if the anti-guerrilla commander and his men are to know their zone sufficiently well, they must stay in it for a long time, and this requirement, in the Portuguese case, led to discontent and demoralisation, so that a good result could not be obtained. Beyond that, Portuguese troops in Angola found it difficult to practise their slogan ('Find, Fix, Attack') because their movements were hampered by (guerrilla) use of land mines, an effective method of dissuading patrols from going very far from their base.

The comment could be generalised; huge numbers of land mines were used by both sides, and with much effect.

Later on, striving to crack this problem of 'finding and fixing', Portuguese commanders in all three territories developed the use of highly-trained and highly-rewarded commandos, many of whom were African volunteers or conscripts who knew the terrain and its peculiarities better than the European troops. Picked 'find and fix' units were sent into the bush for some days, even as much as a week or two, marched on a pre-decided route, and then retrieved by helicopter from a prearranged point of rendezvous. Such patrols could make a lucky hit now and then, but generally they stayed out in the bush for too short a period before going home again, for the strain imposed by such operations was evidently hard to take by men who were conscripts or mercenaries. In this respect, as in others, guerrilla volunteers serving a cause in which they believed were generally able to achieve a powerful moral advantage. A variety of operational methods was tried in combination with helicopters, sometimes with bombing support, and at first with some success; they will be discussed in the section entitled *Weaponry*.

Once fighting units had survived initial offensives, chiefly by evasion but also by rearguard actions, and had then proved that they could regroup and fight back, the Portuguese commanders reverted to another well-tried method; it was one, as we have seen, that the British had introduced to South Africa sixty-five years earlier, and the French lately to Algeria. They began to round up rural populations and confine them within army-guarded camps or settlements, known as *aldeamentos*. This was much easier than chasing elusive guerrillas in the bush, and was practised on a huge scale. Approximate figures show that about one million rural people were corralled in this way in Angola, or perhaps a quarter of the whole rural population at that time. About the same total or rather more (but, of course, a smaller percentage of a larger population) were similarly confined in Mozambique; and the same policy was adopted, on a lesser scale, in Guinea-Bissau.

This enormous effort was justified by an apparently strong argument: confining rural populations behind army-guarded defences would deprive guerrilla units of food, shelter, information, and recruits. Thus isolated, these guerrilla units would gradually collapse, fritter away, accept defeat. But the argument could hold good only upon the fulfilment of two conditions. One was that the Portuguese were able to take and sustain the strategic initiative, driving guerrilla forces from one defensive position to the next and eventually depriving them of their last defences. The other was that the bulk of the confined populations were out of sympathy, or became out of sympathy, with the guerrillas and their liberation movement.

Generally, the Portuguese commanders were able to count on the fulfilment of neither of these conditions. They were seldom able to take the strategic initiative, given the effective leadership on the guerrilla side, or, if they sometimes took it, they proved unable to sustain it. Nor were they able to win over the sympathy of any substantial proportion of the confined populations, partly because of the severely repressive nature of the Portuguese colonial system within which these commanders necessarily worked, and partly because the system in any case lacked the money and ideas with which to embark on 'the winning of hearts and minds'.

The confined populations became more resentful even than before. Crowded into camps or settlements behind barbed wire, taken out daily to work in neighbouring fields under armed guard, poorly fed, often kicked around, always in fear of death or some lesser violence, the uprooted populations of the *aldeamentos* proved no recruiting ground for colonial loyalties. On the contrary, they fell into attitudes which ranged from a sullen hatred of their gaolers to an ardent support for their liberation movement. Yet all these methods of containment and destruction had their huge and steady impact on the peoples of these territories. They imposed much suffering, and accordingly they induced much fear. They had to be met and countered, in their turn, by appropriate guerrilla tactics. What were these?

Principally they were the methods of political warfare. These derived from the ideology of liberation in its various aspects. The first and by far the more important of these emerged from the mass participation in social and political change, and self-transformation, that arose and spread in the liberated zones. Wherever this work could be done well, the resultant comparison between its consequences and the condition of the people in the *aldeamentos* was enormously to the advantage of the liberation movement. People in liberated zones such as those of Cabo Delgado in northern Mozambique might suffer from the war, but they suffered as people who tasted the sweets of self-determination. Seize and confine them then in *aldeamentos*, and even the most paternalist Portuguese administrator became an odious gaoler. They waited only for their guerrillas to release them, or else the more courageous slipped away into the bush and made for the nearest guerrilla unit they could find.

The central strength of this form of political warfare probably lay in its emphasis on unity. What it preached, above all, was that the interests common to every ethnic or regional group were larger and more valuable than any of the interests which might divide these groups. Schools, clinics, an end to traditional as well as colonial abuses, more ready cash, better access to fertile land, the damping of old destructive quarrels: these were what the majority wanted everywhere. Out of their wanting these things, a basis could be made for unity which cut across mental and moral hostilities or doubts: which created, in short, a *culture of unity*.

This was the political warfare which could exercise a powerful attraction on populations in zones controlled or continually harassed by the colonial forces. There evolved a vivid mental contrast between the 'atmosphere' of the enemy's zones and the guerrilla-held zones. In the former there was an accent on hatred, suspicion of neighbours, the grabbing of what benefits one could; in the latter, with these mature movements, there was a quite contrary accent on co-operation, collective solidarity, and the self-respect that comes from high morale. Such became a generalised impression, even if liberated zones could by no means always realise much co-operation and collective solidarity.

The same political warfare was applied as far as possible to the forces of the colonial power, whether by good treatment of prisoners, political agitation in enemy-held zones, or radio broadcasting and the like. This was partly a statement of the principle that the wars of liberation were in no sense race wars, nor could be if their social and cultural objectives were to be fulfilled; and it was partly a method of weakening enemy morale. Repeated attempts were made to win sympathy among Portuguese conscripts or local traders; and not always without success. There were traders who had come to the colonies as radicals exiled for their political views. There were young officers, ex-students for the most part, who grew to understand the ruinous nature of these wars.

Thus the PAIGC, as early as 1962, issued an appeal to local Portuguese which explained that the liberation movement, while determined to eliminate the colonial system, none the less

> makes a distinction between Portuguese colonialism and Portuguese settlers, just as we distinguish between a vehicle and its wheels. A vehicle without wheels will not work. Nor can Portuguese colonialism without settlers . . . If you lack the courage to support our struggle, guard your

> dignity as men by refusing to serve the colonialists: take up a position of neutrality towards our struggle . . . Your position tomorrow will depend on what you do today . . . Long live friendship, equality and peaceful collaboration between all peoples.

For the same reasons of principle and practice, the use of terror against civilians – always, as we have already noted, the weapon of the defeated – was carefully rejected, in this case in a PAIGC manifesto of 1963:

> Our direct action is aimed only at the forces of repression (army, police, and colonial agents) who . . . commit grave crimes against our defence-less populations. Our sabotage actions are aimed only at military objectives and economic targets essential to colonial exploitation. Our fighters have never and will never attack civilians – European or not – unless they oppose our struggle with arms in their hands.

A regular propaganda was later aimed at the enemy's armed forces. Thus a directive of 1965 urged that liberation participants in the enemy's zones should

> Reinforce political work and propaganda within the enemy's armed forces. Write posters, pamphlets, letters. Draw slogans on roads. Establish cautious links with enemy personnel who want to contact us . . . Do everything possible to help enemy soldiers to desert.

Very few Portuguese soldiers came over to the liberation movements, but more African soldiers did. As to the settlers, there were few in Guinea-Bissau, while the many in Mozambique and Angola were strongly organised in fascist associations, generally impervious to democratic ideas, or else, in the mass, eventually panicked by their leaders into fleeing back to Portugal in 1974–75. But an overall effect of liberation politics on the Portuguese armed forces was none the less profound, as was seen decisively in 1974.

Within weeks of the Lisbon *coup* of that year which overthrew the dictatorship and called for democracy and decolonisation, the PAIGC leader Luiz Cabral* affirmed that 'We have fought our war for national independence without hatred for the people of Portugal, and we are now ending it without hatred.' And the truth of this affirmation was seen in the result. For in the following October, with the last Portuguese soldier out of Guinea-Bissau, Luiz Cabral could say with equal truth that the whole process of evacuation had been concluded without the loss by armed action of a single Portuguese soldier. The present writer was in Guinea-Bissau with the PAIGC during that time, and saw that it was true. Though the Portuguese had to evacuate about one hundred and thirty garrisons, as well as a huge force in the capital of Bissau, the last troops left in mid-October without there having been a single clash in this withdrawal. Nothing like that could have been possible without the PAIGC's consistent application of the politics of liberation.

* Younger brother of Amílcar Cabral, he became deputy secretary-general of the PAIGC after the latter's murder by African agents of the Portuguese in 1973, and then the President of the Republic of Guinea-Bissau.

And this politics, in turn, impressed its principles upon the Portuguese. There is much evidence of that. Those who prepared and carried out the Lisbon *coup* were for the most part young officers. Their movement was called the *Movimento das Forças Armadas* (MFA). It was centred in Lisbon, and had branches in the colonies. In Bissau on 29 July 1974, a meeting of the territorial MFA produced and passed unanimously a declaration of no small historical interest. This affirmed that

> The colonised peoples and the people of Portugal are allies. The struggle for national liberation has contributed powerfully to the overthrow of fascism and, in large degree, has lain at the base of the MFA whose officers have learned, in Africa, the horrors of a fruitless war, and have therefore understood the roots of the evils which afflict the society of Portugal.

And so it was agreed, among those officers who had fought long and bravely, that it was not the political warfare of General Spínola which had won 'the hearts and minds' of Africans, but that of Amílcar Cabral which had achieved precisely the reverse.

I have given priority to the politics of liberation warfare because the subject is cardinal to an understanding of what happened, and of why it happened. Yet these were wars; and we now turn to the technical issues of operational organisation, tactics, and weaponry.

CHAPTER FIFTEEN

TACTICS AND WEAPONRY

In the recruitment of volunteers and their organisation, successful liberation movements built their fighting capacity in five well-marked but, of course, sometimes overlapping stages. These stages were:

1 formation and commitment of guerrilla bands, initially very small, for purely localised and small-scale operation;

2 development of combined operations between two or more neighbouring bands, but in elementary forms, and still for localised and small-scale use;

3 division of fighting forces into two types of organisation:
    (a) a full-time fighting force for mobile warfare under strong discipline, also initially small in numbers of fighting personnel;
    (b) part-time militias for purely localised defence, chiefly of liberated zones;

4 further development of mobile forces, with addition of units specialised in mortars, light artillery, etc.; further development of militias;

5 large-scale offensives.

As may be seen, the process was both progressive and protracted. All competent sources stressed these aspects. Thus a commandant of the MPLA, Jaime Morais-'Monty', in the manual noted above, wrote that:

> Guerrilla forces accept the prospect of a prolonged war such as can wear out the enemy and can gradually strengthen guerrilla units in number, weaponry and organisation. Failure to accept the needs for this prospect leads to crass mistakes. To suppose a rapid victory for guerrilla forces is the manifestation of a right-wing opportunism. . . Without much time, it is impossible to organise an army capable of defending the conquests of a war of national liberation.

ORGANISATIONAL DEVELOPMENT

The first stage, as the examples all show, required unusual courage and initiative by 'volunteers of the first hour' – men such as Samora Machel, Hoji ya Henda, João Bernardo Vieira – but relatively little training. The early commanders of FRELIMO and its companion movements had, at best, less than a year's training (mostly in Algeria) in the use of small-arms (i.e. rifles, sub-machine-guns, light machine-guns); elementary use of explosives; and some tactical instruction (use of ambush, etc.). Their task was to return from their training country and practise what they had learned; others then learned alongside them. Most learned 'on the job'.

Much the same applied to the second stage, which meant little other than 'doing more of the same, but doing it better'. This, usually, was when early failures in command became apparent: militarism, 'commandism', regionalism, 'tribalism'. Tough measures were required to make good these failures; but this, usually, was also when the revelation of individual quality and talent confirmed good commanders and enabled others to be picked. In this second stage, moreover, the liberation movement had generally survived the enemy's first major counter-offensives; and, in the wake of these, guerrilla targets could be enlarged: from isolated police posts to minor garrisons, for instance, or from ambush of solitary vehicles to attacks on convoys.

All this, so far, was guerrilla warfare in the strict sense of the term. Its immediate objectives were threefold: to prove to a sympathetic but still frightened or sceptical rural population that action against the enemy could be both possible and successful; to provide battle experience; and, not least, to enlarge the opportunities for political work. As the first colonial counter-offensives were survived and further development became possible, achievement of these initial objectives led into two larger objectives. Each was fundamental. One was to form zones more or less cleared of enemy control, the fully liberated zones of the future; and the other was to develop an organised defence of the populations of these zones from enemy raids and reprisals. Such defence might never become complete; but it had to become increasingly effective if the liberation movement was to grow and develop.

Stage three marked a turning-point, and, partially, the end of guerrilla warfare in the strict sense of the term. This came through the formation of small full-time forces which continued to adopt guerrilla tactics – high mobility, refusal of pitched battles, sudden swift attacks on limited objectives – but which were regular units and not guerrilla-type units. From now onwards the liberation forces consisted of full-time assault units available for action wherever they were ordered, no matter how far from their localities of recruitment; and, secondly, of local militias formed by part-time guerrillas living in their localities of recruitment and defending these whenever required, usually in combination with assault units if large enemy offensives had been launched.

Further development involved steady improvement in organisation and equipment of both types of force, but especially of the assault units. New forms of training became necessary: for example, commanders had to learn the tactical use of combined units, and, as these improved in efficiency and discipline, the handling of more sophisticated weapons. Plans had to be devised and carried through which could enable the liberation army to sustain the strategic initiative which it had now seized. All this belonged to the fourth stage; and this was the period which repeatedly demonstrated that peasant fighters, however previously encased in their 'village universe', could become commanders with a real grip on larger realities. In the military dimension, in short, this was the period when the liberation war could be seen, ever more clearly, as a 'determinant of culture'.

At this fourth stage, or earlier, it was usually found necessary to review and revise basic units of organisation. Thus the PAIGC had based its initial army, formed in 1964, on the *grupo*, a unit of about 25 men. But increasing success led to the coagulation of groups into units of 100 to 150 men during 1965. Portuguese offensives then showed that these were too large and too static. They were broken down into mobile *bigrupos* (double groups) of from 30 to 50 men. By early 1966, with more experience of mobile warfare, combinations of two or three *bigrupos* began to be used. Increasingly thereafter, this army could undertake large-scale operations against major targets or series of targets, and could do this with great speed and strike-power. The fifth stage was now reached.

In this fifth stage, onward from 1968 in the case of the PAIGC, the national armed forces consisted of a variety of well-defined formations. These were, by 1970:

1 combinations of *bigrupos* organised in 'army corps', each of several hundred fighting men but differing in size according to terrain, availability of food, and targets to be attacked. These were under commanders who took their orders from regional commands, the latter being subordinate, in turn, to the high command of the liberation movement.
2 a varying number of *bigrupos* with specific functions, usually the operation of sophisticated weaponry, and available for temporary attachment to one or other of the army corps.
3 local militias strictly attached to defensive work in liberated zones, but available for co-operation with regular units whenever neighbouring targets were to be attacked in force.

This type of organisation was designedly flexible, and of course varied among the different movements. In the MPLA, for instance, the development of large units came in 1970–71; these were known as 'squadrons', several of which could combine together. Generally, in the PAIGC, the initial composition of an 'army corps' consisted of a maximum of four *bigrupos* for offensive commitment, of one *bigrupo* with artillery, and of four specialised units with a small but varying number of men, according to the new weaponry that became available. The initial total of such 'corps', that is, was around 400–450.

These large formations developed great capacity. They moved in on targets at speed, hit hard, and withdrew by plan, carrying their own food, first-aid services, and ammunition. We shall look at some typical operational plans (see *Combined Operations*).

Exactly how these forces were used is part of the detailed military history of these wars, and can have no place here. Much detailed documentation is available, but one example may suffice. A review of PAIGC actions for the eight months of January–August 1971, well into stage five but characteristic of the whole period 1968–73, noted 508 major actions, including 369 attacks on garrisons in urban localities; 102 ambushes and other attacks on enemy road transport (there were no railways in Guinea-Bissau); 15 major landmining operations; 14 actions against river and sea transport; and 8 commando-type actions against especially difficult targets in urban centres, such as airfields, repair-shops and the like. Ninety enemy vehicles were destroyed, 28 rivercraft sunk, and two aircraft and three helicopters shot down. Three entrenched camps were taken from the enemy, and many small encampments were seized and razed.

All this, again, supposed continual and intensive political work designed to raise the level of political understanding in fighting units, and to achieve an ever more consistent tying of military operations to political objectives. This meant, in other words, an unrelenting effort to deepen and extend the political work of transforming mass support into mass participation in liberated zones which became gradually larger; and, in zones still controlled by the colonial power, a steady political penetration.

Two instruments were used. One was the political network of the liberation movement in its non-military manifestations: of representative committees and social services in the liberated zones, of clandestine political workers in the enemy-controlled zones. The second, closely linked to the first, consisted of political commissars in fighting units. Something needs to be said about the second of these instruments.

Political commissars were found to be indispensable, and were appointed alongside commanders at every level of organisation. The need for them was both tactical and strategic. It was tactical because successful units in liberation wars had to be highly democratic units. Such units were composed of volunteers, never of conscripts (at least until late in stage five, when large forces began to be raised within tried forms of organisation), whose motives were primarily political and whose morale and effectiveness depended, invariably, on the development of a unity and understanding which could derive only from well-conducted discussion. Tactically, commissars were there to ensure such discussion, to look after welfare, maintain morale, organise food and other supplies, and safeguard relations of trust and co-operation with civilian populations. Once military decisions were taken, commanders fully commanded their units, including their commissars who were also fighting men; but such decisions were taken only after the agreement of commissars. Strategically, in other words, commissars were there to ensure that politics remained in control of warfare, and that this politics stayed in line with liberation policy. Their task, in this wider sense, was to watch out for militarist or other destructive tendencies, and act against these if they appeared.

An internal PAIGC document of May 1966, dealing with a military reorganisation within stage three (the passage to mobile warfare), went on to say:

> We now clearly separate the action of those who direct the armed struggle, and who from now on will dedicate themselves exclusively to the action of our fighting forces. On the other side, our party committees (the elected people's committees in the liberated zones and their party organs) will dedicate themselves exclusively to political work and the development of civilian life in the liberated zones (as to agricultural production, education, health services etc.). But we emphasise that this separation does not mean that there are now two kinds of leaders, political and military. To think so would be to make a bad mistake.
>
> In our party and our struggle, as repeatedly said before, there are no purely military personnel (*militares: militaristas*). Those who dedicate themselves to the armed struggle are armed militants (*militantes armados*

= political personnel with primarily fighting duties). Those who have overall direction of the armed struggle are the members of the party leadership. Those who direct the struggle in each area are political responsibles (*responsáveis*) of the Party . . . The organisation and re-organisation of our armed forces is a political measure . . . Each re-organisation corresponds to the development of a new phase . . . But in each new phase the military direction of the struggle remains sub-ordinate to the political leadership.

The PAIGC had faced a crisis in the first stage of armed struggle, as we have seen, precisely because certain local commanders rejected political control; they became militarists instead of armed militants. All this was stopped in time, but must otherwise have brought disaster. Other movements – one may even say, I think, all liberation movements in the examples of the last fifty years – faced comparable weaknesses. A commander of the Angolan MPLA, the late Commandant Gilberto da Silva-'Jika' (afterwards killed in action), summed up such weaknesses in reflections written in 1971:

There are those who hide away in the most inaccessible places and who act by orders concerned merely with their own local situation. It is characteristic of comrades imbued with these attitudes that they get as far as possible from the scene of action. Even so, their indifference to or misunderstanding of real problems in no way prevents them from dis-playing the most exaggerated optimism, no matter how unfavourable or disastrous their actual position may be.

They may carry out an occasional attack or ambush, but every time they do it with success there follows an interminable argument about this or that personal merit in what was done, even though no real merits were displayed, along with a lot of fatuous talk . . . Their great preoccupation is to install themselves in command posts, where, surrounded by large units specially detached in order to protect them, they can boost their prestige with military rites and ceremonies.

Such commanders like to gather a regular court of more or less servile persons who pile on easy praise so as to be sure of a share in the privileges to hand. For them, responsibilities suppose no sacrifice, only privilege.

Such criticism came from within the ranks of all the liberation movements at one time or another during early stages of development. It pointed to weaknesses which were evidently inherent in the whole enterprise. The unsuc-cessful movements, notably UPA/FNLA and UNITA in Angola in the period before their outright transfer to the colonial side, were those in which such weaknesses went unchecked, became dominant, and therefore led to with-drawal and betrayal. The successful movements were those which faced and overcame these failings, or at least reduced them to a point of no decisive significance in the balance of development.

The same considerations have applied to the acceptance of casualties. These had to be accepted, however painful they might be, but they had to be kept to a minimum: and for two reasons. First, because these liberation forces were always heavily outnumbered by the colonial enemy; and, secondly, because replacement of fighters with the requisite political as well as military preparation and ability was necessarily a slow process. It appears to have been a feature of all well-conducted liberation wars, at least in recent times, that fighting casualties were relatively few.

After a successful eleven-year war against an enemy overwhelmingly stronger in numbers and equipment, the PAIGC made up its provisional casualty accounts, and found that its severely wounded fighters totalled 345, of whom 150 had suffered amputations. The exact number of killed was still unknown when these figures were obtained in 1976; but there were thought to be some 500 war widows and about 1 000 children who had lost one parent or both in action against the enemy. It seemed unlikely, however, that the number of killed in action was much above 1 000, and may have been considerably less. (These figures, of course, do not include civilians killed or injured by enemy action.)

Portuguese losses were undoubtedly much higher. Official Lisbon figures for the whole war period up to 1 May 1974 admitted a total of 3 265 killed in action, of whom 1 084 were in Guinea-Bissau, 1 142 in Angola, and 1 039 in Mozambique, together with another 3 075 'killed by other means' (landmines, accidents, and so on?); or a total dead of 6 340. Those wounded in action were said to have totalled 12 878, of whom 6 161 were in Guinea-Bissau, 4 472 in Angola and 2 245 in Mozambique, not counting another 15 041 wounded 'by accidents', whatever these may have been. On top of these losses, another 84 286 are listed as 'sick'.

These Portuguese official figures may be taken as an understatement of actual losses in dead and wounded. It was accepted policy by senior Portuguese commanders to admit far smaller losses than they actually received, and seriously wounded men were even sent to Western Germany so as to avoid placing them in hospitals in Portugal. This was partly to enable senior commanders to claim that they were winning the wars, and partly to prevent a collapse of morale on the home front. The evidence on the ground pointed to much higher losses. Shortly after the war in Guinea-Bissau, for one example of such evidence, I counted the names on two memorial plinths in the former Portuguese base of Buba, one of several dozen major bases in that country. One of these plinths, for 1966–68, listed the names of fifty-one dead, and the other, for 1969–71, those of forty-nine dead: in other words, one major base among several dozen such major bases (in Guinea-Bissau alone) had lost 100 dead in six years alone of this eleven-year war. Lisbon's admitted totals were clearly far too small.

This comparison between low losses on the liberation side and high losses on the colonial side offers another aspect of the success of these movements.

AMBUSH TECHNIQUES

Comprising the oldest and most used tactic of guerrilla warfare, methods of ambush varied with objectives, availability of automatic weapons, and levels of organisation. The actual effectiveness of these methods always depended on solving successive problems of anti-ambush defence evolved by the enemy. Given high morale on the insurrectionary side, the evidence suggests that a well-prepared ambush could usually succeed, but a fair measure of good luck could also be required. One needs to look at examples.

The Mulelist rebellion in south-western Zaire (1964) developed the following technique, as described by Belgian observers:

> Ambushes usually follow this pattern: the partisans dig a side trench across a road and cover it with branches and foliage, nets and sand, in such a way that the trap becomes invisible; an oncoming vehicle goes through the covering and is caught in the trench. The partisans come out of hiding and kill the occupants of the vehicle with arrows or machets. . . .

Such elementary methods might succeed against demoralised opponents; they could not be usefully deployed against staunch Portuguese troops. More sophisticated methods had to be invented. These relied, as time went by and better armament became available, on a combination of tactical skills, automatic weapons, and landmines.

Even so, by all the evidence, success continued to depend on inventiveness, high morale, and skilful use of terrain. Some commanders, such as Commandant Kwenhe in eastern Angola, became legendary for ingenuity and courage. Here are four actual examples, drawn from the successive experience of the MPLA in eastern Angola, and recorded by Commandant Jaime Morais. The first relates to 1967, and to a unit commanded by a fighter with the *nom de guerre* of 'Cowboy', a name apparently deserved by his methods of operation:

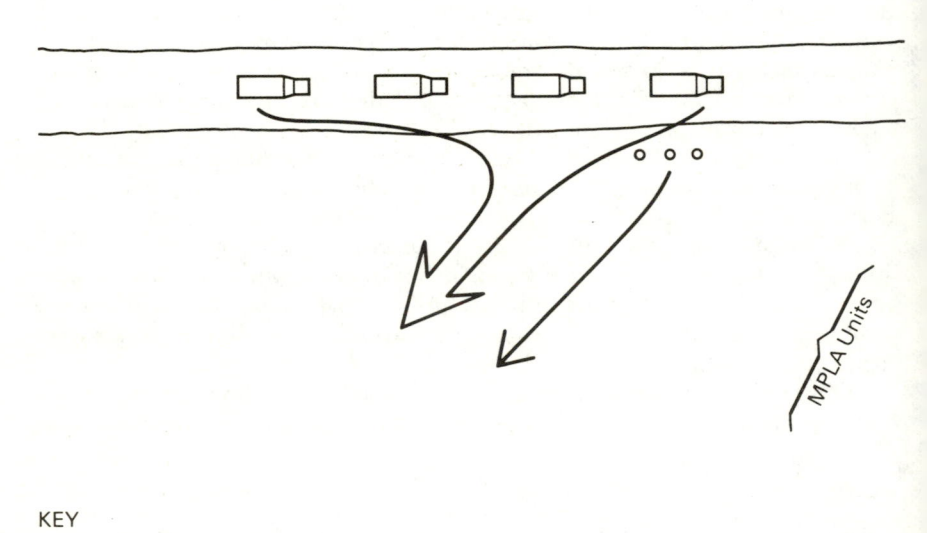

KEY

o o o 'Deception' group

[□□] Enemy trucks

MPLA Units

Map 15.1 *Typical ambush by Commandant 'Cowboy', eastern Angola.*

The scene takes place in the immense grassland plains of the southern part of Region III [district of Moxico] in the middle of the 1967 dry season. This was a time when the Portuguese troops showed a more or less complete disdain for our Angolan forces, knowing we were badly armed [and the guerrilla war in eastern Angola, in 1967, was less than a year old]. So they would leave the roads and launch their Unimogs [large military trucks supplied by West Germany] in veritable charges across that flat and open terrain where trees or bushes are rare or altogether lost in the immensity of a sea of grass.

Cowboy entrenched his men on this occasion about a hundred metres from the road. Their armament consisted of a few sub-machine-guns, otherwise only rifles . . . But he also placed four or six fighters right next to the road with the task of opening fire on an approaching motorised Portuguese force.

Seeing their attackers were few, the Portuguese thought they could capture them and extract information. So they stopped their trucks and jumped down. At which point the little 'deception group' took to its heels, and the Portuguese went running after them.

> Running hard, and eager to seize what seemed an easy prey, the Portuguese were completely surprised by the fire then opened against them on their flank. Panic followed, and flight. . . . And so they fled without firing a shot, leaving their dead and a reasonable quantity of arms and equipment.

This showed what could be done with a very inferior armament. Towards the end of 1970 a somewhat better armament began to become available. On 1 May 1971, as a final exercise in a regional politico-military training course, an ambush of a far more powerful type was mounted on the Ninda–Chiume road. Morais rightly emphasises the unprecedentedly large number of bazookas and machine-guns employed, and that these were combined with small 'fields' of anti-personnel landmines capable of obstructing an enemy attempt at encirclement of the ambuscade:

> The guerrillas were located about ten metres from the road. Very considerable for that period and for what we had been used to, their fire-power caused heavy losses of enemy men and material. From then onwards, the enemy knew that something had changed.

Another variant, again reflecting improved fighting capacity, was exemplified by units under Commandants Xieto and Maninga somewhat to the north but still in eastern Angola, on 22 November 1973. Morais comments on four aspects:

> In the first place, the duration of this action, almost one hour; then the number of troops on each side, each with almost a company but with the colonial forces in slight superiority; next, the decision of our commanders to leave their ambush and attack under enemy fire a part of the

enemy column; and, lastly, the use of a heavy machine-gun under the best tactical conditions.

Late in May 1973 the Portuguese army got ready to launch a 'sweep offensive' in the guerrilla region of Cazombo in far north-eastern Angola.

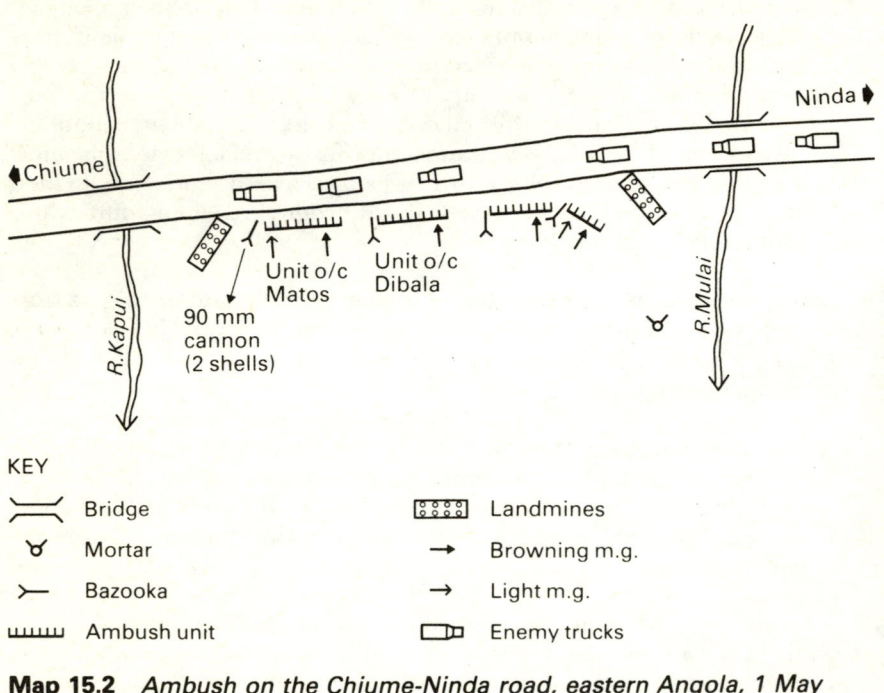

KEY

⟩⟨ Bridge		⊡⊡⊡ Landmines
ϗ Mortar		→ Browning m.g.
⟩— Bazooka		→ Light m.g.
⊔⊔⊔⊔ Ambush unit		⊏⊡ Enemy trucks

Map 15.2 *Ambush on the Chiume-Ninda road, eastern Angola, 1 May 1971.*

N ⬆

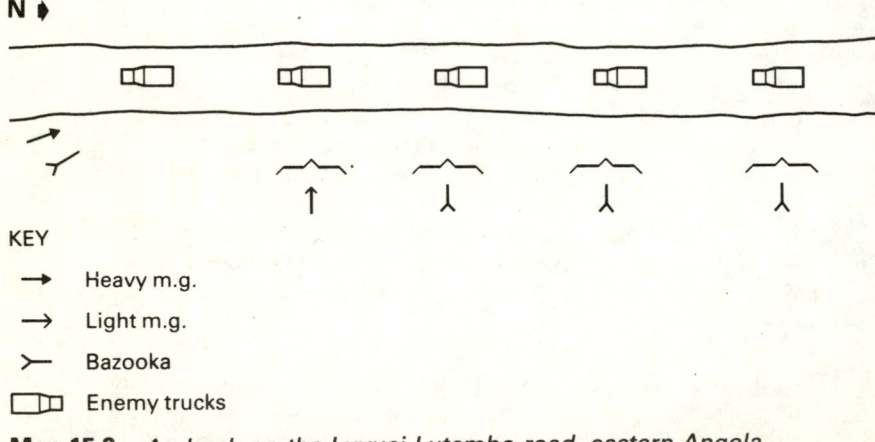

KEY

→ Heavy m.g.

→ Light m.g.

⟩— Bazooka

⊏⊡ Enemy trucks

Map 15.3 *Ambush on the Luvuei-Lutembo road, eastern Angola, 22 November 1973.*

Code-named 'Diáspora', this included the commitment of naval-marine units. One of these units, carrying as it happened the operational plans for 'Diáspora', was ambushed and destroyed on 2 June 1973. The chosen site on the Lute river, Morais records, was almost without any tree-cover anywhere nearer the road than several hundred metres, but there was high grass. MPLA units were disposed in an 'L' formation because the level of the road was higher than the ground on either side, and could have given cover to the enemy if the MPLA had placed units only on one side of the road. Morais records:

> Our forces were placed at eight to ten metres from the road except for the bazooka-man; his task being to stop the enemy column, he was placed at about two metres from the road. A 'field' of anti-personnel mines was sown on the side of the road opposed to the bulk of the ambush force so as to prevent the enemy from taking up positions there. . . . Two 60 mm. mortars completed the circle of fire, their task also being to protect our forces if enemy reinforcements should appear. Two protective positions were also mounted at either end of the ambush with the same object in mind.

A little before 7 a.m. the ambush units heard the sound of trucks approaching from the north, as expected; but almost at once they also heard trucks approaching from the south, which they did not expect. Yet

> everything went as planned. The (northern) column entered the ambush. The truck in front braked hard to go over a deep pot-hole, and when its back wheels were over, and in the fraction of a second when it

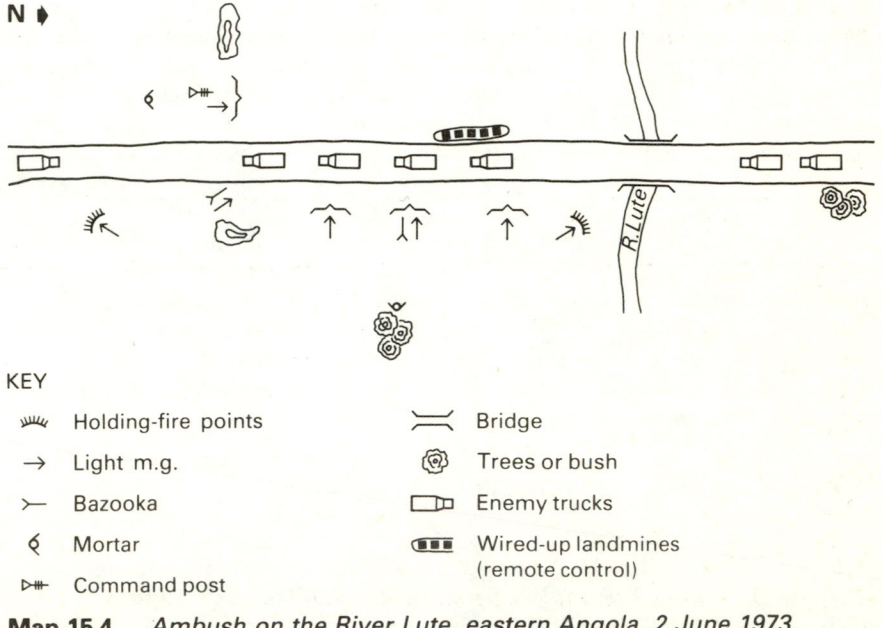

KEY

⁂	Holding-fire points	⊃⊂	Bridge
→	Light m.g.	⊛	Trees or bush
⊱	Bazooka	⊏▯	Enemy trucks
⟨	Mortar	⊟⊟	Wired-up landmines (remote control)
⊳╫	Command post		

Map 15.4 *Ambush on the River Lute, eastern Angola, 2 June 1973.*

halted as the driver changed gear, our bazooka-man jumped on to the road and opened fire, hitting the middle of his target. That gave the signal to begin. As planned, only one side of our forces opened fire immediately, and this caused the enemy to seek shelter on the other side of the road. Then the further side of our forces came into the action, as did the anti-personnel mines.

Two trucks, meanwhile, had not crossed the bridge into the ambush. Their men had no time to organise, however, because our northern protective position opened up at once, as did the two mortars, causing those men to abandon their trucks. The other protective position similarly opened up on the second column (approaching from the south), and forced them to turn back. We then passed to the assault. . . . This action killed 25 of the enemy, a number that was confirmed, twelve being identified. We also took valuable secret documents, various materials of war, and a good quantity of crates of beer.

Harassment of fixed enemy positions was another frequent tactic. Such actions might last only for ten or fifteen minutes of concentrated fire, but, often repeated and always by surprise, they pinned down the enemy, cut into his morale, and helped to ensure the immunity of liberated zones from raids by troops based in these fixed positions. But there came a time when combined operations could be organised so as greatly to strengthen such attacks, and even to eliminate such positions.

COMBINED OPERATIONS

A romantic notion that these wars were won by bearded heroes acting 'freely' in spontaneous enthusiasm, leaving plans and discipline to the enemy, could not be further from the truth. Unplanned guerrilla warfare, commanded by no stern discipline and overall strategic concept, ended always in defeat. Successful operations of this type demanded two planning phases in each case: first, by commanders who thoroughly understood the terrain, the enemy's dispositions, and the objectives to be gained; and, secondly, subsequent discussion of the part that he must play by each fighter in each unit, so that everyone concerned should know exactly what they had to do, and why.

Actual operational plans can document the first planning phase. Here are the general plans for *Operational Fanta*, fairly characteristic of the type of combined operations launched by the PAIGC in 1967. Its objectives were to isolate and attack two strongly fortified enemy encampments and two lesser ones, and thereby enlarge the liberated zones in this particular region. Two *bigrupos* were committed. Their orders were as follows (being copied from originals, place-names retain their coding):

PHASE 1: Destruction of Bridge at M

Closing of access roads:
1 Road 10 (near Bridge M) – comrade Sory Djalo's group will mine this road;
2 Road 11-A (near Bridge B) – comrade N'Bare Tchuda's group will mine this road;

3 Road 11-B (near G) – comrade Kemessene Camara's group will mine this
   road; near T, comrade Temna Kebeque's group will mine this road.

Destruction of bridge
Comrade Malam Sanha, with four others, one from each *grupo*.
Security on roads – Road 10: comrade Malam Numo;
                     Road 11-A: comrade Hilario Rodriques;
                     Road 11-B: comrade Luiz Correa.

After destruction of bridge
Bigrupo Numo-Hilario will safeguard roads 10 and 11 (ambushes). Bigrupo
Sanha-Luiz will withdraw towards sector T, rest, and prepare to attack P.
This attack will be carried out on the evening of the next day.

PHASE 2: Attack on P

Closing of roads
1 Road 10 – Grupo Sory Djalo, with Malam Numo;
2 Road 11-A – Grupo N'Bare Tchuda, with Hilario;
3 Road 11-B (near G) – 4 men of Grupo Temna Kebeque (with 1 light
   machine-gun and 2 sub-machine-guns).

Attack on fortified camp of P
Grupos of Kemessene Camara and Temna Kebeque.
N.B.: the trenched camp at C will be attacked the same night (mortars
commanded by comrade Cirillo).
In attacking P follow *Fanta* detailed plan, having regard to changes imposed by
the reinforcement of fighters and supplies.

After attack on P
Bigrupo Numo-Hilario will safeguard the roads leading to P. Attack on the
Trenched Camp at B.

Closing of roads
1 Road 10 (crossroads at D) – Grupo Sory Djalo, with Malam Numo;
2 Road 11-A (crossroads at C) – Grupo N'Bare Tchuda, with Hilario;
3 Road 12 – 5 men of Grupo Kemessene Camara (1 light machine-gun, 2
   sub-machine-guns, 1 bazooka);
   N.B. – After this attack the roads will be mined.
         After the attack, bigrupo Numo-Hilario will continued to safeguard
         the roads: patrols and ambushes.

PHASE 3: Liberation of OM and other *tabancas* (hamlets) of the zone
Reinforcement of the isolation of C
Attack on trenched camp at OM

Closing of roads
1 Road 10 – Grupo Sory Djalo, with Malam Numo;
2 Road 11-A – Grupo N'Bare Tchuda, with Hilario;

3 Road 12 – Grupo Samba Seydi of the 1st sub-section, with Pedro Ramos.

Attack on Trenched Camp at OM
Grupo Temna Kebeque, with Malam Sanha. Grupo Kemessene Camara, with Luiz Correa.

Liberation of other tabancas
Follow detailed plan for safeguard of roads to P and B – bigrupo Numo.

PHASE 4: Co-ordinate with other forces to attack C

PHASE 5: Co-ordinate with other forces to liberate all *tabancas* of zone, and totally isolate BT

PHASE 6: Co-ordinate with other forces to attack BT
N.B. – Co-ordination of forces in Phases 4, 5, and 6 will be commanded by comrade Domingos Ramos.

   Mission Solidarity offers another example from PAIGC operations in 1967. As with *Fanta*, the orders were drawn up by the central command and signed by Amílcar Cabral. They concerned enemy-held zones in the north-eastern grass-land country, a region not then under PAIGC control. The objectives were to hem in enemy positions there, reduce the troops in them to a purely defensive role, and isolate these troops from ground contact with other regions. The units assigned to these tasks were to undertake long-term operations, and seize arms and ammunition from the enemy as they went along. The plan provided for the commitment of:

> 3 units (A, B, and C), each composed of at least 11 fighters without counting porters of material.
> *Responsible:* Pedro Ramos, leader in the zone and member of the central committee [of the PAIGC].
> *Co-responsibles:* Amadu Alpha Diallo, Abubakar Barry, Humberto Gomes, each commanding under Ramos's command the three groups A, B and C.
> *Each group will take*
> 3 sub-machine-guns with 300 rounds for each;
> 5 rifles with 200 rounds for each;
> 8 pistols with 50 rounds for each.
> *The Mission will also take*
> 1 boat [inflatable rubber: for crossing rivers];
> a quantity of money (in notes and coins);
> 1 first-aid kit;
> a quantity of explosives, detonators and fuse;
> 'incendiary bottles' and detonators;
> 50 hand-grenades for each group.

Each small group would move separately, for better security and surprise, but keep in touch with Ramos, responsible for the whole mission, by means of couriers. Similar liaison would join the mission to the central command of the PAIGC. The orders continued:

The Mission must organise its own food supply, light food simple to carry and keep, for 5 to 8 days. After 5 to 8 days, each group must obtain food from our people. It must explain to the people why the struggle is necessary and why it is in defence of the interest of the people. If food is refused, it must be obtained at any cost (*custe o que custar*). Mission must carry first-aid supplies. Wounded must be sent back (to the rear). Mission must avoid sheltering in villages except where absolute security can be guaranteed and guards are placed. In general, Mission will overnight in the bush.

Detailed cartographical instructions followed for each of the three groups. Its actions were to be

(a) to sabotage and put out of action, as much as possible, the road Contabini-Madina;
(b) to sabotage the ferry-raft on the Corubal river at Canda Mandim;
(c) to ensure our passage of the Corubal by our own means or by canoes;
(d) to attack Madina by surprise and dominate its garrison [a major tactical point for the enemy]. Avoid making victims among Africans, unless they are in arms against us [i.e. in enemy service];
(f) capture the enemy's weapons;
(g) mobilise the people for our struggle.

Lastly, the orders concluded with a summary of crucial points:

(a) Never lose to view the object of the Mission: to isolate the Gabu-Boé region from the rest of the country;
(b) Throughout its action the Mission must make propaganda among African troops in the colonial army so that they come over to our side with arms and ammunition;
(c) If African troops in enemy service outnumber Portuguese troops in any locality, Mission must work to persuade them to turn their arms against the enemy and dominate the enemy. if necessary with our help;
(d) Maintain liaison with the command and send a complete report on progress.

Solidarity was an example of the use of small numbers of highly dependable fighters for long-term operations in regions of particular difficulty; and again emphasises the attention to detailed orders. In the event, *Solidarity* worked so well that the PAIGC were able, a year later, to evict all Portuguese forces from the region of Boé and press them harder than before in the neighbouring region of Gabu.

Large combined operations with improved weaponry became possible in 1968 and after. One of these, *Tenaz*, was a complex dual operation of mid-1969 against enemy positions around Bafata, again north of the major river of Guinea-Bissau, the Corubal. The general orders are too lengthy for reproduction here, running to some 2 000 words, but their main lines may be set forth; they were, as usual, signed by Amílcar Cabral, who continued to play a central role in military as well as political planning.

Preliminaries included the making of clandestine and generally underground ammunition dumps at suitable points in the rear of areas of actual engagement; the detailed instruction of fighting units detached for the operation; and the inspection of enemy dispositions. The latter was to be ensured by two *bigrupos* whose task was to infiltrate the area of operations but, to begin with, avoid all contact with the enemy until his dispositions were known, and landmine the roads that could deliver enemy reinforcements. Two strong strike forces, each of several hundred men, were given separate but convergent duties. Each successive phase was worked out, naming the commanders of all units, and the various tasks they were to perform.

Besides ambush, harassment, siege, and capture operations, inventiveness produced other ways of retaining the strategic initiative over a far more powerful enemy. One of a somewhat special nature may be mentioned: the exemplary exploit. Its object was to strike a blow that would raise morale on the insurrectionary side and depress it on that of the enemy. Its method was to attack targets thought by the enemy to be so well protected and so difficult to reach as to be immune from any danger.

In the case of the PAIGC – and I continue to examine actual examples – such exploits could be useful in relation to the capital of Bissau, around which the

Fig. 15.1 *Men of a* PAIGC *bigrupo in action with a 75mm. recoilless (and portable) cannon against the major Portuguese military base of Buba, in southern Guinea-Bissau, during February 1968. Taken by the British TV director, John Sheppard, this 'frame' was part of an outstanding documentary film produced by British Granada Television. Buba was about one kilometre distant, and the attackers, while this rare 'action shot' was taken, were under heavy fire.*

enemy stood in what appeared to be unassailable strength, and within which there lived perhaps an eighth of the country's whole population. In March 1968 a PAIGC commando of thirteen men, all of whom had volunteered for the mission, was successful in the extraordinarily hazardous enterprise of infiltrating to the very periphery of the principal airport of the colonial forces, situated on the edge of Bissau and heavily protected by wire, minefields, and blockhouses. Firing into the airport at short range, this commando damage planes on the ground, hangars, and other installations.

Several points should be noted. Such operations were aimed at hitting the enemy, but, still more, at proving to urban populations held behind enemy defences that this could be done even at points of greatest enemy strength. It was therefore important that the proof should be a very patent one: this commando, for instance, took 60 mm. mortars and bazookas with it, even though these were very hard to carry on such clandestine missions. It fulfilled, moreover, another crucial condition of success: it withdrew without casualties, proving that immunity lay on the guerrilla side, not on that of the colonial forces.

WEAPONRY

The weapons used by these movements remain to be examined, even if briefly and in a non-technical way. They fell into three types, each appearing in the measure of advances in the tactical situation, in training facilities, and in supply. They were small-arms (i.e. rifles and sub-machine-guns), light machine-guns, grenades, landmines; secondly, portable artillery; thirdly, a small armoury of sophisticated weapons.

Initial supply, in all known cases, was by whatever means came to hand. The Algerians, as we saw, began with a small quantity of old Italian rifles of World War Two vintage or older. The 'Mau Mau' fighters had to buy or take whatever they could lay their hands on, chiefly .303 British army rifles and settlers' shot-guns. It was much the same in the Portuguese wars: the 'fighters of the first hour' made do with the few weapons they could buy or purloin, and then went on to capture more from ambushed enemy police or patrols.

The capture of further quantities of weapons and ammunition remained a prime objective, but at least with the development of stage three, that of mobile warfare by regular units, sources of outside supply became indispensable. For even if guerrilla forces could still capture small-arms, machine-guns, bazookas, and a little ammunition, it remained generally impossible to capture enough ammunition. Besides which it became important that mobile guerrilla forces, as distinct from static guerrilla militias, should develop at the point of action a fire-power at least equal to that of the enemy.

This meant the use of new automatics developed since World War Two. Experience of insurrectionary warfare in World War Two had already shown, in fact, that the rifle was an outmoded weapon. Its precision could still be useful against individual targets, especially if used with a telescopic sight. But generally, whether in ambush, harassment, or siege-and-capture operations, the sub-machine-gun with its ability to fire very rapid volleys and its ease of reloading was much superior.

Yet it was hard to get hold of, and its ammunition harder still. At the outset of the Portuguese wars, for example, the colonial forces had relatively few of these highly portable automatics, and the guerrilla forces had none. Moving into stage three and mobile warfare, outside supply of such weapons and ammunition became entirely necessary. Apart from a few bought on the international market (but very expensive), or obtained through the Liberation Committee of the Organisation of African Unity, early sub-machine-guns in any quantity derived mostly from dumps of German weapons captured by the Soviet Army during World War Two, or else of outmoded Soviet stock. Among these were the German Schmeisser and its heavier but still effective Soviet equivalent, the so-called 'Pepesha' with its circular magazine.

As hostilities developed further, and the colonial forces acquired increasing quantities of new automatics and other weapons from NATO sources, so also did the quality of weapons supplied by the friends of the insurrectionary movements. Decisively useful in this context was the Soviet Koleshnikov sub-machine-gun; this had improved range, precision, and volleying capacity, and could meet the latest NATO sub-machine-gun on equal terms.

Landmines were used by both sides and sometimes in very large numbers. The guerrillas found them especially effective on dirt roads where they could be laid with a high degree of concealment. Discovering this, the Portuguese commanders were driven to the expense of laying hard surfaces on many hundred miles of road, partly to speed up movement but partly, too, in counteraction to landmines.

Grenades could sometimes be manufactured in guerrilla workshops; incendiary bottles ('Molotov cocktails') invariably were.

Light machine-guns, firing rifle-calibre ammunition, became a regular feature after stage two. Heavy machine-guns became part of the armament of specialised units or large formations after stage three.

Light artillery was valued according to its portability. Fixed-wheel guns could be of little use, because very hard to shift, and impossible to shift at speed. Smaller and portable types much used were:

1 the bazooka, first developed during World War Two but repeatedly improved afterwards, and usually easily portable by one man, proved very useful against transport and, whenever they appeared, armoured fighting vehicles (AFVs).
2 small and middle calibre mortars (i.e. 60 mm. and 82 mm.) became important in the phase of mobile warfare and then, especially, in combined operations and large-scale ambushes. They required (a) some specialised training in their use; and (b) their attachment to formations which were large enough to afford special mortar units for porterage, assembly, firing, and withdrawal.
3 portable cannon, notably the recoil-free 75 mm. gun which began to become available for the first time in 1968, usually from Soviet sources or by way of the Liberation Committee of the OAU. The 75 mm. cannon or its near equivalents could be broken down into parts portable by three men, to whom others had to be attached to carry shells. This again was possible only with the development of specialised units available for attachment to infantry formations.

As specialised units developed the capacity to handle weapons such as mortars and light cannon, the introduction of more sophisticated weapons became feasible. Prominent among these was the 122 mm. Soviet long-range 'missile launcher' known by various names in the African movements. This weapon became available in 1971 (so far as I have been able to ascertain) and initially to the PAIGC, who named it *grad*. It proved a notable addition. Capable of a range of some eleven kms., though never very accurate at the top of this range, the *grad* gave the guerrilla forces some compensation for their lack of air-bombing capacity, for it could hit distant targets with devastating effect from distances which gave the users a practically complete immunity from any immediate counter-strike. Aimed at enemy positions whose defending troops had never had to fear any attack from the air, *grad* undermined enemy morale and strengthened 'siege-and-capture' capacity.

But every advantage in a new weapon was found to have its possible disadvantage. In the case of the sub-machine-guns, for example, this was a double one: it could lead to a neglect in precision aiming, and to a huge waste of ammunition. In the case of *grad*, for another example, it could lead to a loss of aggressiveness. In an internal directive of September 1970, explaining the use of *grad*, Cabral listed its advantages and went on to note that:

> But it is well to remind our fighters, with insistence, that it is not the *grad* system which will win the war against the colonialists: only our fighters themselves can do that.

This being so, the *grad* system must be used in reinforcement of attacks using other weaponry, including mortars, portable cannon and heavy bazookas. To organise this, an initial six specialised units were formed, each with two *grad* launchers and eight men for each, or a unit total of sixteen. These groups were 'to act independently against well-defined targets, but be able to act whenever necessary in combination' with infantry units. Their action 'must always be co-ordinated with other artillery weapons. Infantry actions must follow the use of *grad* whenever possible and convenient . . . [while *grad* must be used] exclusively against the principal enemy fortified camps and his airfields', preferably by daylight when the greatest effect could be obtained.

Anti-aircraft defence posed insoluble problems till very near the end of the Portuguese wars. Little or nothing effective could be done against aerial bombardment, especially by fast-flying jets, before ground-to-air rockets became available in 1973. Meanwhile the Portuguese, from 1967 onwards, introduced new helicopter tactics. These enabled:

(a) machine-gun harassment at low levels of altitude;
(b) rapid commando raids;
(c) combined operations with bombing support.

As developed by about 1970, (b) and (c) could be fairly effective, but especially by way of the landing of commando units. These were provisioned and equipped to stay on the ground for a given number of days, doing as much damage as they could, before being retrieved from a pre-arranged rendezvous. Such operations depended on short-wave radio communications, but this presented no problem so long as the radio operators remained intact.

The problem of dealing with these raids was partly the problem of hitting helicopters. But it was soon realised that helicopters were by no means invulnerable to well-directed small-arms fire by men who kept their nerve. A 24-page directive on dealing with helicopters was drawn up by Cabral as early as June 1967, and the companion movements of the PAIGC made corresponding dispositions. Drawing on experience, the Angolan commander Jaime Morais wrote somewhat later that

> Whenever the surprise factor is partly absent, because guerrillas have become used to this form of attack and oppose it with a well organised fire, this arm (helicopter) at once loses much of its effectiveness.
>
> To be really effective (the helicopter) must be used in large numbers as by the Americans in Vietnam . . . But, as is evident, such concentrations can only help the work of a well organised anti-aircraft defence. They have, too, the disadvantage of being very expensive, and their massive use by poorly-financed armies such as the Portuguese becomes prohibitive. Apart from being very vulnerable (to anti-aircraft fire), a helicopter also needs two pilots and other highly trained crew, and depends for its effectiveness, in any case, on co-operation with ground forces.

But if dealing with helicopters proved increasingly possible, defence against aerial bombardment had to await the SAM-7 'heat-seeking' ground-to-air rocket. This was first committed in March 1973, by the PAIGC, and proved immediately successful. Almost within weeks the last Portuguese superiority – in the air – was overcome; not even Portugal's jets, bombing and machine-gunning at 500 kms. per hour or more, could escape these deadly rockets. They were weapons, moreover, which could be used by two-man teams without prolonged training, and they were as mobile as the men who carried and used them, requiring no kind of fixed firing pad.

Somewhat earlier, in 1972, the PAIGC command reached the conclusion that it might have to assault the chief military centres of the colonial forces, and, to that end, acquired a number of Soviet AFVs (including amphibians) and trained PAIGC crews to use them. In the event, however, they were scarcely needed.

CONCLUSION

In bringing this short history to a close, the author would like to stress a few points. He has intended to select some of those examples which can be most instructive, but without prejudice to others of the same type. He has wished to emphasise that all wars have been evil, but that a well-directed war of self-defence – as distinct, always, from every terrorist adventure – could extract good from the most adverse circumstances. He has tried to show that any such well-directed war of self-defence has been governed by an overall political and moral concept which was always paramount. He has hoped to explain, by the examination of real examples, the nature and meaning of that concept in recent times: the strategy and ideology of people's war.

GUIDE TO SOURCES

A full guide to relevant writings would be impracticable here because it would be far too long. For further reading I therefore offer a short list of works, most of them introductory or expository, and many with their own bibliographies; these are mentioned by chapter or section according to my page numbers. I have kept to English and French books as far as possible, with a few necessary exceptions where translations into English or French are not available. So as to avoid the irritation of reference numbers in the text itself, or of expensive footnotes, I also give source-references alongside page numbers below.

PART ONE

There are many books about the subject of guerrilla warfare, but rather few are of much value, many being the work of authors little acquainted with the realities of this admittedly difficult subject. Several of the most notable exceptions are mentioned in the following pages.

For the background to the Moroccan invasion of Songhay, see essays by J. O. Hunwick and J. E. Willis in J. F. A. Ajayi and M. Crowder (ed.), *History of West Africa*, Longman, London 1971, vol. 1. The little that is known of Askia Nuh and his guerrillas I have taken from the 17th century Timbuktu chronicles, *Tarikh al-Fattash* and *Tarikh as-Sudan*, sources all the more valuable for having been compiled so soon after. The quotations here (in my translation) are from the French renderings of Houdas and Delafosse first published in Paris during 1913–14, but taken here from the reprintings published by Adrien-Maisonneuve, Paris 1964. On the battle of Mbwila, see D. Birmingham, *Trade and Conflict in Angola*, Oxford 1966. General histories which provide a wide background to these and other subjects include B. Davidson, *Africa in History*, Weidenfeld, London, and Macmillan, New York, 1968, and (paperback) Paladin, London 1972; R. Cornevin, *Histoire de l'Afrique*, Payot, Paris 1975; P. Curtin, S. Feierman, L. Thompson and J. Vansina, *African History*, Little, Brown and Co., Boston, and Longman, London, 1978; J. D. Fage, *A History of Africa*, Hutchinson, London 1978; J. Ki-Zerbo, *Histoire de l'Afrique Noire*, Hatier, Paris 1972; R. Oliver and J. D. Fage, *A Short History of Africa*, Penguin, 5th edn., 1975; and J. Suret-Canale, *French Colonialism in Tropical Africa, 1900–1945*, Hurst, London 1971.

Page
1 Both quotations are drawn from C. Hill and E. Dell, *The Good Old Cause*, Lawrence & Wishart, London 1949, introduction.
4 For Caribbean and other trans-Atlantic slave revolts, the 'maroon' wars in Jamaica, the black republics, etc., see a brief overview in B. Davidson, *Black Mother*, Penguin,

Page

London, revised edn., 1981; or, extensively, a superbly detailed history in R. Hart, *Slaves Who Abolished Slavery*, Community Education Trust, 8 Manor Gdns, London N.7, 2 vols, 1979–81; and, for a classic study of Toussaint L'Ouverture and the San Domingo revolution (later Haiti), C. L. R. James, *The Black Jacobins*, Vintage, New York 1963. Within the context of Caribbean history, the whole subject continues to be fruitfully explored, and the available historical literature is already very large.

10   *Tarikh al-Fattash*, 264.

11 ff. On Askia Nuh, *Tarikh al-Fattash*, ch. 16; *Tarikh as-Sudan*, ch. 22.

12   *Tarikh as-Sudan*, 239.

13–14 *Ibid*, 223.

18–19 King Antonio's call to arms: Visconde de Paíva Manso, *História do Congo, Documentos*, Academia Real das Sciencias, Lisbon 1877, 244.

21   Masemba: Reichskolonialarchiv (Potsdam 747, Masemba to Wissmann) quoted by F. F. Müller, *Deutschland – Zanzibar – Ostafrika*, Rütten & Loening, Berlin 1959, 456.

21   Baule: T. C. Weiskel, *French Colonial Rule and the Baule Peoples*, Oxford 1980.

22   For Nana (Olomu), O. Ikime, *Merchant Prince of the Niger Delta*, Heinemann, London 1971. Admiral Bedford's report, *Correspondence Respecting the Disturbances in Benin*, etc., A/CG Moor to FO, C/7638, 1895.

25–26 Mackinnon *v.* Sandile: R. Godlonton and E. Irving, *Narrative of the Kaffır War 1850–52*, repr. Struik, Cape Town 1962, 48, 50, 75 ff.

27   Fynn: J. Bird (ed.), *The Annals of Natal 1495–1845*, repr. Struik, Cape Town 1965, vol. 1, 64 ff.

28   Bird, vol. 1, 80.

30–31 South African (Anglo-Boer) War, reliance of both British and Boers on Africans: P. Warwick, 'African Societies in the South African War, 1899–1902, D.Phil. thesis, York University, 1978. In general, P. Warwick (ed.), *The South African War*, Longman, 1980.

31   C. R. de Wet, *Three Years War*, Constable, London 1902, 264.

32–33 *Ibid*, 323, 321. For material in footnote on p. 32, see Warwick, thesis, p. 55.

36   D. of Orleans, *Campagnes de l'Armée d'Afrique, 1835–39*, Paris 1870, 226: quoted here, in my translation, from Z. Pečar, *Alžir do Nezavisnosti*, Prosveta, Belgrade 1967, 679–80.

41   *Maji maji*: J. Iliffe, *Tanganyika under German Rule, 1905–12*, Cambridge 1969; G. C. K. Gwassa and J. Iliffe (ed.), *Records of the Maji Maji Rising*, Tanzania Publishing House, Dar es Salaam 1968.

42 ff. The indispensable work on the German war against the Herero and the Nama is H. Dreschler, *Süd-West-Afrika unter Deutscher Kolonialherrschaft*, Akademie, Berlin 1966; like Müller's (page 21 above), it draws on the otherwise unpublished German imperial records in the Reichskolonialarchiv, Potsdam; Eng. edn., Zed Press, London 1981.

43   Cabral, in a pamphlet of that name, MAGIC, 34 Percy St, London W1, 1971.

45   M. Bayer, *Mit dem Hauptquartier in Südwestafrika*, Berlin 1909, 229.

47   B. W. Andrzejewski, personal communication.

49   D. Jardine, *The Mad Mullah of Somaliland*, Jenkins, London 1923, 308, 315.

49 ff. Abd al-Krim: much research remains to be done, but two good recent books are: D. S. Woolman, *Rebels in the Rif*, Oxford 1969; and Colloque internationale d'Etudes historiques, Paris 1973, *Abd el-Krim et la République du Rif*, Maspero, Paris 1976. For the Moroccan background, see esp. Charles-André Julien, *Le Maroc Fâce aux Imperialismes, 1415—1956*, Editions 'J.A.', Paris 1978, a very outstanding work. *Abd el-Krim* (see p. 54), 112–13.

54   Ho Chi-minh's opinion, *Abd el-Krim*, 149. The *Abd el-Krim* volume also contains an excellent account of Libyan guerrilla resistance to Italian aggression before and after World War One (an example I am especially sorry to have had to omit for reasons of space): R. Davico, 'La guérrilla libyenne 1911–1932', *Abd el-Krim,* 402–39.

PART TWO

Page

55 Sayyid Mohammed: for English translations of some of his verse, B. W. Andrzejewski and I. M. Lewis, *Somali Poetry*, Oxford 1964; Tillion, in A. Horne, *A Savage War for Peace: Algeria 1954–62*, Macmillan, London 1977, 115.

58 J. Morley, *The Life of William Ewart Gladstone*, Macmillan, London 1903: vol. 3, 144, 557, 148 (Morley's comment towards end of paragraph).

58 Tawara: A. E. and B. Isaacman, *The Tradition of Resistance in Mozambique*, Heinemann, London 1976, 164; Maji Maji: Gwassa and Iliffe (see p. 41 above), 3–4;

59 S. Nigeria: T. N. Tamuno, *The Evolution of the Nigerian State: The Southern Phase 1898–1914*, Longman, London, 1972, 35, 42; Fr. W. Africa: M. Crowder, *West Africa under Colonial Rule*, Hutchinson, London 1968, 111.

59 Belgians: Min. des Colonies, *Recueil à l'Usage des Fonctionnaires et des Agents, etc.*, 4th edn, Brussels 1925, 151.

62 R. Pélissier, *Les Guerres Grises: Résistance et Révoltes en Angola 1845–1941*; *La Colonie du Minotaur: Nationalismes et Révoltes en Angola 1926–1961*, Ed. Pélissier, Montamets, France 1978.

62 Isaacman (see 58 above), 104 (on Mapondera), 111 ff., on Barue rebellion, 166 ff. Cuanhama: R. Pélissier, 'Campagnes Militaires au Sud Angola (1885–1915)', in *Cahiers d'Etudes africaines*, Mouton, Hague, IX, 1, 1969.

63 J. A. Atanda, 'The Iseyin-Okeiho Rising of 1916', *Journal of Historical Society of Nigeria*, IV, 4, June 1969; see also A. Osuntokun, *Nigeria in the First World War*, Longman, London 1979, 120 ff.; and, for further comment, A. I. Asiwaju, *Western Yorubaland under European Rule, 1889–1945*, Longman, London 1976, ch. 6.

64 Atanda, 505.

65 Atanda, 503–4.

65 'Women's Riots': A. E. Afigbo, 'Revolution and Reaction in Eastern Nigeria 1900–1929', *Jnl. of Hist. Socy. of Nigeria*, III, 3, Dec 1966; Afigbo, 'The Warrant Chief System, etc.', *loc. cit*, iii, 4, June 1967; and Afigbo's longer study, *The Warrant Chiefs*, Longman, London 1972; French interpretation: 'Notes sur les activités de l'internationale communiste dans la domaine coloniale', III/56 SLOTFOM, Archives Nationales, Paris.

66 Afigbo, 1966, 553.

67 For US motives and policies, W. R. Louis, *Imperialism at Bay 1941–45*, Oxford 1977.

69 The notion that the 'European model' could be made acceptable by means of reforms was widely denied by radicals at this time. But even so conservative a commentator as Prof. Ali Mazrui could tell the world (BBC Reith Lectures 1979) that 'the Westminster model' was among European 'artifices' which had not worked in Africa: A. A. Mazrui, *The African Condition*, Heinemann, London 1980, 7. For a less restricted discussion, see B. Davidson, *Africa in Modern History*, Lane/Penguin, London 1978/79, at various points; US edn.: Atlantic Boston, *Let Freedom Come*, 1978.

70 ff. Copious materials: for background, begin with Charles-André Julien, *L'Afrique du Nord en Marche*, Julliard, Paris, 1952; and J. Berque, *Le Magreb entre Deux Guerres*, Seuil, Paris 1962; and, in English, B. Davidson, *Africa in Modern History*, (p. 69 above), chs. 18 and 23 (US title: *Let Freedom Come*, Atlantic-Little, Brown, Boston, 1978).

73 Deaths in Morocco: Julien, 1978 (p. 49 above), 385/note 100.

73 French historian: Julien, 1978, 461.

74 Algeria: abundant French sources. The best history in English of the Algerian war, though much stronger on the French than on the Algerian side of the story, is Alistair Horne, *A Savage War for Peace*, Macmillan, London 1977. For the Algerian side of the story, the best all-round history in any European language (I do not have the advantage of reading Arabic) is by the Yugoslav historian and Arabist, himself an eyewitness, Zdravko Pečar, *Alžir do Nezavisnosti*, Prosveta, Belgrade 1967; an English translation is greatly needed. I am grateful to Dr Pečar for allowing me to draw several long passages from his book.

74 Julien, *Marche*, 330.

Page
77 Origins of rising, Pečar, 346 ff. See also an interesting book by M. Harbi, *Aux Origines du FLN*, Bourgas, Paris 1975.
77 Rising against élitism, Pečar, 410.
79 Tillion, Horne, 115.
83 Base of pyramid holds firm, Horne, 229.
83–84 Mohand al-Hadj, Pečar, 731 (interview of 1964); Laribi, Pečar, 401–2 (interview of 1964).
84 Ahmed ben Sharif, Pečar, 726–30.
85 OAS terrorism, Horne, 531.
87 Writings on the Kenya Emergency are many but of greatly varying quality; it seems that final judgments, in any case, have still to be made. Meanwhile the most perceptive analysis, to my knowledge, is R. Buijtenhuijs, *Le Mouvement 'Mau Mau'*, doctoral thesis, Ecole Prat. des Htes. Etudes, Paris 1969. A legal view is in P. Evans, *Law and Disorder* (in Kenya), Secker & Warburg, London 1956. The white-settler standpoint can be found in a multitude of works: see, for example, D. Holman, *Bwana Drum*, Allen, London 1964. The police have their say in I. Henderson, *The Hunt for Kimathi*, Hamilton, London 1958. Karari Njama's invaluable testimony is in D. L. Barnett and K. Njama, *Mau Mau from Within*. MacGibbon & Kee, London, 1966: and three other testimonies of participants in the insurrection are available in pamphlet form from LSM Information Center, Richmond, Canada: Ngugi Kabiro, *The Man in the Middle*, 1973; Karigo Michai, *The Hard Core*, 1973; and Mohamed Mathu, *The Urban Guerrilla*, 1974. There are many other works on various aspects of the subject.
87 R. Meinertzhagen, *Kenya Diary 1902–1906*, Oliver and Boyd, London 1957, 41, 60, etc.
91 Dr L. Mair, quoted from *The Listener*, London, 28 November 1963.
96 Barnett and Njama, 335.
97 Barnett and Njama, 487–8.
98 On some of the worst detention conditions brought to light, see Colonial Office reports on Hola Camp, Cmds. 778, 795, and 816 of June–July 1959, HMSO London. Generally, conditions were less bad; for a wider view, see J. M. Kariuki *'Mau Mau' Detainee*, Oxford 1963, with an interesting foreword by (Dame) Margery Perham.
100 ff. Congo rebellions: indispensable is the documentary series assembled and edited by B. Verhaegen, perhaps most notably *Rébellions au Congo*, CRISP., Brussels, 2 vols, n.d. (but dealing with 1964). Add R. B. Fox, W. de Craemer and J. M. Ribeaucourt, 'The Second Independence: a case study of the Kwilu rebellion', in *Comparative Studies in Society and History*, Mouton, Hague, VIII, 1965–66, 78 ff. An overview by Verhaegen is his 'Les Rébellions Populaires au Congo en 1964', in *Cahiers d'études africaines*, VII, 1967, 345 ff. For background, begin with: R. Lemarchand, *Political Awakening in the Belgian Congo*, Univ. of California Press, 1964; R. Anstey, *King Leopold's Legacy: The Congo under Belgian Rule*, Oxford 1966; C. Young, *Politics in the Congo: Decolonization and Independence*, Princeton 1965; and C. Hoskyns, *The Congo Since Independence*, Oxford 1965.
100 Hoskyns, 27; Lemarchand, 220.
103 'Assassins', Verhaegen vol. 1, 454.
103 Verhaegen, 504 ff.
105–6 Verhaegen, 319, 320–21, 437.
107–8 Verhaegen, 111.
109 Verhaegen, 167.
111 *La Libre Belgique*, 5 March 1964, quoted here from Verhaegen, 118.
112 Verhaegen, 132.
112–13 Fox *et al.*, 31.
113 On the Cameroun events, R. A. Joseph, *Radical Nationalism in Cameroun*, Oxford, 1977, and bibliography.
119 National liberation movements in Portuguese Africa: for background and sources, B. Davidson, *The Liberation of Guiné*, Penguin, London, 1969, and enlarged edn., Zed, London 1981, *No Fist is Big Enough to Hide the Sky*; and *In the Eye of the Storm: Angola's People*, Longman/Penguin, 1972/75; Eduardo Mondlane, *The Struggle for Mozambique*, Penguin, London 1969.

Page

Of volumes so far devoted to the writings/teachings of the principal leaders of these movements, the fullest is (posthumously) A. Cabral, *Unity and Struggle*, Heinemann, London, and Monthly Review Press, New York 1980 (also available in a fuller edition, *Unité et Lutte*, Maspero, Paris 1975, 2 vols).

120 Cabral: in *La Lutte de Libération Nationale dans les Colonies Portugaises*, CONCP, Algiers, 1967 (records of a conference of 1965), 152.

120 Mondlane (see p. 119 above), 125.

122 Machel: interview with B.D., 14 May 1979. See other published statements: e.g. interview with *Tempo*, Maputo, 7 Jan 1979; *Report* of Standing Political Committee of 4th Session of Central Committee of FRELIMO, Agencia de Informação de Moçambique, 2 Aug 1978; and much else to same effect. Two important statements of Machel's available in pamphlet form in English, and bearing on the standpoints discussed here, are: *Mozambique: Sowing the Seeds of Revolution*, MAGIC, 34 Percy St, London W1; and *Establishing People's Power to Serve the Masses*, Tanzania Publishing House, Dar es Salaam 1977.

127 Quoted by A. Cabral in his 'Brief Report on the Situation of the Struggle, Jan-Aug 1971', PAIGC, 8.

134 Frelimo in 1968: see B. Munslow, *Frelimo and the Mozambique Revolution*, doctoral thesis, Manchester 1980, forthcoming.

137 ff. I have described these events in detail in *No Fist Is Big Enough to Hide the Sky*, Zed, London 1981.

139 Machel, interview with *Tempo*, see p. 122 above.

140 For a general background review of Eritrean developments, see papers by various writers in B. Davidson, L. Cliffe, and B. H. Selassie (eds.), *Behind the War in Eritrea*, Spokesman, Nottingham 1980.

140–141 R. Sherman, *Eritrea*, Praeger, New York 1980, 41. For opinions on some of the international aspects, see, e.g., T. J. Farer, *War Clouds on the Horn of Africa*, Carnegie Endowment, New York, 2nd edn, 1979; and C. Legum and B. Lee, *The Horn of Africa in Continuing Crisis*, Africana, New York and London, 1979.

142 ff. A useful survey of the armed struggle in Zimbabwe down to 1975 is A. R. Wilkinson's contribution to B. Davidson, J. Slovo, and A. R. Wilkinson, *Southern Africa*, Penguin, 1976.

144 Early efforts: see Wilkinson, 226.

145 A Vietnamese opinion: Nguyen Van Tien, 'Notre Strategie de la Guérrilla', in *Partisans*, Paris, 40 of 1968, 67. This statement is as brilliant as it is brief, and is a vital item in the dossier of 'people's war'.

147 On the Black Consciousness movement, posthumously published writings of S. Biko, *I Write What I Like*, Bowerdean, London 1978. On Soweto, B. Hirson, *Year of Fire Year of Ash*, Zed, London 1979.

149 Sources available on all of these: see, for example, R. Buijtenhuijs, *Le Frolinat et les Révoltes populaires du Tchad, 1965–76*, Mouton, Hague 1978; and much journalism since.

150 Pharaonic upsets, in A. Gardiner, *Egypt of the Pharaohs*, Oxford 1961, 109–10.

151 E. J. Alagoa, *A History of the Niger Delta*, Ibadan 1972, 19 ff.

152 'Charter', in Buijtenhuijs 1969; O. R. Tambo (Acting President, African National Congress of South Africa), statement to AAPSO conference, Lusaka, April 1969, in *Documents*, AAPSO, 35–6.

153 Cabral: in Havana address 1966, see *Unity and Struggle*, Heinemann, London 1980, or Davidson, *Liberation of Guiné*, above, and new edn. of 1981, *No Fist is Big Enough to Hide the Sky*.

PART THREE

155 Machel: in *Report* of Standing Political Committee (see p. 122 above).

157 Mao Tsetung, *Selected Works*, Lawrence & Wishart, London 1954, 4 vols, vol. 1, 175 ff. For Mao's comment on Abd al-Krim, see the Colloque papers, *Abd el-Krim . . .*, *supra*, p. 401.

157 V. N. Giap, *Guerre du Peuple, Armée du Peuple*, Maspero, Paris 1967. J. B. Tito: some of his many writings and addresses are available in English: see, in context of our

Page

subject, *Selected Military Works*, Vojnoizdavački Zavod, Belgrade 1966. Huk guerrillas: W. Pomeroy, *The Forest*, Seven Seas, Berlin 1965. For a wide selection of important writings about guerrilla warfare and national liberation, see also W. Pomeroy, *Guerrilla Warfare and Marxism*, Lawrence & Wishart, London 1969. For an extended discussion of 'the politics of armed struggle', Davidson in *Southern Africa*, Penguin, London and Baltimore 1975.

158   Machel, 1973.

159   Cabral in his *Palávras Geráis*, 1965: English trans. in *Unity and Struggle*, above.

160   Cabral, PAIGC seminar of 1969, see also *Unity and Struggle*.

161   Cabral on strategy: quoted here from *Afrique-Asie*, Paris 1974, no. 66, xxv.

161   Rodrigues: in (Generals) J. da Luz Cunha, Kaúlza de Arriaga, Bethencourt Rodrigues, Silvino Silvério Marques, *A Vitória Traída*, Intervenção, Lisbon 1977, 130.

162   For detailed account of PAIGC strategy and tactics in removing all these garrisons, see Davidson, *No Fist is Big Enough to Hide the Sky*, Zed, London 1981.

    PAIGC sources: interviews with B.D. quoted here from Davidson, *Africa in Modern History* (see p. 169 above), ch. 30.

166–168   Cabral, Syracuse lecture, *Unity and Struggle*.

169   J. Morais-Monty, *Luta de Libertação, Exercito Nacional e Revolução*, União dos Escritores Angolanos, Luanda 1978. I wish to express my thanks to Monty for allowing me to reproduce these passages from his book, as well as the ambush sketches on 180 ff.

171–172   PAIGC, in Davidson, *Liberation of Guiné*, 1969 edn., 96, 97, 127.

177, 184 ff.   PAIGC documents, operational orders, etc.: I wish to thank the PAIGC for their permission to reproduce extracts from a selection of their documents in my possession.

178   'Jika', *Reflexões sobre a Luta de Libertação Nacional*, Luanda 1976, but written in 1969–71 and published posthumously.

179   These Portuguese military casualty figures are quoted here from *A Vitória Traída* (see p. 161 above) which states that they have been drawn from official Portuguese sources.

180 ff.   Ambushes: reproduced from J. Morais-Monty, *Luta de Libertação, op. cit.*

184 ff.   Operation Fanta, etc.: see note to p. 177 above.

INDEX

(Note: Alphabetical arrangement is word-by-word; a single letter in an abbreviation is treated as a single word, but acronyms are indexed as one word. Page numbers in italics refer to maps and figures.)

ALN (Algerian Army of National Liberation) (*see also* FLN)
  defeats, 82–4
  early successes, 78–80
  size, 80
APL (Armée Populaire de Libération), 102, 104–6
Abdullah, Muhammad Ahmad ibn, 37, *38*
Abdullahi, Khalifa, 37
Aberdare Mts, 92, 95
Adowa, battle of (1896), 21
aerial bombing, 49, 60, *82*
African National Congress, 144, 148
Africans
  in colonial armies
    Boer war, 30–1
    British, 25, 30–1, 98
    Portuguese, 18, 169, 172
Afrikaans, 28
Afrikaners
  defeat of British (1881), 29–30
  development of national consciousness, 28
  in Anglo-Boer War, 29–33
aid, military, 122, 126–7
aircraft, 53, 126
  defence against, 191–2
al-Hadj, Col. Mohand, 83
al-Kader, Abd, *34*, 35–6, 151
al-Kattabi, Abd al-Kader, *50*
al-Krim, Abd, 51–4
Albertville, APL in, 102, 106
aldeamentos, 170
Algeria (*see also* ALN; CRUA; FLN; MTLD; OS)
  army reorganisation, 36
  European settlers' revolt, 85

French invasion, 33–7
independence, 85
insurrection, 70, 78–84
  mass support for, 76–7, 78, 80
  rejected by older nationalists, 74, 77
modernising leadership, 113
nationalism, 35, 71, 76–7
nationalists, disagreement amongst, 74–5, 77
racism, 74
support for liberation movements in Portuguese colonies, 122, 136
support for POLISARIO, 149
weapon supply, 189
Algerian Army of National Liberation, *see* ALN
Algerian Front of National Liberation, *see* FLN
Algiers, battle of (1956), 80–1
Alvaro III, *16*
ambush techniques, 179–84
ammunition, 23, 189–90
Angola (*see also* Kongo kingdom; MPLA)
  ambush techniques in, 180–4
  Cuanhama uprising, 62
  declared a sovereign republic, 132
  imprisonment of civilians, 170
  insurrection in, 120, 129–32
  invasion by South Africa, 132, 146–7
  Portuguese casualties in, 179
  Portuguese military expenditure in, 125
  unity in, problems of, 128
  support of Congo and Zambia for, 122
Antonio, King, 18
Anual, battle of (1921), 51

apartheid (*see also* racism), 143
  uprisings against, 142, 147–8
Armée Nationale Congolaise, 102, 104
  attack on by *jeunesses*, 105
  success of Mulele's troops against,
    108
Armée Populaire de Libération (APL),
  102, 104–6
armies
  colonial, dispersal of, 161
  imperial, 13, 16
  Land and Freedom Armies, 95, 96,
    97, 98, 113, 152
  long-service, 27
  of kings and chiefs, 23
  of national liberation movements
    (*see also under individual countries
    and movements*), 123, 175
Army of Liberation, 73
Arriago, General Kaulza de, 8, 127,
  128
Asante
  conquest by British, 21
  defence of by king's army, 6
Askia Iskaq II, 10
assault units, 175
Atbara river, battle of (1898), 37
Atlantic Charter (1941), 67–8
Aurès Mts, 78
automatic weapons, 189–90

Bafata, 187
Bamiléke people, 113
Bantu peoples, 24–6
Barue rebellion, 62
Bassa people, 113
Basuto nation, emergence of, 28
bazooka, 190
Bedford, Rear Admiral, 23
behaviour, Mulele's code for, 109–10
Belgium
  colonial rule in Congo, 101
  Congo's independence granted, 100
  military displays in colonies, 59
Ben Bella, Mohammed, 75, 78, 81, 82
Ben Bulaid, assassination of, 80
Benin river, 22, 23
Berbera, British base at, 47, 48
Berne, formation of FLN and ALN at, 78
Bey, Ahmed, 35
Biafra, 135n
bigrupo, 176
Bissau
  PAIGC infiltration of airport, 189

support for PAIGC in, 128, 136
'black consciousness' movement, 147
blockhouses, 32–3
Boé, eviction of Portuguese from, 187
Boer War, 29–33
Boers, *see* Afrikaners
bombing, aerial, 49, 60
  destruction of forest cover by, *82*
Borgawa people, 15, 16
Boumédienne, Co. Houari, 84
Bourghiba, Habib, 73
Brazzaville
  Lumumbists in, 102
  MPLA base in, 130
Britain
  Atlantic Charter with USA, 67–8
  Boer War, 29–33
  colonial rule (*see also* British colonies)
    Kenya, 87, 89, 91
    Nigeria, 59
    'pacification', 59, 87
    Rhodesia, 143
  colonial troops, Africans in, 25, 30–1,
    98
  conquest of Asante, *20*, 21
  conquest of Niger Delta area, 21–3
  control of Eritrea, 140
  desire for overall control in South
    Africa, 29
  imprisonment of Jacob Morenga, 44
  involvement in 'Kaffir Wars', 24–6
British colonies (*see also* Kenya;
    Nigeria; Rhodesia)
  insurrection in, 63–6, 92–9, 116
British Kaffraria, *24*, 25
British Somaliland
  establishment of, 45–7
  reoccupation of, 48–9
British troops
  counter-insurgency techniques, 31–3
  defeat by Afrikaners, 29–30
  defeat by Zulus at Isandlwana
    (1879), 21
  defeat of guerrillas in Malaya, 168
  defeat of Khalifa Abdullah's troops,
    37
  withdrawal from warfare with
    Somalis, 47
Browning, John M., 60
Bugeaud, Marshal, 36
Bukavu, 102
Bulawayo, strikes in, 144

Cabinda, MPLA in, 130

Cabo Delgado, support for FRELIMO in, 133, 135
Cabral, Amílcar, 135, 173
  comment on realities of guerrilla warfare, 117
  comments on Portuguese economy, 120
  directives on weapons, 191, 192
  military planning, 187
  murder of, 137
  political training by, 136
  teachings, 159–60, 165, 166–8
Cabral, Luiz, 172
Cairo, FLN/ALN in, 78
Cameroun insurrection in, 71, 113
camps, rural population confined in, 31–2, 96–7, 98, 170
cannon, 23, *188*, 190
Cape of Good Hope, colonisation of, 23
Cape Verde, 124–5, 135, 136, 137–8
capitalism, rejection of, 69
capitalists, 109
casualties
  Algeria, 75, 81, 85
  Kenya, 98
  kept to a minimum, 178–9
cattle
  in battle of Tondibi, 10–11
cavalry, 13
Cazombo, Portuguese sweep offensive in, 182–3
Challe, General Maurice, 83
chiefs, *see* kings and chiefs
China
  guerrilla warfare in, 157
  military help from, 122
China, General (Waruhio Itote), *94*, 95
Christianity, 151
  Calvinist, 28
civilians
  colonial reprisals against, 42–3, 80
  imprisonment in camps, 31–2, 96–7, 170
  terror against rejected by PAIGC, 172
class conflict, 68–9, 116, 141
Clausewitz, Karl von, 5
clinics, 165
combined operations, 174, 184–8
Comité Révolutionnaire pour l'unité et l'Action (CRUA), 75
command, failures in, 162, 175, 178
commandos
  Afrikaner, 30
  Portuguese, 169–70

compromise
  association with defeat, 121, 133–4
Conakry
  murder of Cabral in, 137
  PAIGC base in, 136
concentration camps, 31–2, 96–7, 170
Congo
  'Central Government'
    failure to control country, 100
    independence from aimed for, 102–3
  colonial administration, 101
  independence
    chaos after, 101
    lack of preparation for, 100
  nationalism, 100, 103
  rebellions against 'central government', 101–12
    causes of failure, 106–7, 110–12, 113
Congo republic (Brazzaville), 102
  support for Angola, 122
Congolese National Army, *see* Armée Nationale Congolaise
Conseil National de la Libération, 102, 103, 107
coordination, lack of, 101
cotton cultivation, forced, 58
counter-insurgency techniques, 168–70
  Algeria, 36
  Boer War, 31–3
  Kenya, 96–7
'Cowboy', Commandant, 180–1
crops, defence of, 169
CRUA, 75, 76, 77
Cuanhama people, uprising by, 62
Cuba, military help from, 122, 132, 136
cultural development, 66, 113, 124, 139, 160, 166–7, 168

Dar es Salaam, formation of FRELIMO in, 132
dawa, 105
de Gaulle, Charles, 83, 85
decolonisation, Atlantic Charter agreement on, 67–8
defence, *see* self-defence
Dembos forests, MPLA support in, 131
democracy, PAIGC establishment of, 163–8
Dervishes, army of, 47–8
Destour party, 71
diamonds, discovery of, 29, 30n
Difaqane, 28

Dingiswayo, unification of Nguni by, 27
discipline, 26, 105, 109–10
  lack of, 162
divorce, Yoruba reaction against, 64–5
Dongola, 37
Dub Madoba, battle of (1913), 48
Dutch East India Company, 23

ELF (Eritrean Liberation Front), 141
ELM (Eritrean Liberation Movement), 140
EPLF (Eritrean People's Liberation Front), 141–2
Ebrohemi, British conquest of, 22–3
education, 165
Egypt, Pharoahs', 150
elephant, Congo compared to, 112–13
Embu people, 116
endurance, 8
English history
  quoted by Land and Freedom Armies' leaders, 152
Eritrea
  civil war, 141
  insurrection in, 140, 141–2
  nationalism, 140
Eritrean Liberation Front (ELF), 141
Eritrean Liberation Movement (ELM), 140
Eritrean People's Liberation Front (EPLF), 141–2
Ethiopia
  annexation of Eritrea, 140
  establishment of Ogaden, 46–7
  invasion of Somali lands, 45
  resistance to in Eritrea, 140–2
  victory over Italians at Adowa (1896), 21
expenditure, military, 124–5
exploit, exemplary, 188–9

FLN (Algerian Front of National Liberation), 78, 80
  leadership, 81, 82
  provisional government in Tunisia, 84, 85
FNLA (UPA), 128, 129, 130, 131, 132, 178
Fanta, Operation, 184–6
fellaghas, 72–3
fences, isolation of guerrillas by, 32–3, 82, 83, 84
Fez, 53

fighting units
  organisation of, 3–4, 51, 95, 174–8
  political commissars in, 177
  size, 3–4
folk heroes, 150
food supplies, destruction of, 31, 169
forced labour, Yoruba uprising against, 63–4
forest cover, bombing of, *82*
forts, construction of by Sayyid Mohammed, 47–8
France
  anti-colonial protest in, 54, 73
  colonies (*see also* Algeria; Cameroun; Madagascar; Morocco; Tunisia)
    administration, 70, 71, 74
    colonisation, 33–7, 50–1
    European settlers in, 71
    independence, 73, 74, 85
    insurrection in, 52–3, 54, 70, 72–84, 113
  conquest of Western Sudan, 21
  defeat in Vietnam, 73
  Napoleonic Wars, 3
  OAS bombings, 85
FRELIMO (Frente de Libertação de Mocambique), 8, 121, 127–8, 132–5, 145, 158
Fynn, Henry, 27, 28

Ganda king, 21
Gao, 11
Gatling machine-gun, 60, *61*
Gbenye, Christophe, 103
general elections
  Guinea-Bissau, *164*, 166
  Zimbabwe, 145
Geneva, conference in, 145
genocide, 42
Germany
  colonial oppression, 58
    resistance to, 41, 42–5
  invasion of Tanganyika, 21
Ghana, ancient empire of, 12, 13
Giap, V. N., 157
Gizenga, Antoine, 107
Gladstone, W. E., 58
gold discoveries, 29, 30n
Gomes, General Costa, 9
'Gordian Knot' offensive, 127–8
Gorenjama, 62
grad, 191
Great Depression, 71, 151
grenades, 190

Griqualand West, diamonds in, 29, 30n
ground-to-air missile, 137, 191, 192
grupo, 176
guerrilla warfare
  defensive motive, 4, 5, 6
  definitions of, 3–6
  development into regular, disciplined
    warfare, 123
  duality of theme (restoration and
    reorganisation) (*see also* reformist
    movements; revolution), 36–7,
    38, 40, 41, 77, 116, 152–3
  duration, 174
  guides and manuals, 157
  methods (*see also* strategy; tactics), 4
  realities of, 117
  similarities with regular warfare, 5,
    6, 16
  subjective aspects, 7–8
guerrillas, early usage of, 3
guerrillas, first English usage of, 4
guides and manuals, 157
Guinea
  support for PAIGC, 122, 136
Guinea-Bissau (*see also* PIAGC)
  confinement of rural population in
    camps, 170
  establishment of self-government,
    163–8
  general election, *164*, 166
  independence declared, 137
  insurrection, 120, 135–8
  peaceful evacuation of Portuguese,
    172
  Portuguese casualties, 179
  Portuguese military expenditure in,
    125
  support of Guinea and Senegal for,
    122, 136
  unity in, 128

Harar, 45
hardships, 7, 117
Hasan, Mohammed Abdille (Sayyid
  Mohammed), 47–9
Haartebeestmund, 42, 43
health, public, 165–6
helicopters, 191
herbicides, 126
Herero people
  resistance to colonial rule, 42–5
Horn of Africa (*see also* Somali state)
  partition, 45–7
hospitals, 165

Huk people, 157
hunger, 169

ideology, 113, 117, 141
ideology of liberation, *see* liberation,
  ideology of
imperialists, 109
improvement (*see also* modernisation)
  as aim of armed resistance, 88
innovating change, phase of, 151, 152
intelligence, 36
International Court of Justice
  declaration on South Africa's
    occupation of Namibia, 146
Isandlwana, battle of (1879), 21
Iseyin-Okeiho region, uprising in, 63–5
Islam, unity of, 117
isolation (of guerrillas), 96, 97, 110,
  168, 170
Italy
  colonisation of Eritrea, 140
  defeat by Ethiopians at Adowa
    (1896), 21
  invasion of Horn of Africa, 45
    establishment of Somalia, 46–7
  peace treaty with Sayyid
    Mohammed, 47
Itote, Warihiu (General China), *94*, 95

Jamaica, slave revolts in, 4
Jebba, *63*
jeunesses, 104–6, 111–12
Jijiga, 45
Judar, 10, 11, 12

KAU (Kenya African Union), 90–2
KCA (Kikuyu Central Association),
  89–90
Kabila, Laurent, 107
Kabylia, saturation offensive in, 83–4
Kadungure, 62
'Kaffir Wars', 24–6, 27
Kamanyola, 105
Katanga (Shaba), 102–3
Kenya
  early anti-colonial resistance, 116
  European settlers, 89, 90, 91
  nationalism, 87–8, 89–92
  pacification, 87
  rebellion against colonial rule, 92–9
    leaders, 94–5, 113
    mass support for, 93
    political aspects, 95–6, 98
    preparation for, 88–92

Kenya, Mt, 92, 95
Kenya African Union (KAU), 90–2
Kenya African National Union, 98
Kenya Defence Council, 95
Kenya Parliament, 96, 97, 98
Kenyatta, Jomo, 91
Khoi people, enslavement of, 23–4
Kikuyu Association, 89
Kikuyu Central Association (KCA),
    89–90
Kikuyu Independent Schools
    Association, 89
Kikuyu people, 87, 89–99
  detention in camps, 96–7, 98
  internal division among, 92–3, *94*
  leadership, 95
  magic and superstition amongst, 97
  rebellion against colonial rule, 92–9
  preparation for, 89–92
Kimathi, Dedan, 92, 95, 96
kings and chiefs
  interests of not shared by troops, 23
Kinshasa (Leopoldville), 100
  escape of MPLA nationalists to, 130
Kisangani (Stanleyville), 101, 102, 106,
    107
Kitchener, Lord Horatio, 33
Kivu, rebellion in, 102
Kongo kingdom, *16*, 17, 18
Kongo people, regionalist movement
    among, 128, 129
Kumasi, entry into, *20*
Kwenhe, Commandant
  ambush techniques, 180
Kwilu region, rebellion in, 107–14

land competition, 26
Land and Freedom Armies, 95, 96, 97,
    98, 113, 152
landmines, 82, 97, 169, 181, 190
Laribi, Capt. Alexander, 84
latrines, Iseyin reaction against, 65
leaders and leadership (*see also names of
    individual leaders*, e.g. al-Kader;
    Cabral; Machel; Mulele etc.),
    40, 94–5, 115–16, 121–2, 160–1
  contact with peasantry, 166–7
  effects of removal of, 91–2
  modernising, 113
  political, 177–8
  training for, 174–5
Lenin, V. I., 158
Leopoldville (Kinshasa), 100
liberated zones, 161–8, 175

contrast with enemy zones, 171
liberation, ideology of, 115, 116–17,
    122, 143, 153, 159–61
liberation politics, 137
liberation movements (*see also* EPLF;
    FRELIMO; MPLA; PAIGC; ZANU;
    ZAPU etc.), 121–4, 139–40
Lisbon, 173
local issues, ideological development
    from, 160
London, Zimbabwe conference in, 145
Luanda, uprising in, 129
Lumumba, Patrice, 100, 103
Lumumbist movement, 100–1, 102,
    105, 107
Lusaka, Zimbabwe conference in, 145
Lute river, ambush on, 183–4
Luvuei-Lutembo road, ambush on,
    181–2

MFA (Movimento das Forças Armadas),
    173
MNC (Mouvement National Congolais),
    100
MPLA (Movimento Popular de
    Libertação de Angola), 121, 128,
    129–32, 147
  ambush techniques, 180–4
  organisation of armed forces, 123,
    176, 177–8
MTLD (Mouvement pour le Triomphe
    des Libertés Démocratiques),
    75
Machel, Samora, 8, 122, *134*, 135, 158,
    160
machine guns, 60, 61, 181, 190
Mackinnon, Lt-Col., 25
Madagascar, insurrection in, 71, 113
Maghrib, *see* Algeria; Morocco; Tunisia
magic and superstition, 97, 104–6,
    111–12, 117, 124, 162
Magna Carta, 152
Mahdia, 37
Mahmud, 12
maize war, 169
maji maji movement, 41
majority rule
  as aim of Kenya African Union, 90
Malawi, Mozambique nationalists in,
    132
Malaya, defeat of guerrillas in, 168
Mali empire, 12
Maniéma, rebellion in, 102, 106
Maninga, Commandant, 181–2

Mao Tsetung
  teachings on guerrilla warfare, 107, 109, 157
Mapondera, 62
Mariam, Mengistu Hailé, 142
Marxism–Leninism, 158
Masemba, 21
Mathenge, Stanley, 95
'Mau Mau' movement, 90–1
Mauritania
  fighting with POLISARIO, 149
Maxim machine gun, 60
mbunda people, 108, 111
Mbwila, battle of (1665), 18
Meinertzhagen, Col. R., 87
Melilla, 50
Menelik, 45
mercenaries, 13–14
middle class (see also class conflict)
  support for Algerian insurrection, 76
middle-class values
  rejected by young Algerian nationalists, 77
migration, rural-urban, 66–7
Mindelo, support for PAIGC in, 136
minority rule, white, 143, 145
missile-launcher, 191
mobile warfare, 123, 137, 161, 174, 177–8
  weapons for, 190
Mobutu, General, 100, 101
  formation of Armée Nationale Congolaise, 102
  hostility to MPLA, 129, 131, 132
  visit to army unit at Kamamyola, 105
modernisation (see also reformist movements; revolution), 151
  conflict with traditional ideas/beliefs, 97, 110–11, 113, 117, 124
Mohammed V, Sultan, 73, 74
Mombassa, 90
Mondlane, Eduardo, 120, 132, 134, 135
Morais-Monty, Jaime, 169, 174, 192
morale
  raised by successful exemplary exploits, 188–9
morale, enemy
  undermining, 5, 8, 14, 171
Morenga, Jacob, 42–5
Morocco (see also Rif, Republic of)
  colonisation of, 50–1
  fighting with POLISARIO, 149
  independence, 74
  invasion of Songhay empire, 10–12

mercenary army, 13–14
  nationalism, 71, 73–4
  war for independence, 73–4
mortars, 190
Moshweshwe, King of Basuto, 28
Mouvement National Congolais (MNC), 100
Mouvement pour le Triomphe des Libertés Démocratiques (MTLD), 75
Moxico, ambush in, 181
Movimento das Forças Armadas (MFA), 173
Movimento Popular de Libertação de Angola, see MPLA
Mozambique (see also FRELIMO)
  confinement of rural population in camps, 170
  development of nationalism, 132–3
  independence, 135
  insurrection, 62, 120, 132–5
  obstacles to national unity, 128–9
  Portuguese casualties in, 179
  Portuguese military expenditure in, 125
  South African policy against, 147
  success of Machel's strategy and tactics in, 8
  support of Zambia and Tanzania for, 122
Mugabe, Robert, 145
mujahiddin, 37, 38
Mulele, Pierre, 107
  attitude to magical beliefs, 111–12
  teachings, 107
muskets, 13, 14, 22
Muslim reforming movements, 37–8
Muzorewa, Bishop Abel, 145

Nador, 51
Nairobi, 89, 92, 93, 96
Naivasha, trial at, 90
Nama people, resistance by, 42–5
Namibia
  nationalism, 145–6
  resistance to colonial rule, 42–5
Nana, Chief of Ebrohemi, 22–3
Nandi people, 116
Napoleonic Wars, Spanish guerrillas in, 3
Nasser, Gamal-Abdel, 78
Natal, 26
nation-state European
  as model for African nationalists, 67

national liberation, *see* liberation movements

nationalism (*see also under individual peoples and countries*), 67–9
development as a response to colonialism, 20, 29, 116
distant origins, 15–16, 19
foreshadowed by unity of neighbouring peoples, 41

nationalist movements
development into liberation movements, 121, 153, 161

NATO, military aid for Portugal from, 126–7

Ndebele people, 40, 41

Nembe people, 151

neo-colonialism, 68–9, 120

Néo-Destour party, 71, 72, 73

Neto, Agostinho, 130

neutralism, positive, 103

Nguni people
resistance to colonists and troops, 24
unity of, 26–7

Niassa, support for FRELIMO in, 133, 134

Niger Delta
British invasion of, 21–3
new god in, 151

Nigeria, Eastern
women's riots against taxation, 65–6

Nigeria, 'pacification' programme in, 59

Nigeria, Western uprising in, 63–5

Ninda-Chiume road, ambush on, 181, *182*

Njama, Karari, 95, 96, 97

Nkavandame, Lazar, 134–5

Nkomo, Joshua, 145

North Atlantic Treaty Organisation (NATO), 126–7

Northern Rhodesia, *see* Zambia

Nuh, Askia, 11–12, 13, 150

Nyasaland, Mozambique nationalists in, 132

Nyobe, Rueben Um, 113

OAS (Organisation de l'Armée Secrète), 85

OAU (Organisation of African Unity)
support for liberation movements, 137, 145

OS (Organisation Secrète), 75

oath of unity, *see* 'Mau Mau' movement

Ogaden, 46–7

Olenga, Nicolas, 106

Omdurman, battle of, (1898), 37

Orange Free State, war for control of, *see* Boer War

Organisation de l'Armée Secrète (OAS), 85

Organisation of African Unity (OAU), 137, 145

Organisation Secrète (OS), 75

Ouandié, Ernest, 113

Ovimbundu people, 128

PAIGC (Partido Africano de Independência de Guiné e Cabo Verde), 121, 135–8
casualty figures, 179
establishment of liberated zones, 161–8
exemplary exploits, 188–9
mass support for, 128, 163–8
operational planning, 184–8
organisation of armed forces, 123, 137, 161, 176
political warfare, 171–2
weapons, 191, 192

'pacification'
Kenya, 87
Nigeria, 59

parliamentary institutions
rejection of 'European model', 69

participation, 6, 76–7, 78, 80, 115, 116–17, 122, 123, 136, 141, 143, 158, 159, 163–8, 171

Partido Africano de Independência de Guiné e Cabo Verde, *see* PAIGC

patriotism (*see also* nationalism), 40

peasantry
contact with leaders, 166–7
imperial exploitation of, 12–13
mass support for Algerian insurrection, 76–7, 78, 80
support for PAIGC, 136

Pende people, 108, 111

Pharoahs, 150

Philippeville, 79, 84

Philippines, Huk guerrillas in, 157

plantation workers, uprising of, 129

planning, importance of, 184

plans, operational, 184–8

POLISARIO, 149

political commissars, 177

political consciousness, raising of, 123, 124, 139

political core, lack of, 106

litical instruction, 108–9, 136
olitical preparation, lack of, 144, 145
olitical victory
  military victory ineffective without,
    85
political work
  link with military operations, 177–8
political warfare, 171–3
politics, war as continuation of, 5, 36,
    139
Pomeroy, William, 157
Portugal
  African allies, 128
  colonialism (*see also* Portuguese
    colonies), 119–20, 123
  dictatorship
    overthrow by *coup d'état*, 8, 121,
      135, 173
    support of Western powers for,
      122–3
  economy, 120
  invasion of Kongo kingdom, 18
  military commanders
    counter-insurgency techniques,
      168–70
    inability to wage political warfare,
      168
    prejudices, 127
  military power and expenditure,
    124–7
  troops
    Africans in, 169
    casualties, 179
    helicopter tactics, 191–2
    peaceful evacuation from
      Guinea-Bissau, 172
Portuguese colonies (*see also* Angola;
    Cape Verde; Guinea-Bissau;
    Mozambique; São Tomé and
    Principé), *119*
  insurrection in, 8, 62, 120–38
    obstacles to success, 124–7, 128–9
    strategy of, 159–73
    support for from other countries,
      122–3
  nationalist movement, 120, 123
  oppression in, 58
  PAIGC appeal to settlers in, 171–2
  political warfare in, 171–3
power, post-imperial dispersal of, 15
Praia, support for PAIGC in, 136
Principé, see São Tomé and Principé

Quitáfine, PAIGC congress in, 162

racism
  Algeria, 74
  as policy instrument of colonialism,
    60
  Portuguese colonies, 127
  Rhodesia, 143, 144
  South Africa, 28, 33, 148
Ramazani, Joseph, 102
reactionaries, 109
reforming movements, Muslim, 37–8
reformist movements (*see also*
    modernisation)
  development into revolutionary
    movements, 109, 121, 142, 143,
    152–3
resistance, armed
  as determinant of cultural change, 66
  capacity for, 110
  combined with reorganisation and
    revolution, *see* guerrilla warfare:
    duality of theme; reformist
    movements; revolution
  ideology of, *see* liberation, ideology of
  improvement as primary aim, 88
  phases of, 150–3
  primary, 19–20, 45, 151
    duration, 21
  secondary, 19, 39, 40–54
    motives, 63
restoration (*see also* reformist
    movements; revolution), 20,
    36–7, 38, 63, 77, 150, 151, 152
Réunion, Abd al-Krim deported to, 54
revolution, 37, 77, 109
  and traditional beliefs, 113
  development from reformist
    movements, 121, 142, 143, 152–3
Rhodesia
  European settlers, 143
  insurrection in, 144–5
  Mozambique nationalists in, 132
  nationalism, 142–3, 144
  Ndebele and Shona resistance to
    colonialism, 40, 41
  South African influence and
    protection of regime, 147
  unilateral declaration of
    independence, 143
Rhodesia, Northern, independence, 142
Rif, Republic of, 51–4
rifles, 61, 189
rockets, ground-to-air, 137, 191, 192
ruling groups, clashes between and
    against, 19

rural population (*see also* peasantry)
    confinement in camps, 31–2, 96–7, 98, 170
    influence of colonialism on, 66–7
rural-urban conflict, 16

Sahroui people, 149
SAM-7 rocket, 137, 192
Sandile, 25–6
São Tomé and Príncipe, 124–5
Sayyid Mohammed (Mohammed Abdille Hasan), 47–9
schoolchildren, *see jeunesses*
schools, 165
Selassie, Haile, dethronement of, 141
self-defence, wars of (*see also* resistance, primary), 4, 5, 6, 16, 19
self-government
    establishment of by PAIGC, 163–8
Senegal
    support for Guinea-Bissau, 122
Shaba (Katanga), 102–3
Shaka, 27–8
Sherif, Ahmed ben, 84
shield, hide, 28
Shona people, 40, 41
shot-guns, 60–1
Silva-Jika, Gilberto da, 178
simba (*see also jeunesses*), 104, 105
Simango, Uriah, 133, 135
slave revolts, 4
slave trade, 19
social organisation
    influence of colonialism on, 66–7
    traditional, 26
social reorganisation (*see also* modernisation; revolution), 37, 38, 40, 41, 51–2, 77, 108–9, 116, 161
socialist system, 69
socio-economic crisis, 151
Solidarity, Mission, 186–7
Somali clans
    resistance to colonial control, 45–9
Somali state
    Sayyid Mohammed's attempts at creating, 47–8, 49
Somalia, 46–7
Songhay empire
    collapse of, 14–15
    exploitation of peasant labour, 12–13, 40–1
    invasion by Moroccans, 10, 150
    rural-urban conflict, 16
Soninke people, 13

Sotho people, 24
Soumialot, Gaston, 102
    nationalist aims, 102–3
    problems with *jeunesses*, 104–6
South Africa
    African National Congress, 144, 148
    apartheid system
    Rhodesia modelled on, 143
    uprisings against, 142, 147–8
    attitude to African nationalism, 142, 146–7
    domination by, 146
    early racism, 28, 33
    invasion of Angola, 132, 146–7
    occupation of Namibia declared illegal, 146
    policy towards Mozambique, 147
    suppression of African protest within, 146, 147
    white supremacy guaranteed by Boer War, 30, 33
South West Africa (Namibia), 42–5, 145–6
South West African People's Organisation (SWAPO), 146
Soviet Union, *see* USSR
Soweto, uprising in, 142, 147–8
Spain
    colonisation of northern Morocco, 50–1
    defeat by Abd al-Krim's troops, 51
    guerrillas in Napoleonic Wars, 3
    warfare against Rif Republic, 54
spears, 27, 28
Spinola, General, 168, 173
Stanleyville, *see* Kisangani
starvation, 169
strategic initiative, 159, 167
strategy, 7, 8, 157–73
students, African, black consciousness movement among, 147
sub-machine-gun, 189–90
Sudan, resistance to colonisation in, 37
success, factors contributing to, 115–18
superstition, *see* magic and superstition
support
    transformation into participation, 159, 163–8, 177
SWAPO (South West African People's Organisation), 146
Swazi nation, emergence of, 28

tactics, 4, 7, 8, 174–89
    in Boer War, 31, 33

tactics, cont.
  of Abd al-Krim, 51
  used by Dervishes, 47
  used by MPLA, *131*
Tale fortress, 47, *48*
Tall, Racine, *14*
Tambo, Oliver, 152
Tanganyika
  invasion by Germany, 21
  maji maji movement, 41
Tanzania
  support for Mozambique nationalists,
    122, 132, 133
taxation
  women's riots against in Nigeria,
    65–6
Taza, 53
Tenaz, Operation, 187–8
terrain
  influence on guerrilla warfare, 41, 42,
    52
terrorism, 115
theory
  development from practice, 122,
    158–9, 160
Thuka, Harry, 89
Timbuktu, 11
Tondibi, battle of (1591), 10–11
Touré, Sékou, 122
trade, 18, 22
trade unions, 67, 71
traditional ideas and beliefs
  conflict with modernisation, 97,
    110–11, 113, 117, 124
traditional structures, breakdown of,
  151
training (of guerrillas), 107–8, 136,
  174–5
transitional phase, 150, 151–2
Transvaal,
  gold discoveries, 29, 30n
  war for control of, *see* Boer War
Tunisia
  nationalism, 71–2
  war for independence, 72–3
Turkish empire, Algeria as province of,
  34–5
UPA (FNLA), 128, 129, 130, 131, 132,
  178
USA
  Atlantic Charter with Britain, 67–8
  strategy in Vietnam, 168
USSR, military help from, 122, 136, 142,
  190, 191

UNITA, 128, 132, 147, 178
unity (*see also* participation), 116–17,
  139, 171
  as forerunner of nationalism, 41, 116
  effect of defeat on, 15
  lack of, 47
  obstacles to, 128
Uvira, 102

vaccination, Iseyin objection to, 65
Vereeniging, Peace of (1902), 33
Vietnam
  American strategy in, 168
  anti-colonial war in, 73, 157
village committees, 163–4
violence, colonial, 57–60
  counter-violence against, 40, 41,
    57–8, 62
    related to size of white-settler
      population, 68
    underlying motives, 63
volunteers (*see also* jeunesses), 23, 78,
  123, 136
  moral advantage over conscripts, 170
  political motivation, 177

Wachanga, Kachniga, 97
warfare
  inter-African, 27
  irregular, *see* guerrilla warfare
  mobile, *see* mobile warfare
  regular
    similarities with guerrilla warfare,
      5, 6, 16
  von Clausewitz's definition of, 5
warrior oath, 92
wars of wandering, 28
wealth, accumulation of, 150
weapons (*see also* ammunition; cannon;
    landmines; machine guns;
    musket etc.), 13, 53, 60–2,
    189–92
West Germany
  sale of aircraft to Portugal, 126–7
Western countries
  equivocal attitude to South Africa,
    147
  support for Portuguese dictatorship,
    122–3, 137
Western Nigeria, uprising in, 63–5
Western Sahara, independence
  movement in, 149
Western Sudan, French conquest of, 21
Wet, Christiaan Rudolf de, 31, 32, 33

Wilhelm, Kaiser, 44
Windhoek, strikes in, 146
women
    participation in liberation, *164*
    revolt against colonialism, 65–6
World War Two
    anti-colonial resistance during, 151–2
    colonial violence during, 59

Xhosa-speaking people
    resistance to colonisation, 25–6
Xieto, Commandant, 181–2

Yao people
    resistance to German invasion, 21
Young Kikuyu Association, 89
Yorubaland, uprising in, 63–5

Zaire (*see also* Congo)
    ambush techniques, 180

hostility to MPLA, 129, 131, 132
Zambia
    independence, 142
    support for Angola and
        Mozambique, 122, 130
ZANU (Zimbabwe African National
    Union), 144, 145
ZAPU (Zimbabwe African People's
    Union), 144, 145
Zigut, Yussef, 80
Zimbabwe (*see also* Rhodesia)
    independence, 145
Zimbabwe African National Union
    (ZANU), 144, 145
Zimbabwe African People's Union
    (ZAPU), 144, 145
Zulus
    methods of warfare changed, 27–8
    victory over British at Isandlwana
        (1879), 21